AF335095

DO THE RIGHT DEAL
DO THE DEAL RIGHT

Do the Right Deal
Do the Deal Right

35 Success Factors
for Mergers & Acquisitions

B. BARRY MASSOUDI

Seattle, Washington
Continental Publishers
2006

Library of Congress Control Number: 2005908064
ISBN-13: 978-0-9765173-0-6
ISBN-10: 0-9765173-0-2

Includes References and Index.

Printed in the United States of America on acid free 50% post consumer recycled paper.

Additional copies can be ordered from Continental Publishers LLC by visiting www.continentalpublishers.com or by writing to Continental Publishers LLC, P.O. Box 1279, Mercer Island, WA 98040-1279. Discounts are available for bulk purchases.

To my parents

CONTENTS

PREFACE

It is widely noted in today's media that the majority of mergers and acquisitions (M&As) will fail to create their expected value. However, despite such failures, thousands of small and large M&A deals still take place in the U.S. and worldwide each year. Skeptics tend to view M&A deals as signs of self-indulgence, inflated egos, or simply as games of chance played with shareholder wealth. Supporters, on the other hand, see in M&As opportunities to create value and to gain a stronger competitive position. It seems as if most people, whether in the business world or not, have some sort of opinion formed about the efficacy, viability, or the ethics of M&As—especially considering the globalizing climate. No one should deny, though, that understanding the M&A process is an important part of thinking through the economic realities of the times. And therefore no one should either facilely accept or dismiss their potential value without first getting the fundamentals involved right. This 'getting the fundamentals right' so that one can ultimately 'do the deal right' is the main impetus of the present book, which attempts to enter into this conversation about the present, past, and future state of M&As and the important business issues they generate.

Studies have suggested that odds for a successful M&A are not much better than those in a coin toss. So the question remains for company leaders: what can one do to overcome the prevailing odds and increase the chances of success in M&A deals? I would like to take up this question concerning the success of mergers and acquisitions in such a way that some of the answers will hopefully emerge in clear relief. Having been involved in numerous post-deal integration projects, ranging among Fortune 500 companies in a number of industries in the U.S. and Europe, I have a great deal of experience working closely with clients to make their newly combined entities a success. I have, in all of this, witnessed the challenges of integration first-hand as an employee in two organizations that underwent mergers, one of which was at the end of the day a painful failure. Despite various difficulties, including cultural clashes, processes that would not mesh together without great difficulty, IT systems that could not talk to one another, and synergy goals that could not be achieved in a timely fashion, the people in the organizations worked hard to make the deals successful and to realize the expected value. Regardless of all the hard work and sacrifices of hundreds of employees, some of these deals, though, still could not be considered a success, as ultimately shareholder value was lost. Time and time again, the daunting obstacles that had to be overcome during integration were a direct result of the unsatisfactory decisions made at earlier stages of the deal—decisions that could have been made otherwise. This book, then, would hope to help prevent such breakdowns in decision-making and aims at aiding in seeing the M&A process as clearly as possible.

The questions that the management and board of directors need raised and answered at the earlier stages of the M&A process include the following: Are we prepared to walk away from the M&A deal if we find it to be a weaker fit than expected? Can we stick to the price range that would create strategic value and break off negotiations when the other side demands more? Are considerations of organizational culture being given similar weight as financial and operational considerations? Are sufficient resources being dedicated to a thorough due diligence and to the development of detailed integration plans? Are synergy benefit estimates, in terms of magnitude and timing, realistic and can the organization realize them? These are some of the major issues, among others, that this book explores in depth. If such important questions are considered superfluous to the pursuit of an M&A deal, or if the answers to the above questions ever are no, then any management should expect a loss in value to occur, and they should be prepared to face a cardinal business problem: the giving away of owner or shareholder wealth to the other side. Therefore, when one is involved with companies conducting M&A deals, it is the responsibility of the senior management to consider these crucial issues in depth, and it is the role of advisers then to raise the awareness about them. This book will, along these lines, attempt to consider just such issues in order to raise the awareness of those who find themselves involved in M&A deals.

In *Do the Right Deal / Do the Deal Right*, the M&A process is shown to be a series of steps with intermittent key decision nodes. Each step in the

M&A process requires pre-planning to focus efforts on critical activities. The quality of and the timeliness of the decision making by senior leadership can either create or destroy value in the M&A process. Good decision making therefore requires clear decision criteria and the gathering and analyzing of reliable information as well as making realistic assumptions after gaining a thorough understanding of the risks associated with the deal and their implications on the deal value. Finally, there should be a focus on key stakeholders, especially on the customers and employees. The book guides one along this process in careful steps that illustrate just how to go about getting the job done right in this respect.

The primary purpose of writing *Do the Right Deal / Do the Deal Right* is in this way to recount some of the lessons that were learned from various mistakes in judgment in previous deals that were less than successful and to share them with readers who might be in a better position to avoid similar mistakes as well as some of the more frequent pitfalls and errors that can inhibit the success of an M&A. As a result, *Do the Right Deal / Do the Deal Right* offers 35 success factors for mergers and acquisitions that provide a disciplined focus on the fundamentals of M&A deal making in order to create deals that are more successful and have a better chance of finally creating value. Not surprisingly then, most of the book's focus is for this reason not on the post-deal integration phase, but is centered chiefly on all of the events and activities that occur prior to the closing of the deal, those which will lead to the integration phase. The stress is placed upon these pre-closing activities for obvious reasons: when the deal is set up for success from the start, it is naturally more likely that the integration phase will be made a success and that the expected value will be realized. In addition to offering the success factors, the book also discusses some of things that might prevent decision makers from following sound M&A practices along with ways to overcome these obstacles.

After getting started with the basics in chapter one, the book's main tour of the M&A process starts in the second chapter with a review of each process step and its ensuing key decision. The remainder of the book then covers the key concepts in the mergers and acquisitions process and the major success factors associated with them. The book in this way takes its approach from the perspective of managers in the acquiring or target firms—irrespective of the size of the firm—who are accountable for the success of the M&A deal. It is my hope throughout that *Do the Right Deal*

/ *Do the Deal Right* will become a useful reference guide for managers and business leaders, who are planning on or are currently undergoing M&A deals, but also for any students of business culture who may find themselves in a future position that will require sound knowledge of the ins and outs of the M&A process.

ACKNOWLEDGEMENTS

Rarely an effort is entirely the work of one person. A number of individuals have generously contributed to this book through their ideas, input, encouragement, support, research, and helpful comments. My appreciation goes to Anjali Crawford, Lisa Flexner, and Gigi DeVault for their generous help. Special thanks go to Thomas Stuby for his valuable input and insightful comments. Thank you all. My gratitude goes to clients past and present with whom I've had the privilege to work with and to learn from and to many of my ex-colleagues at Gemini Consulting with whom I had the pleasure to work on many M&A projects.

35 Success Factors for Mergers & Acquisitions

1. Measure M&A success based on the creation of competitive advantage and real shareholder value

2. Gain insights into industry challenges and future trends before pursuing a deal

3. Pass up acquisitions in non-related businesses

4. Understand the M&A process and clearly establish owners, deliverables, and timetables

5. Anticipate and focus on key M&A decisions

6. Drive every aspect of the M&A deal from the senior leadership level

7. Be prepared to walk away from a deal that does not show potential

8. Choose strategic moves that strengthen the company

9. Seek out attractive targets in alignment with the deal rationale

10. Consider the limitations of valuation methodologies

11. Pay the right price

12. Do your homework with the best available information

13. Promote the deal rationale from first contact

14. Know the seller's intents

15. Pursue tough but fair discussion criteria

16. Assess the quality of the target's management

17. Verify that synergies will result in real value

18. Develop a clear M&A business case

19. Align the two businesses based on sources of value

20. Conduct a timely and effective due diligence

21. Assume nothing

22. Evaluate and assess cultural dissimilarities

23. Utilize the power of the information technology to accelerate the due diligence process

24. Know the added risks of cross-border mergers and acquisitions

25. Name an integration manager at the time of the announcement

26. Develop detailed integration plans prior to the closing

27. Retain the best people by treating them as the company's most valuable asset

28. Maintain a strong focus on customers

29. Transition to an integrated management team quickly

30. Maintain a fast integration tempo

31. Communicate the integration priorities

32. Define a common operating philosophy and consistent practices

33. Realize M&A deal benefits tangibly and in a timely manner

34. Tie employee incentives to synergy realization and to the fulfillment of integration requirements

35. Develop in-house M&A skills

Part 1

Getting Started

CHAPTER 1

MANAGING THE ELEMENT OF CHANCE

Success Factors:
- Measure M&A success based on the creation of competitive advantage and real shareholder value
- Gain insights into industry challenges and future trends before pursuing a deal
- Pass up acquisitions in non-related businesses

Two questions should immediately grab our attention within the discussion of M&As: that is, what drives companies to engage in M&A deals, and what are the odds that a particular M&A deal will bring success? It is noteworthy to remember at first that every M&A deal is different. Deals differ by the circumstances driving them, the deal-making environment surrounding them, and the motivations of the managers and decision makers involved. Because of the variance in factors, success in mergers and acquisitions[1] is certainly not guaranteed; however, the success of a merger and acquisition is also not a matter of chance. Management and private owners of firms undertaking mergers and acquisitions do indeed have a number of levers at their disposal that they can use to affect the outcome of and realize the value in their deal.

The debate about whether or not mergers and acquisitions should be considered as a strategic option for creating real shareholder value has a long history. From the vantage point of those who believe in simply sticking to a basic business model that attains growth through organic means, M&A deals are best avoided. M&A deals, from this perspective, cause a disruption to ongoing business and consume huge amounts of energy, especially during the integration activities. M&A deals, in this respect, can distract companies from paying attention to customer needs, competitor moves, and evolving trends, thus increasing the risk of declining shareholder value.

On the other hand, few American corporations have grown to occupy an industry leadership position without undertaking mergers and acquisitions. At any given point in time, a large percentage of growth-oriented companies in the U.S. are considering mergers and acquisitions as a means for attaining growth[2]. One major concern about M&A deals for companies stems from what is called the 'mega deal syndrome' — which is a firm's sole dependence on one large M&A deal that is pursued with the hope that it will overcome all future challenges and provide the firm with all it needs to attain its growth objectives. A successful growth firm, by contrast, will keep a diversified portfolio of growth opportunities and an internal growth engine so that it is not wholly dependent on the mega promises of an M&A deal. In either case, a company properly attuned to various opportunities for continued growth will have carefully considered the various strategic options and their own potential for M&A deals.

FRAMING THE DEBATE: MERGER OF HEWLETT-PACKARD COMPANY AND COMPAQ COMPUTER CORPORATION

The deal between Hewlett-Packard Company and Compaq Computer Corporation is a good place to begin the M&A debate as it highlights the cases both in favor of and against M&A deals. The deal between these two corporations set up one of the greatest proxy fights within any industry. In September 2001, the management of the two companies announced their merger agreement to form a global diversified technology company. The mutual goal of H-P and Compaq was to provide a wide range of technology products and services to both businesses and consumers. The merged entity would become the industry leader in diverse areas of technology, including imaging and printing, servers, personal computers, and handheld devices. Soon after the deal announcement, Walter Hewlett, an activist H-P board member and son of H-P's late co-founder William Hewlett, took the unusually strong step of opposing the deal by filing a proxy. Mr. Hewlett was joined in his opposition by members of the family foundation and co-founder David Packard.

In M&A deals between publicly traded corporations, both the Board of Directors and the majority of the two firms' shareholders must approve the deal. Reaching out directly to the shareholders, the proxy asks them to cast their vote in favor of or against the deal. H-P and Compaq management teams, led by H-P CEO Carly Fiorina, decided to move ahead with the deal despite the opposition. The management, as a result, engaged in the proxy fight by working to convince investors of the positive aspects of the M&A deal. In a similar fashion, those opposing the deal met with major shareholders in order to emphasize the drawbacks of the M&A to win support for a rejection of the deal. The battle therefore took shape around the different visions H-P management and Mr. Hewlett had for H-P and the perceived risks that would be associated with such a large 'mega' deal. The Hewlett and Packard family foundation members' main concern was whether Compaq would in fact create additional value through the combination over and above the value of H-P as a stand-alone company.

THE CASE AGAINST THE MERGER

Those who opposed the deal raised concerns that previous high-technology mergers had not generally been successful and that melding two technology companies had proven difficult at best. They drew on failed examples from the recent experience of both companies: H-P's deal with Apollo Computer Inc. and Compaq's deal with Digital Equipment Corporation. The opposition specifically based its position on arguments drawn from the factors that follow. H-P's crown jewel, subsequently the center of the proxy battle, was the highly profitable imaging and printing business, which delivered the majority of H-P's profits. The deal making effort and its ensuing integration, as well as placing greater emphasis on the PC business, would distract management from running its core businesses and focusing on their future growth. The integration of the two technology giants would require a huge effort, and the cultural differences between the companies would increase the risk of failure for the deal significantly. H-P had only mixed experience with major change efforts, and so it remained unclear whether the company could pull off such a merger. H-P also at the time had a strong and ingrained culture, which had become known for its bureaucratic and slow decision-making. In addition, the two companies had been rivals for years, and now their employees would be expected to work side-by-side. These complications and others, it was argued, would therefore hamper the potential for success in the merger.

Neither company was considered completely healthy though, and both companies were struggling with internal restructuring efforts. Compaq's business outlook was lagging, and H-P suffered from product delays. What the deal with Compaq certainly would do is increase the combined entity's share of the very competitive, lower-growth, and low-profit personal computer market. But this new exposure would also dilute the value of H-P's imaging and printing business while increasing H-P's business risk. H-P's return on capital would diminish because the combination would not significantly strengthen H-P's market position in the more profitable and growing high-end servers and services business, and the deal could potentially cause concern for customers about product discontinuities, and some might defect to competitors. Therefore, the question became whether H-P would in the end be paying too much for the deal.

The immediate way to avoid these potential problems, according to those who opposed the merger, was for H-P to refocus its efforts on fixing its own business and rejuvenating itself through the more traditional means of focusing on people, creativity, and technical innovation. These arguments against the merger received an additional boost when the H-P stock price rose as the media became aware of the opposition and Standard & Poor's lowered H-P's credit rating in anticipation of the deal risks.

THE CASE FOR THE MERGER

H-P management, though, believed that the H-P-Compaq deal was necessary since the high-technology industry's growth rate had been diminishing, and the industry needed to consolidate. By reacting to these trends early enough, the deal could create a major force in the industry. Management attributed H-P's performance issues to a more general economic malaise. They believed that the deal would ultimately leverage H-P's current business and make inroads into new markets. Management's position was based upon arguments drawn from the following points.

The deal would provide H-P with a more balanced portfolio of products by expanding both the profitable servers-and-storage-devices and consulting-and-services businesses. H-P and Compaq, in this regard, could compete better by leveraging their common strategies and capabilities against IBM and other key industry players. The deal would supply the combined company with an increased production capacity along with better service and support in the personal computer business to compete better against industry leader Dell. Compaq's personal computer and software businesses would, in turn, also benefit H-P's printer and imaging unit. The deal would offer $2.5 billion in synergy opportunities, resulting from cost savings and job reductions, which would then increase earnings and boost H-P's post-merger share price.

In anticipation of the time and effort necessary to integrate the two company cultures, to coordinate staff, and consolidate product lines, detailed integration plans were developed and integration teams were formed. In January 2002, the Commission of the European Communities cleared the deal, and in early March 2002, the U.S. Federal Trade Commission closed its investigation of the proposed merger and imposed no restrictions on the deal. As added support, the Institutional Shareholder Services recommended support for the deal, all of which combined to strengthen the position of management.

THE OUTCOME OF THE PROXY BATTLE

In March 2002, the investors narrowly approved the management plan for the merger, tacitly agreeing that the growth opportunities would override the added risks of integration. Investors at the time also expressed concern about the ensuing effects of uncertainties on both H-P and Compaq if the deal were to fall through. The eight-month proxy battle cost over a quarter of a billion dollars. The CEOs of H-P and Compaq were drawn away from their primary responsibilities of taking care of customers and preparing for integration as they concentrated their efforts on gathering support for their case. All stakeholders were affected by the protracted nature of the proxy battle. Many day-to-day executive tasks had to be delegated to others, and employee productivity suffered as individuals became preoccupied with the complications of the deal and its potential to result in significant changes and job losses. The anxiety over the merger trickled down even to customers, some of whom became concerned with the future of the company's products, which sometimes caused a delay in purchases or defection to competitors.

A positive outcome of the proxy battle was that management had commissioned integration teams to develop more detailed plans that would address the cultural and organizational challenges, resulting from the integration of the two companies. In April 2002, before closing the deal H-P named 150 senior managers from both companies to executive positions. Once the deal was closed in May 2002, H-P attempted to move forward by focusing once more on employees, customers, partners, and investors. Management could now implement integration plans, which included: discontinuing some product lines, cutting jobs, eliminating redundant office space, leveraging purchasing, repairing customer confidence, and calming employees in order to restore productivity. As a result, management was able to communicate more clearly with customers, employees, and industry partners about the future direction of the combined entity. To this end, more high and mid-level managers were appointed, and large groups of managers were brought together to learn about each other's culture.

The detailed planning combined with the fast pace of its execution helped H-P exceed its cost reduction synergy targets by trimming $3.5 billion from the costs. Over the next few quarters, H-P's overall performance was affected by the slowdown in technology spending as well as by an overall hi-tech industry slowdown. Looking back at the merger over two and a half years after its completion shows that the advantages of size have not yet paid off to the level that H-P's investors had hoped they would. Today, the printing and imaging business is still the crown jewel of the company and generates the vast majority of its profits. There are now calls by some industry experts and institutional investors for H-P to spin the unit off as a stand-alone business because it is still not clear that the other parts of the business are sufficiently generating network synergies by being a part of the technology conglomerate. Main competitors, Dell and IBM, are continuing to outperform H-P. Dell, with its direct sales, is the number one PC maker, and IBM recently spun off its low margin PC business to Lenovo, China's leading computer maker, so that it could focus on higher growth technologies.

Carly Fiorina, H-P's CEO, continued to believe that the size of H-P would allow it to compete in the converging technology arena, in part because its cash flows would allow the firm to continue funding its growing businesses. She even had her eye on further acquisitions to strengthen the higher margin businesses such as software and services. In February 2005, though, Carly Fiorina was ousted from her job by the board of H-P, and it still appears that the deal's ultimate success is a matter of debate. Such an example illustrates many of the main stakes involved in evaluating a certain company's potential risks in M&A deals, while also highlighting certain key factors that one should look for when considering moving forward on an M&A. It is for this reason that looking briefly at the H-P example will provide a general reference point for the specifics in the discussion of M&A success factors.

SUCCESS FACTOR #1

MEASURE M&A SUCCESS BASED ON THE CREATION OF COMPETITIVE ADVANTAGE AND REAL SHAREHOLDER VALUE

A variety of metrics are used to gauge the success of mergers and acquisitions, and each acquirer may apply its own set of success criteria to its M&A deal. Although an M&A deal may enable the firm to survive and take part in the uncertain future of a changing industry, survival cannot be the only measure of deal success. The owner and shareholder expectations extend beyond mere survival: the owners and shareholders of the acquiring firm expect to realize value from the acquisition in line with industry performance and other key competitors. The combined entity should demonstrate that it has the potential to create value when compared to its industry competitors and to broader market indices. If this were not the case, then the investors could simply diversify their own portfolios. Studies conducted by researchers along with major consulting and accounting firms have found that the majority of acquisitions do not create significant new value for the acquirers. These studies in general show that chances of M&A success are about even—no better than a coin toss. Over time, about one half of the deals fail to meet expectations concerning return on capital invested and end up destroying value.

Despite these less than favorable odds, pursuing success in mergers and acquisitions should not be reduced simply to a coin toss or a game of chance. Unlike a coin toss where, after the initial flip, the outcome is inevitable, throughout the merger process, the management of a firm can intervene and undertake actions in target selection, valuation, and negotiations that will enhance the chances of deal success and influence the outcome in their favor. Management can acquire and use good information continually to estimate the deal outcome and re-evaluate the deal value and other deal criteria throughout the M&A process. In an M&A deal, the seller has asymmetric knowledge about its own firm and can use this knowledge-advantage to gain most of the value created by the deal. As the M&A deal moves forward, though, the acquirer is constantly learning and analyzing new information about its target, and may uncover new surprises in the target's business such as hidden liabilities, environmental issues, or unusual business practices. Assumptions made at an earlier stage about the M&A business case may prove to be incorrect or biased, providing acquiring managers with a fresh understanding of the risks at hand who can re-evaluate their chances of getting a successful deal. Subsequently, the acquirer can modify its approach to valuation and negotiations, which may help turn the outcome of the deal into a more favorable direction; or it may be that the acquirer will choose to stop the deal if it is seen that the outcomes will not meet expectations. Since the acquirer must gain the seller's assent to reach a friendly deal, an assertive yet patient seller with an attractive business model and sources of strategic value can wait for a price and terms that will be most advantageous. When the acquirer succeeds at closing the deal, but does so by giving away so much value that its future becomes uncertain and its shareholders are threatened with lost value, it has suffered the winner's curse. While it is true that withdrawing from the M&A deal also has associated costs, one should bear in mind that the costs of withdrawing could in the end be less than the costs of a failed deal. Therefore, from the deal maker's vantage point, simply closing the deal cannot be the primary measure of success because closing a poor deal will certainly result in destruction of shareholder value. For these cautionary reasons, thus, a universal measure of M&A deal success should be the attainment of competitive advantage and a higher economic profitability over and above the acquirer's base performance as a stand-alone entity.

CONSIDER ALL STAKEHOLDERS

Multiple stakeholders—shareholders, employees, customers, and suppliers to say the very least—are affected by a merger or acquisition. Each of these groups has its own interest in mind, and so naturally measures deal success by its own criteria. Management, in order to evaluate properly the M&A, must be attuned to the perspectives of these various stakeholders and address them both during the lead-up to the deal and also once the deal is underway. What follows, then, is a short consideration of the particular interests of the main players and stakeholders in an M&A as factors to be weighed carefully by management.

Acquiring CEOs wish to see their companies grow and prosper; they perceive mergers and acquisitions as a way to achieve a desired end. For the acquirer's **owners and shareholders**, the goal is to get an attractive return on investment in the form of dividends and to realize an appreciation in the value of the firm and the price of the security. The shareholders assert their considerable influence in that they must approve the deal in a publicly traded firm. Generally, most owners and shareholders take a long term view by looking at sustainable growth for their investments, which would encourage shareholders to maintain or increase their investment in the company.

Creditors look for the ability of the firm to generate stable cash flows without any additional risk of default. For a company in Chapter 11 bankruptcy, the deal must be adequately financed and the creditors should do at least as well with a deal as they would if the company's assets were liquidated. The alternative for the creditors would be to auction off the company or to wait and see if an alternate suitor will emerge.

The **customers** desire, first and foremost, a reliable and stable source for their needs. They expect to receive added benefits from the M&A deal through lower costs, broader product and service offerings, and higher quality. Customers might worry that the resulting entity from an M&A will obtain more bargaining power after the deal to squeeze the customer margins or to reduce the ease of purchase by discontinuing certain products.

Suppliers want to receive payments during the M&A process, and wish to continue and even expand their relationship with the combined entity. In a merger or acquisition situation, any given supplier may be in danger of losing a long-standing strategic partnership. For some suppliers, these relationships have been their main source of survival; therefore, some suppliers might begin to worry that the combined entity may consolidate its supplier list. Suppliers are wary that the new entity may obtain a more concentrated buying power and be capable of dictating new terms of the future relationship.

The desired outcomes for **employees** are stable employment, opportunities for career advancement, and better pay and benefits. Employees are, for these reasons, usually enthusiastic about a merger upon its announcement because it might promise greater opportunities and rewards for them just as it does for the growth of the resulting company. However, many employees might also become distracted as they worry about potential job cuts, new uncertainties about career advancement, the loss of personal networks, and working for a new boss. Employees will likewise become anxious about the possibility of relocating if a facility is made redundant and learning the new procedures and processes of the resulting culture. These concerns are at their height during the integration phase as the reality of the merger begins to affect the day-to-day work environment.

Competitors look to exploit any perceived weaknesses or opportunities for their own benefit. If the acquirer takes its eyes off the customers during the intense period of a merger or acquisition, it may become vulnerable to its competitors through discontinuous levels of service and product offerings. When an M&A is in the works, savvy industry competitors will execute their own strategies in order to respond with their own deal activity. It is common to see a cluster of M&A activities occurring in one industry as it consolidates. Management therefore should consider the impact of the deal on the competitive landscape in the industry by asking: how will competitors respond and retaliate with their own deals, or how might the deal lower the barriers of entry for new and nimble competitors. Competition factors for this reason should be a key concern; and, if one considers the reach of global deals, which comprise additional stakeholders in international equity markets in countries that the firm will operate, the competitive complexities are increased even more.

SUCCESS FACTOR #2

GAIN INSIGHTS INTO INDUSTRY CHALLENGES AND FUTURE TRENDS BEFORE PURSUING A DEAL

A firm that wants to maintain its long term profitability must gain knowledge and insights into the future changes that can affect the industry and its competitive structure, its growth potential, and regional and global market changes—the evolution of customer needs as well as the future requirements for winning in the marketplace. It is important in this respect to study the emerging and evolving trends along with their pace of development, which includes consideration of these trends: macroeconomic, political and geopolitical, industry and competitive, demographic, societal and social, technological, and legal and regulatory. Such an evaluation can help the firm gain a better understating of the future, realistic strategic options that it can pursue.[3]

In an M&A deal, the target and the acquirer should hold common assumptions about how future events will shape their business and the industry at large. These assumptions about the future will affect the direction of the business (its vision, strategic decisions, research and development), and its practices (its operating philosophy, allocation of resources, and the rate of technology adoption). If the two parties in the deal diverge in assumptions about the future then they will have a hard time reaching alignment around key objectives and their leadership teams will likely clash on key decisions and time will be lost. Such delays will prove a hindrance to moving the business along effectively, as there will be more difficulty in decision making about synergy realization and business direction. This will end up complicating business trajectories to say the least, but more often than not, it will end up destroying value. A lack of real alignment at the leadership team level sends mixed messages to the organization and confuses the employees. So it is crucial to focus on shared assumptions about the future because they will in the end enhance the strategic fit and facilitate the coordination of goals, the development of business priorities, and the exchange of know-how.

A leadership team with drive and initiative, which is also wary of the dangers discussed above, sets challenging and motivating goals for the organization based upon a combination of creative insights and good judgment. Enterprising objectives that create an atmosphere of aspiration also challenge the status quo, and therefore they demand the thoughtful alignment and commitment of the organization. Management's role in all of this is to set the objectives and to communicate them broadly in order to gain a common understanding as well as commitment from key resources towards a timely implementation. It is important, though, to note that some employees inside the firm will resist ambitious objectives by labeling them as unrealistic and undoable. The role of the leadership team is to overcome such resistance through counter arguments, by emphasizing the positive aspects of the objectives. Leaders can best achieve a buy-in by demonstrating personal commitment and communicating a consistent message. They must, in a productive way, challenge the employees to live up to that vision. Bringing everyone on board with such a forward-looking vision, along with the required critical mass (potentially gained through mergers and acquisitions), a strong commitment to the stated business objectives, and with discipline and tenacity during the implementation will help management achieve and maintain a strong industry position. The deal maker needs to have a solid understanding of the future trends while also appraising their impact on the M&A deal's ability to create sustainable value and a competitive edge.

Effect of Economic Cycles on the Rate of M&A Activity

From the early twentieth century to current times, the pace of merger and acquisition deal making showed cycles of high and moderate activity. During the nineties, which was called the "deal decade", a record number of mergers and acquisitions were struck, coinciding with a steadily growing economy. In the United States, these growing trends culminated in the year 1999, when the value of announced deals exceeded $1.5 trillion. After this peak, though, the bursting of the high-tech bubble, coupled with an overall slowdown in economic activity and the emergence of new geopolitical uncertainties, brought dramatic changes to the M&A climate. The period running from the end of 2000 to the second half of 2003 was marked accordingly by a slowdown in the rate of mergers and acquisitions. M&A deals during this time were noticeably absent from news headlines. Both the number of and also the value of M&A deal announcements dropped significantly. Yet with the rebound of certain economic fundamentals, this brief but deep slowdown once again gave way to a more robust deal-friendly environment. Deal makers are now returning to the scene, and M&A deals are again considered to be key strategic tools for growth. Firms are undertaking M&A deals in pursuit of larger size, broader product portfolios, entry into new markets domestically and globally, and in response to the pressures of global competition. Today, there is frequent M&A deal activity across multiple industries; it recurs in the field of financial services, healthcare, consumer products, airlines, high technology, telecommunications, manufacturing, and so on. As M&A activity picks up, the pressure will mount for those sitting on the sidelines to push for deals of their own, and what might typically be self-control may give way to sense of urgency about joining the ranks of the deal makers.

The number of deals that are inked each year is affected by the inherent risks involved with particular economic cycles. An unfavorable economic outlook and uncertainties about the future depress the pace of M&A deals. Corporate leaders tend to keep their capital in the company's coffers, or they distribute their cash in the form of dividends and focus on enhancing the business fundamentals of the company. Depressed equity markets and high interest rates limit the acquirer's access to needed funds, and so most corporate leaders avoid mergers and acquisitions even though in the unfavorable climate lower valuations may make the targets more affordable. Shrewd acquirers who engage in M&A deals during this period of uncertainty tend to negotiate harder and are quicker to abandon a weak deal.

In similar fashion, the target's board and management receptivity towards an acquisition is impacted by the conditions of the industry and the marketplace as well as by the target's security valuation and its business performance. When sellers find the valuations less than to their liking and the rigorous bargaining too cumbersome, they are more likely to reject offers. In such situations, they will likely maintain their independence if they can afford to and focus on improving the business performance of their firm. A high security valuation then is the strongest deterrent against becoming a takeover target.

In terms of the alternative picture, a strengthening economy and a favorable economic outlook create optimism and trust in fundamentals as earnings get back on track and the stock market rises. In this climate, corporate executives gain more confidence about the future and are more willing to take on M&A deals. Mounting stock market valuations can offer buyers and sellers a stronger hand with which they can make deals. Buyers have access to more capital from their rising equity values, and sellers have more bidding suitors to drive up the price of the deal.

Boards and managers today are also learning more about the effect of the Sarbanes-Oxley Act of 2003 and other corporate governance requirements on merger and acquisition deals. Corporate governance reforms and personal liabilities have driven the boards to scrutinize targets more closely for signs of regulatory compliance, lawsuits, and any problems in financial reporting.

The final point to keep in mind here then is that history has repeatedly demonstrated that despite variations in the pace of M&A deal activity, major acquisitions continue to occur every year. CEOs continue to see mergers and acquisitions as a key instrument in gaining competitive advantage and creating sustainable shareholder value. So it remains important that deal makers take into account the lessons of various economic cycles and the favorability of prevailing and future economic conditions in terms of how they might advantageously position an M&A deal for value creation.

SUCCESS FACTOR #3

PASS UP ACQUISITIONS IN NON-RELATED BUSINESSES

Companies that have diversified into unrelated businesses have not succeeded historically on a broad scale due to the fleeting nature of a key ingredient: the realization of network synergies achieved from disparate parts of the combined business. Studies show that horizontal acquisitions[4] perform better than acquisitions in unrelated businesses. Diversified companies were in vogue during the merger wave of the nineteen sixties, and periods of high and low inflation and unpredictable economic cycles, combined with the need for a stable and predictable cash flow to fund growth activities, had compelled management to diversify by bringing cyclical and counter-cyclical businesses together in order to balance out the unpredictability. In these diversified businesses, management teams must extend their management competencies across multiple industries and gain network synergies from a range of unrelated businesses. Many of these diversifications were for this reason later reversed. For example, USX Corporation acquired Marathon Oil Company to balance the cyclical trends in the steel industry with oil, but the acquisition was reversed in 2001, leaving the steel business vulnerable to global competition. Network synergies rarely materialize in these kinds of conglomerates comprised of unrelated businesses, and without the realization of network synergies, the shareholders are better off investing their own cash and diversifying their own portfolios of security holdings. General Electric has been a notable exception, demonstrating sustained earnings growth by gaining significant synergies between its diverse businesses.

Industry convergence appears on its surface to justify these acquisitions in unrelated businesses and brings the promise of great network synergies. The America Online Inc. and Time Warner deal was intended to lead an era of convergence between Internet and traditional media and entertainment businesses. The network synergies were expected to be realized from running the combined entity as an operating company with cross-cooperation between the divisions; the brand recognition and content of Time Warner, such as CNN News, could be delivered to the Internet and made available for AOL subscribers. Time Warner programming could, in turn, be promoted on the web, and Internet services could be neatly woven into the fabric of Time Warner's business. Deals justified based on such a need for industry convergence, tend on the whole to create a greater business complexity along with their diversity, and since the expected technological advances and customer interest and acceptance may be slow to develop, they have shown mixed success.

Some deals in unrelated businesses, however much they present certain risks, are an attractive option for some owners. In particular, when a firm is owned by an entrepreneur or a privately held firm, the owners may decide to diversify their portfolio of holdings through the acquisition of non-related businesses. Since the owners may have all or a major portion of their wealth in the company, they may want to diversify in order to reduce their risks of being exposed to a single line of business. Owners then should be thoughtful about these sorts of deals, and they must fully understand the industry and its success drivers for new businesses prior to undertaking any deals in unrelated industries.

NOTES

[1] Acquisition is defined as taking-over a company through purchasing a controlling stake of the target's shares. Merger is defined as combining two business entities when one entity acquires the net assets of the other and no new entity comes into being. Consolidation is combining two or more entities into the formation of a new corporate entity. Section 368 of Internal Revenue Code defines a statutory merger or consolidation when the surviving company inherits all the assets and liabilities of the target. In this book, mergers, acquisitions, and M&A deals are used interchangeably to refer to a business combination.

[2] As reported in *Quality* in April 1996, Coopers and Lybrand Trendsetter Barometer survey found that almost half of the U.S.'s growth companies are considering acquisitions seriously over the following three years.

[3] Sources for trends data include the Federal Reserve Bulletin and the Survey of the Current Business developed by the U.S. Department of Commerce.

[4] Horizontal deals take place in the same industry with a business similar to the acquirer's core business. Vertical acquisitions are with businesses up or down the value chain.

CHAPTER 2

MAKING VALUE-ADDED DECISIONS

> **Success Factors**
> - Understand the M&A process and clearly establish owners, deliverables, and timetables
> - Anticipate and focus on key M&A decisions
> - Drive every aspect of the M&A deal from senior leadership level
> - Be prepared to walk away from a deal that does not show potential

It is difficult to assign a definite starting or end point to the M&A process. Merger ideas may incubate for a long time before the conditions are ready for realization. Based on the degree of fit, consolidating two large entities can take months as companies struggle to achieve true integration. People in organizations that have undergone a merger or acquisition with significant cultural differences see themselves as members of one parent company or the other for years after the deal closes; thus the felt experience of an M&A continues long after the deal is made.

What remains definite, though, is that the M&A process involves a number of key decisions that come with highly interdependent outcomes. The M&A process starts with the acquirer's decision about whether to pursue a deal as a viable option for the attainment of its growth objectives. As it screens candidates, it should decide if it has identified potential candidates that would be a good fit. When involved in deal discussions, it should decide whether the two sides can reach an agreement on the price and terms of the deal and if it can close the deal and accept the associated deal risks. Finally the firm should decide if it is achieving the desired integration and expected deal synergy benefits or if it needs to make course corrections. The quality of decision outcomes depends on the acquirer's knowledge about the industry, its ability to gather reliable information about the target, defining clear roles in the decision process for key players, and reaching clear decision criteria. Time pressures, the lack of good information, and conflicting personalities are all factors that can affect the decision process negatively. Senior leadership's visible commitment and direction is necessary at each step of the deal process; they should also be prepared to walk away from an M&A deal that does not show potential for value creation based on its price and risks. A thorough understanding of the M&A process and its underlying deal drivers therefore will reduce these uncertainties, will enhance decision outcomes, and will improve the chances that the acquirer may create value.

This chapter will, along these lines, review the M&A process and its intermittent key decision nodes while presenting suggestions for enhancing M&A decision quality.

SUCCESS FACTOR #4

UNDERSTAND THE M&A PROCESS AND CLEARLY ESTABLISH OWNERS, DELIVERABLES, AND TIMETABLES

The merger or acquisition process consists of five steps and five key decision nodes. The steps in the M&A process are depicted in figure 1. A detailed description of each M&A process step and its key decision node follows. The remainder of this book covers the salient elements of the M&A process in more detail, moving from a basic awareness of general issues affecting an M&A to a more specific discussion of how this understanding begins to be implemented in a high quality decision-making process for management.

STEP 1. DEFINING A VISION AND STRATEGY FOR GROWTH

The M&A process commences in the defining of a vision and strategy for growth. Here, the leadership's insights and aspirations combine with a sober understanding of future trends to set the firm's vision and objectives

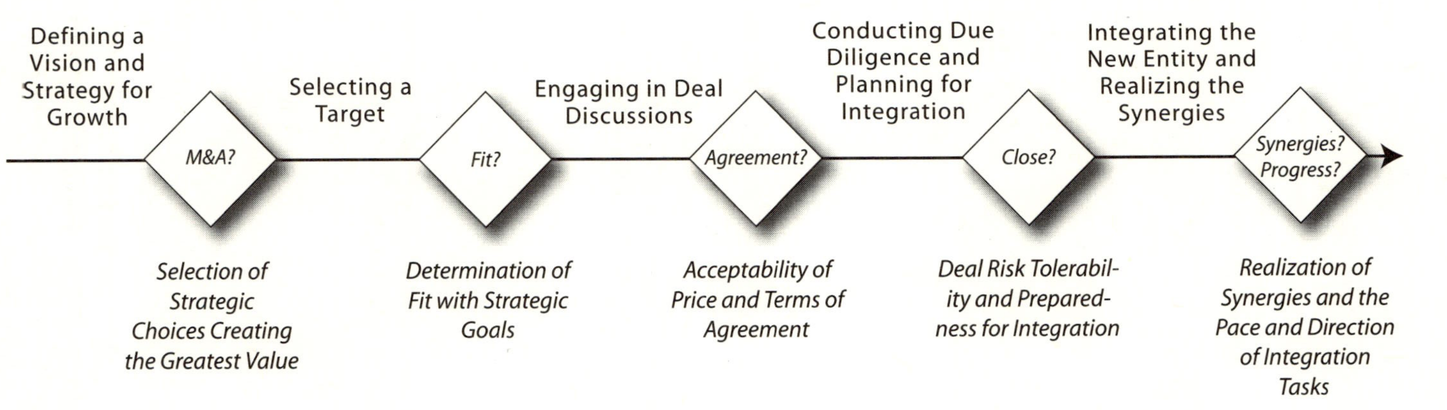

Figure 1. The M&A Process

as guideposts for future success. To achieve its objectives, then, the firm will devise a strategy to overcome its performance gap between the desired future state and its current state. The firm's strategic options may include mergers and acquisitions. Firms at such times may also pursue costs restructuring and divest themselves of non-core businesses that no longer fit into their long-term strategy, or they may spin off businesses in initial public offerings in order to capture their fundamental value. The firm's ability to realize value in this way depends upon its capability to carry out and implement effectively such a strategy and vision.

DECISION NODE 1. SELECTION OF STRATEGIC CHOICES CREATING THE HIGHEST VALUE

Initially, the firm's key decision is to choose a suitable combination of strategic options to pursue. Its strategic options include: internal growth initiatives, joint ventures, partnerships, alliances, and licensing. It can also pursue mergers and acquisitions concerning whole or parts of a company. The pursuit of each strategic option requires a sufficient amount of funds and effort, and it also involves certain risks. If the decision makers conclude that it would be too complex or that it would take too long to achieve the firm's strategic objectives and close the strategic gap through the implementation of internal initiatives, then mergers and acquisitions are a viable option for the firm to gain access to the resources that offer particular advantages for a company at various times, including quick access to size, a new national and global market share, access to new brands and services, and getting a foothold in growth businesses as a base for its own growth. The overall decision making outcome and its implementation will become the firm's primary strategic framework for the realization of its growth objectives.

STEP 2. SELECTING A TARGET

If the firm decides to pursue mergers and acquisitions, it needs a list of candidates, candidate profiles, and screening criteria for identifying a good fit. The list of candidates is compiled from external and internal sources. The target selection criteria for identifying a good fit are defined by the senior leadership in alignment with the requirements of the firm's strategic framework and the deal rationale. Each M&A candidate is investigated in detail, and a profile, along with an initial business case, is developed for those candidates under serious consideration.

DECISION NODE 2. DETERMINATION OF FIT WITH STRATEGIC GOALS

The screening of acquisition candidates is done iteratively, resulting in a shortlist of candidates. Through its list of candidates, the acquirer is looking for its needed strategic capabilities that may be acquired through an acquisition. Strategic, synergy, and integration criteria are all used to determine the degree of fit with the acquirer's gap closing needs. Strategic criteria include the size, profitability, the asking price, and the return on investment from the deal. Synergies result from this compatibility between the acquirer's and target's business drivers and the improvements in overall business performance. The level of complexity associated with the integration of the two entities and the impact of the M&A deal on customers are part of the selection criteria.

STEP 3. ENGAGING IN DEAL DISCUSSIONS

The acquirer approaches the firms on its shortlist of candidates to determine the feasibility of making a deal. Once the target is amenable to further pursuit of the deal, the acquirer conducts an initial high level due diligence involving various facets of the target's business as it negotiates the terms and conditions of the M&A agreement, including the price.

DECISION NODE 3. ACCEPTABILITY OF PRICE AND TERMS OF AGREEMENT

The goals of acquirer and target diverge in deal discussions: the acquirer's goal is to arrive at mutually acceptable terms that would create value for its owners and shareholders while the target's objective is to capture as much of the value for itself. Both sides have to decide whether they can accept the deal and the terms of the agreement, or if they will abandon the deal. In publicly held companies, the board of directors and the shareholders of both companies must approve the deal. Deciding upon approving such a deal involves asking questions about the fit of the deal and the degree of risk involved considering the time required for integration, the deal's complexity, the deal price, and its financial structure. The M&A agreement contains all of the terms of the transaction: its closing requirements, its timing, the articles of incorporation, the directors and officers of the new entity, how the securities will be exchanged or converted, how to handle employee stock options, agreements on promotion of products, and warranties and representations. Once the two sides agree to the deal they announce it to the outside world. Prior to the announcement, the two sides should determine a communication strategy and name an integration manager.

STEP 4. CONDUCTING DUE DILIGENCE AND PLANNING FOR INTEGRATION

The acquirer must inquire as to the soundness of the target's business and must consider its own assumptions about the target's fit, its potential for value creation, and the accuracy of warranties and representations made in the M&A agreement. The acquirer must also investigate the various aspects of the target's business including: financial, operational, supply chain, legal, regulatory compliance, environmental, customers, markets, technology, human resources, and management quality. It should also assess the target's culture and the availability, magnitude, and timing of synergies, as well as the ease of integration. The role of the integration manager in all of this is to develop detailed transition and integration plans in conjunction with the due diligence teams.

DECISION NODE 4. DEAL RISK TOLERABILITY

If the acquirer uncovers unexpected practices or unrealistic assumptions based on the due diligence investigations that would affect the deal value, then the acquirer must consider whether the risks posed by the deal can be accepted. The acquirer can at this point decide to close the deal and accept all risks, or to close the deal only under certain conditions, which may include the transference of some risks to the target, adjustment of deal price commensurate with deal risks, or it may finally decide to abandon the deal outright and simply pay the termination fees.

STEP 5. INTEGRATING THE NEW ENTITY AND REALIZING THE SYNERGIES

If the deal closes, the goal of the acquirer must be to implement its transition and integration plans in a prompt and efficient manner. The acquirer needs to move rapidly with a sense of urgency so that the new entity may soon be up and running, capturing the deal's expected synergy benefits. The acquirer should implement a disciplined program management, regular reviews and lookbacks, and synergy realization tracking and reporting. It is important then that its leadership must be visibly committed to the integration success.

DECISION NODE 5. REALIZATION OF SYNERGIES AND THE PACE AND DIRECTION OF INTEGRATION TASKS

Leadership should also determine if the synergies are being achieved in a timely manner and are having a direct effect on the bottom-line. At this point, it can be determined whether or not additional actions are required to increase the scope and pace of the integration and the synergy realization activities. To meet the integration objectives, the leadership should decide on the effectiveness of the activities and the tempo of the integration. It may decide to apply additional resources or reprioritize in order to accelerate the tempo of integration.

THE M&A PROCESS steps and decision nodes are interdependent and decisions carry important consequences. The need for information grows as the process progresses and as a result some activities stretch through multiple steps. Figure 2 depicts some of the interdependencies of the M&A process viewed as a system.

The outcome of each step and its key decision node has a direct influence on future choices in the M&A process. When the acquirer defines its vision and growth strategy by deciding to pursue mergers and acquisitions, the outcome will drive the deal rationale, the criteria for identifying a good fit, and the sources of the deal value. The criteria for a good fit and the sources of the deal value creation, in turn, will affect the strategic value of a target for the acquirer as well as how the two entities will be aligned in terms of separation, sharing, and integration. Assumptions used in the deal valuation and in the business alignment determine the risks posed to the combined entity. The M&A business case impacts the due diligence requirements, the extent of the integration planning, and along with the degree of assimilation and sharing required, it affects the complexity of the integration phase.

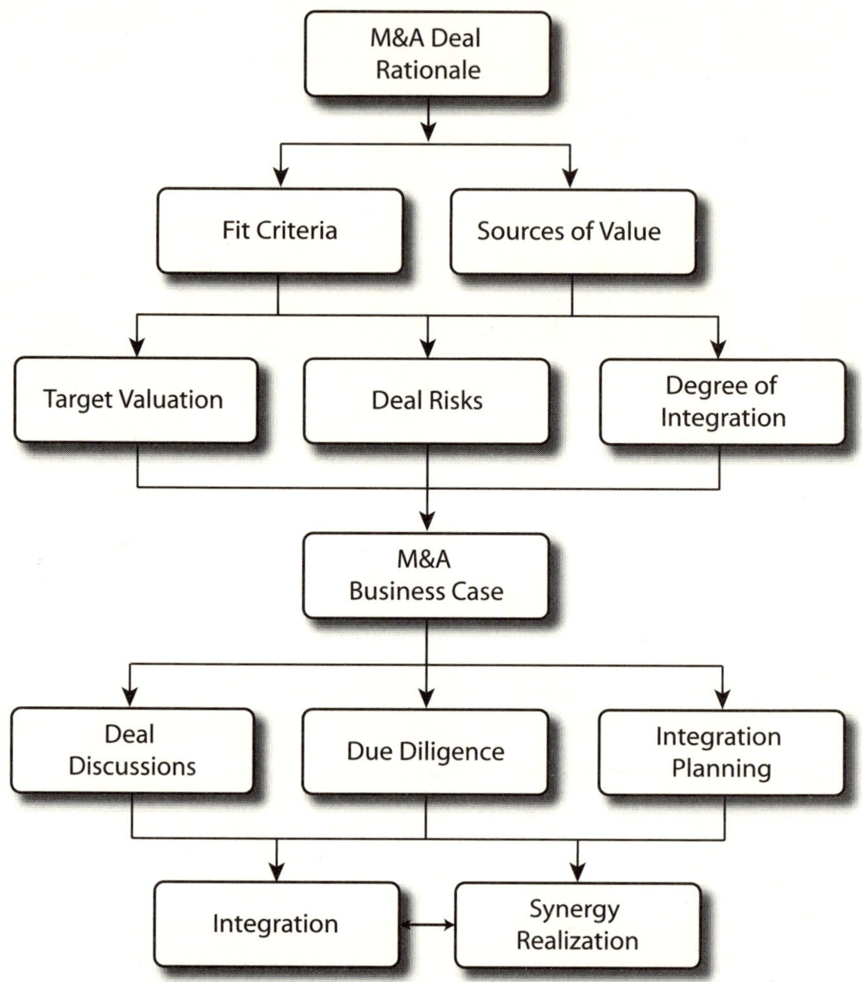

Figure 2. A System View of the M&A Process

As the deal progresses, the acquirer knowledge evolves about the target's business. Quality decision making requires that each succeeding key decision receives more refined information about the target. The timely availability of this needed information for the decision makers requires careful planning and personnel continuity in order to avoid unnecessary rework and in order to ensure that the information is relevant to the decision at hand.

Some of these activities extend over several of the M&A process steps.

Due diligence activities start as early as the time of the identification of an acquisition target. Data collection about the target's stability and integrity starts with review of external resources. After signing a confidentiality agreement, and with the target management's consent, the acquirer conducts a high level internal assessment of the target's business. After the M&A agreement and until closing, a detailed internal and external assessment of the target's business practices and organization takes place. Some due diligence activities may even continue after the closing. Similarly, the M&A business case, which documents estimations, assumptions, and valuation methodologies, underwrites deal discussions and the negotiation steps. The business case assumptions are likewise thoroughly examined during due diligence activities prior to close. After the close, the business case supports the integration planning, its goals, and all synergy realization activities. Activities such as senior leadership oversight, senior leadership decision making, customer management, and people management activities extend throughout the M&A process.

SUCCESS FACTOR #5

ANTICIPATE AND FOCUS ON KEY M&A DECISIONS

The goal of the leadership is first and foremost to make sensible decisions. In the M&A process, a key decision node is a critical juncture at which the decision owner, key analysts, and subject matter experts review the available information and conclusions about the deal in order to consider the implications of each alternative path forward. The success of the M&A deal depends on the quality of decisions made at each key decision node.[1] Quality M&A decision making requires clear roles and responsibilities, good planning for work activities, clearly articulated decision criteria, an understanding of underlying assumptions, reliable information, knowledge of the industry, and a continuity of personnel across decision nodes.

Considering the complexity of the decisions and the time constraints that go along with the M&A process, planning for and establishing certain responsibilities and timelines for activities such as data gathering, data analysis, risk based evaluation of decision criteria, recommendations for path forward, and decision making is critical. A decision owner is a senior leader (and may include his/her executive leadership team which constitute the final decision owners) who takes responsibility for each decision node, defines and prioritizes the decision criteria, has final accountability for making the decision, and so owns the decision results. The appropriate subject matter experts and analysts participate in a timely manner in order to support the decision owner define the process outcomes and decision criteria—as agents they collect and analyze all relevant data, present findings in a usable format, and, at times, they support the ensuing discussions and the decision making. Areas of needed expertise may include, but are not limited to: financial analysis, auditing, legal, manufacturing, human resources, tax laws, environmental regulations, contracting, cross-border legal and financial regulations, public relations, and communications. Many of these skills may be needed regardless of the size of the M&A deal.

Since there needs to be good information input into quality value-added decisions, the activities of each step are focused on identifying, compiling, and refining the necessary information and delivering it in a useful format so that it supports the decision owners. Each step in the M&A process starts with an understanding of the next key decision. By focusing all of the data gathering and analysis at each step of the process on the next decision node, one can ensure that the best use of decision owner's time is made. Understanding the decision criteria and the leadership's expectations before moving on, creates focus on key activities, reduces unnecessary activities, and diminishes the potential for rework that may delay the process. It should be noted, though, that a number of groups may work simultaneously on the M&A activities and will have to join their outputs together to present an integrated depiction of the results to the decision owner. Outside experts or other sources of information are additionally consulted for information gathering and a more objective analysis.

Expectations and criteria for decision making are based on their priority. Some criteria could become deal killers that may halt the process, and others may pose barriers that have to be overcome with innovative solutions. At the decision node, depending on how well the decision criteria are satisfied, the acquirer may decide to continue the deal process, abandon the deal entirely, repeat some analysis steps, delay making the deal, or change the scope of the deal.

In order to make quality decisions, managers must understand the underlying assumptions used for arriving at the recommendations presented by analysts and subject matter experts. To better understand the decision background, the decision owner must be presented with a discussion of assumptions used in the analysis alongside any potential risks posed by the deal prior to making a decision. Analysts and subject matter experts own the data that they use for their analysis and must understand the data's reliability and sources. They can then document and explain the assumptions made in the analysis. Appropriate and diverse perspectives should be provided for each key decision. To ensure a uniform understanding of the findings and to enhance the overall M&A decision quality, the analysts and the decision makers should review the following prior to arriving at a decision:

- Analysis assumptions.

- Sources, reliability, and the quality of data.

- Methodology used for the interpretation of data and baselines for quantitative analysis.

- Scenarios and alternatives considered.

- Key uncertainties and risks.

- The interdependencies between various parts of the target's business and their effect on the deal and post-deal integration.

It is critical that a continuity of oversight is maintained across all of the key M&A decision nodes. Changes in analysts and subject matter experts can cause hand-offs and reduce effective communication; this, in turn, can affect the overall efficiency of information gathering and analysis. People who have not been involved in the deal process or who are unfamiliar with decisions and activities in the previous steps would have to climb the learning curve and rework some of the analysis. Levels of accountability here can also become an issue. The continuity of key resources—particularly when moving from deal making into integration—is critical to the deal's success.

Wherever possible, decision needs should be prioritized prior to starting the activities in a step in the M&A process. Once a decision is made, the data gathering and analysis activities, timetables, and accountabilities for key players for the next step are established. After a decision is made, the subject matter experts and analysts review the decision making process and its effectiveness, and then they apply their learning to the next key decision.

Success in these terms is based on access to reliable, relevant, and timely information as well as on maintaining commitment to the deal's strategic objectives. As the deal progresses and as the acquirer makes new key decisions, additional time and resources are dedicated to the M&A deal. With the progressed commitment of personal time and the application of resources, making an M&A deal may appear inevitable. However, a time and resource commitment to the M&A process should not be confused with a commitment to closing the deal. The acquirer should consider these resources as sunk costs; it should abandon the deal at any time if the acquirer finds it to be no longer commercially viable or if the deal involves risks and complexities that could destroy long term value.

DON'T YIELD LONG-TERM VALUE

A senior executive at a major corporation who had recently masterminded the acquisition of a line of business from a competitor told me that he had made the go-ahead decision for the global acquisition because of a "gut feeling." The company had also followed a truncated M&A deal process, closing the deal after just a few weeks. He went on to explain that his company had sought to take the leading global position in this line of business (with products that were close to thirty years old) because they were committed to it strategically. At that time, the leadership team had been considering a major acquisition for the previous four to five years, and the senior executive had been in discussions with his counterparts in other companies over the years. When the other side was finally ready to sell out, he had seized the opportunity and with the blessing of the board, his company made an offer that it considered reasonable.

It is the quality of the decision-making that determines the acquirer's ability to realize long term value from mergers and acquisitions as well as their continued effects. Ineffective decision-making will undoubtedly result in the destruction of shareholder value. The acquirer in our story selected a target that appeared to be a good strategic fit at a high level; it was a U.S. company that was expanding globally. The target was a European company with facilities, people, and customers in Europe and Asia. Yet, the problem was that the acquirer was working from an outdated mindset. The product line was old and was under attack from new product substitutes, with barriers to entry getting lower as emerging economies began to acquire the technology. The deal valuation was based on a set of high-level assumptions, and the deal benefits were poorly understood. The acquirer for this reason was overly optimistic about the magnitude of the synergies that could be created from the deal, and thus it paid an excessive deal premium. The due diligence activities focused on the financial aspects of the business along with a few site visits. Because of an incomplete due diligence, the acquirer failed to uncover the hidden financial, operational, and human resource risks: issues with target's distribution network, the condition of plant and equipment starved for investment and plagued with quality issues, highly unprofitable customers, organizational culture differences, and differences in national regulations affecting various aspects of the business given their international locations.

The acquirer, though, did not sufficiently plan for integration and underestimated the difficulties that would be faced in the integration process. After the close, the challenges posed by differing applications of technology, difficulties merging IT systems, different accounting practices, challenges in implementing change, and barriers to cost management bogged integration down. In the end, some of the plants had to be shut down since the management had not expected the level of complexity that the integration would create. The achievement of desired synergies, expected to be over one hundred and fifty million dollars, was delayed for years in some cases. Thus, the acquirer never realized the value expected from the deal because there was the assumption that it would be a walk in the park. Those who were making the deal were of the mindset that they could treat the merger as an event rather than as a process; they had rushed through the process and pushed forward to close the deal so that they could then get on with the usual business of managing budgets, people, and customers. This sort of thinking in the M&A process proves risky and will likely lead to significant problems, as it did in this case.

THERE ARE NUMEROUS barriers to quality decision-making and no shortcuts. Poor decision making can generally explain much of the variance between the intended objectives of the M&A deal and the actual end results of the deal. The M&A process is shrouded in uncertain and ambiguous circumstances that create decision timetables that may unpredictably fluctuate. Changes in the acquirer's or target's business performance, security valuation, overall market conditions, breaking media stories, the threat of litigation, or the entry of new suitors represent just a few of these variable circumstances. Complex and time-sensitive M&A decisions require good information, input from specialist experts, and strong management judgment. Each decision has the potential to create or destroy value. Under time pressures, the decision makers may be tempted to arrive at key decisions with whatever information is immediately at hand—not taking the requisite care to make more thoughtful decisions about the process.

Throughout the M&A process, information about the target company and its business practices may be difficult to find or may remain incomplete, and the acquirer may at this point have to rely on the target's management or on third party sources for information. With incomplete or unreliable information and limited resources, a systematic, data driven decision process may be discarded as too time-consuming, too information-intensive, and too involved. It is at such moments, as shown in the previous story, that managers may be tempted to revert more so to intuition, and rely upon past knowledge and gut feelings to make key decisions. Such modes of decision making, it may go without saying, are in of themselves risky and can threaten the results of an M&A deal because management may fail to notice the consequences of their decisions on the outcome of the M&A. The worst-case scenario in this sort of decision making entails managerial decisions based simply on trial-and-error, best guesses, and individual ambitions. Depending solely on a manager's knowledge base for decision making poses a challenge in that the decision situations may be new and unfamiliar; therefore the decision owner's assumptions may be drawn from outdated information or may be founded on facts that no longer reflect current realities. All of these points reinforce the reminder that decisions are going to be affected by the decision owners' risk tolerance as well as the organization's culture and norms.

Managers, if they are to make patient and thoughtful decisions, must then fight the temptation to act presumptuously. With a number of key M&A decisions to make over a brief timeframe, managers may become preoccupied with taking decisive actions to get things moving. As a result, managers can tend to get impatient with lengthy discussions and can appear frustrated with certain ambiguities in the information they receive. Thus, quick decisions and judgments carry with them the promise to alleviate immediate needs and keep the process moving; yet these quick decisions can significantly alter the outcomes of the deal and impact the long-term performance of the firm. Managers will need to balance the need for timely action-taking with careful analysis and use the best information available to consider the future consequences of their decisions on future results.

Resource limitations can overburden individuals and limit their ability to collect and analyze a wide array of M&A deal data and to prepare the information for use by the decision makers. It is for this reason that predefining some of the information needs for decisions makers and discussing the formats for reviewing information greatly contribute to eliminating unneeded activity. Part of the challenge here is that the leadership team may have difficulty articulating their information needs, and so they may recognize their desired criteria only after they see it. Thus they can appear indecisive and cause unintended rework for the analysts.

Understanding the risks associated with the M&A deal and forming opinions about the issues takes time, and the leadership team may be unable to spend the necessary time to delve into details. Therefore, they may overlook sources of risk and may underestimate the magnitude of the risk. Senior leadership may underestimate the degree of change needed for the deal and its impact on the organization culture, and they may overestimate their own ability to institute significant change after the deal closes. Most managers are underprepared for the effort required to combine two large entities, and they often fail to create a sense of urgency regarding the magnitude and timing of synergy capture immediately after the deal closes. Unrealistic expectations of a large payoff as a result of the deal may also affect the judgment of the leadership team. The way that information about the target business is conveyed to senior leadership can also affect the senior leadership's understanding of the M&A challenges and the risks facing them. The acquirer should then only accept risks in line with the deal's expected pay-off and the potential for long-term value creation.

Quality decisions require a substantive knowledge of the industry and its future trends, along with a sense of the evolving state of technology and an inclusive approach to decision making.

SUCCESS FACTOR #6

DRIVE EVERY ASPECT OF THE M&A DEAL FROM THE SENIOR LEADERSHIP LEVEL

Senior leadership creates a vision for the future and a growth strategy. The management team must at first decide what industry position it wants to attain and what actions it is willing to undertake in order to achieve its objectives. A worthwhile strategic vision will result in business objectives that will determine the criteria for longer-term successes, which will require the organization to extend itself in fruitful ways. The long term vision and the M&A deal rationale, which involves a sense of how the two firms will fit together, must be commonly understood by those involved in the deal. The leadership communicates that vision to key stakeholders, so that they can procure an involved commitment towards implementation, and ultimately achieves a buy-in for employee participation in seeing it come to its realization. Tying strategy implementation to employee rewards and incentives in this way will enhance the prospects of an initial buy-in as well as strengthening a commitment to attaining the objectives. A successful M&A deal implementation depends on the commitment of the organization toward such an understanding and realization.

The full commitment and engagement of senior leadership is necessary for the implementation of the M&A process. They bear the final accountability for each step and each key decision node: the M&A deal and its decisions are too important to be delegated down to others in the organization. As decision owners, the responsibility of senior leadership is to provide continued accountability across each decision node throughout the M&A process: they ought to participate in the deal discussions, clearly understand the assumptions, recognize the risks associated with making the deal, and make the final judgment for each key decision. Senior leadership will also assign responsibilities and provide the resources for each step in the M&A process.

During the M&A process, executives should manage time appropriately. Experience tells us that senior leadership spends too much time on organizational structure discussions and people selection, while spending insufficient time on deal planning and execution. When focused on the deal, as well as its emotional and political outcomes, leadership may get distracted from its day-to-day business and overlook the impact of the deal on customer satisfaction and retention. It is imperative that senior leadership be conscious of and take steps towards meeting its ongoing business needs while carrying out the M&A deal.

Most organizations lack previous M&A experience and must depend on the experience of outside advisers. M&A advisers provide their best available advice, but it should be kept in mind that they also have their own self-interests. Although one must rely on advisers, a successful deal depends on an informed CEO and senior leadership team—one which knows what it is looking for and is prepared to execute its strategy. Previous experience with M&A deals or major efforts to bring change is a gauge for M&A success. Senior leadership with M&A experience has better skills to make successful deals. Firms, if they are to be best prepared for future growth opportunities in this respect, must develop their own in-house M&A expertise and be ready for the time when they will be able to use these skills.

SUCCESS FACTOR #7

BE PREPARED TO WALK AWAY FROM A DEAL THAT DOES NOT SHOW POTENTIAL

The acquirer should not undertake a deal that cannot create value for its owners and shareholders. Rational decision-making requires that decision makers consider various strategic choices carefully and choose a course of action based on its cost-benefits. The firm should consider a deal only when it perceives that the deal benefits exceed its downsides, and thus it represents a worthwhile undertaking that will result in a stronger combined business and greater ability to compete. A decision to move forward with a deal should be based on an analysis of the facts and not founded on emotion or bias. If the deal does not make rational sense, the acquirer should walk away from the deal. However, a number of factors may prevent an acquirer from walking away from a deal even though it may appear to be a losing proposition.

There is a strong drive to close the deal once the M&A process has been initiated due, at least in part, to all the pre-close effort. Deals that do not close are viewed as failures by outside observers and can affect the acquiring CEO's reputation as a deal maker. For the acquirer, the time, resources, money, and energy dedicated to the deal for such activities as data gathering, data analysis, candidate screening, business case development, and negotiations are all sunk costs and should never be an excuse for pursuing a deal that is a poor fit.

The personal benefits and rewards to managers associated with a successful M&A close may be substantial and may reinforce the drive for closing the deal. A company's compensation and incentive program is often tied to factors such as the firm's earnings growth, its security value, and the return on equity. Managers will act to maximize their incentives and their personal wealth at times without realizing, or perhaps in spite of, the negative impacts of those decisions on the company's long-term results[2]. In a similar way, the incentives paid to outside professionals may be contingent upon the deal closure and could present themselves as complications to a deal that appears to be a poor fit.

A commitment to embarking on an M&A deal introduces certain biases into the decision maker's judgment. Once senior leadership has made a solid commitment to pursuing the deal, they may find it difficult to abandon the deal and may try by various means to justify the choice. The CEO may have made the decision to pursue the M&A prematurely prior to understanding thoroughly the cost-benefits of each strategic alternative with which he or she was presented. However, having made the decision, the CEO who is in this position might dismiss any negative information about the target and accept only supporting information that emphasizes the deal benefits, and he or she might actively seek ways to overcome its deficiencies. It is not unheard of for executives to decide to make a deal with a particular target and then try to justify the deal strategically. Sellers may similarly become biased by their own goals and may not be prepared to accept a fair deal. A commitment to a selling price may also bias the seller's judgment. The seller who has a figure in mind for the proceeds from the sale of the business may not accept a realistic offer at a lower price, and so might walk away from a good deal. Biased by a high offer that was rejected, the seller at times might be likely to reject all lower offers as well.

Mergers and acquisitions may be conceived as a way out of a firm's current shortcomings and as a substitute for lagging internal growth initiatives as well as for new product development shortcomings and a declining competitive edge. The rationale for making the deal could hinge solely on the hope that the combination could pay off in the long term and save the firm from further decline. The acquisition, seen in this way, could be a way to circumvent the firm from becoming an acquisition target itself. On the other hand, when the company is going strong and has a strong equity valuation and cash reserve, management may feel comfortable taking on a deal knowing that they have a cushion of high security valuation to fall back upon. Undertaking an M&A deal under such conditions may give management a sense of accomplishment, personal satisfaction, and the prestige of being at the helm of a large and growing firm. Other influential managers within the firm may also push for the deal and strongly support it as a way to gain visibility and promote their own careers.

Understanding these common challenges of M&A deals will greatly enhance the likelihood of success. Often, the underlying causes of issues which arise during an M&A integration phase are symptoms that can be attributed to an insufficiently compelling M&A rationale. Where M&A activity is driven only by ambition and ego without solid insights about the future the outcome may cause years of difficulty and loss for shareholder value in the acquiring firm. The acquirer and sellers should always look towards the future and consider the risks, costs, and benefits of their decisions about any potential M&A deal.

Common Characteristics of Successful Deal Makers

Successful deal makers are mythologized as having utmost confidence in their own vision and trusting in their own instincts. Deal makers with a successful track record of value added deals, though, have a strong focus on the specifics of deal fundamentals. Deal makers are always scanning the horizon for new M&A opportunities as they keep their strategic goals in mind and hone their M&A skills for recognizing a good deal and capturing its value quickly. Successful deal makers will not go after deals simply for the sake of making one happen; they will have the patience to wait for the right deal. They learn what the target has to offer by conducting significant amounts of quantitative and qualitative analysis of their targets prior to making a deal. They are also quick to reject deals that appear to be a poor fit.

Successful deal makers intimately know their own business, its value drivers, and its success factors. This knowledge, combined with the skills and hard work it takes to make the M&A deal successful, allows them to be educated risk takers by trusting their own knowledge and value expectations for a deal. They are realistic about what they are getting into and make the needed commitment in terms of time and resources in order to bring about success and to go about making the deal in the right way. Once they make a deal, they focus on realizing value from it, and they do not spend much time wringing hands and second guessing.

Successful deal makers are for these above reasons competitive individuals with a desire to win in the long run, and who possess the ability to undertake bold action to do so. Their carefully obtained reputation as successful deal makers helps them win over their targets by resisting their opponents and securing the trust of their investors.

NOTES

[1] See Robert G. Cooper in References for a discussion of new product development process and quality decision making.

[2] Companies use a number of methods to tie executive incentives to long term firm performance. One example is contingent pay-outs where the executives get rewarded based on the performance of the combined entity over a period of time after the deal close. Some companies have also experimented by issuing stocks or options to executives but prohibiting them from selling the stocks as long as they hold their executive positions in the combined entity.

Part 2

Do the Right Deal

CHAPTER 3

DEFINING A WINNING RATIONALE

Success Factors
- Choose strategic moves that strengthen the company
- Seek out attractive targets in alignment with the deal rationale

Attaining growth in order to create long term shareholder wealth should be *the* business imperative and the highest priority for companies in this new millennium. Yet, this growth is not achieved without certain difficulties as firms seeking to increase revenue and size are faced with an accelerating rate of change in the business environment as well as with increased global competition. Businesses are adapting to these changes through a combination of building internal resources and acquiring what is needed from the outside. In less than two decades, industries such as energy, telecommunications, automobiles, pharmaceuticals, and media have all been transformed through mergers and acquisitions, each based on its own specific business drivers. Some companies have closed tens of deals in pursuit of growth.

Attaining growth begins with defining a strategic framework. Within that framework, mergers and acquisitions provide the firm with an increased market share and access to new products, new markets, needed technologies, and other resources. Mergers and acquisitions may be the primary tool for responding to rapid external environmental changes caused by industry life stage and deregulation, or for taking advantage of investment opportunities presented by the target. The firm's strategic objectives define the criteria for a good fit and the parameters for screening for attractive candidates. Screening criteria are used to assess the target firm's fit based on strategic compatibility, synergism, and ease of integration. The screening process consists of compiling a candidate list, gathering needed information about each candidate, and comparing candidates against the selection criteria to arrive at a candidate shortlist. This chapter will cover in detail these various drivers of mergers and acquisition deals, and it will look closely at the screening and selection process.

SUCCESS FACTOR #8

CHOOSE STRATEGIC MOVES THAT STRENGTHEN THE COMPANY

The allocation of the firm's resources among its various growth opportunities begins with the process of self-evaluation. The firm must define its strategic priorities and understand its strategic gaps. In order to attain a sustainable advantage, an assessment of the firm's external environment including a thorough examination of the immediate and long term opportunities and threats (industry evolution, the development of customer needs, changes in regional and global markets, possible competitor actions, new emerging competitors, the evolution of methods and channels of distribution, and technological transformations), its current performance, and what it can realistically achieve considering its current and developing internal resources and capabilities (research and development, manufacturing, services, logistics, sales and marketing, and management qualifications) will need to be undertaken to define the magnitude of and the root causes of the firm's performance gap. By better understanding the current and future threats and opportunities, the firm can better answer questions about which markets and customer segments to choose and how exactly to position its products. The findings are then weighed against what the firm requires in the way of its specific internal capabilities, strengths, and weaknesses in order to determine its potential performance gap and for a winning strategy in the marketplace.

It should go without saying in this regard that it will take the firm both time and money to adapt the firm's internal capabilities to a level at which they can meet the evolving external requirements surrounding the firm and its industry challenges. The internal development of the next generation of products and services requires the availability of skilled people and intellectual capital as well as an appropriate organizational structure, the construction of new physical assets, new product research, design, and development, and the adoption and leveraging of needed technologies. New distribution networks may need to be developed, and new products and services must be promoted to gain acceptance. All of these tasks take significant time to achieve; they may require the firm to start from scratch so that it can ascend the learning curve.

Alternately, a firm can look to the outside to accelerate its development time and share the know-how and risks associated with the effort through forming alliances, partnerships, or joint ventures. In a similar way, forming joint licensing agreements with other firms can provide greater access to innovation. A company can pursue mergers and acquisitions to buy what it needs as it is in pursuit of its growth objectives. The firm can acquire its needed resources and assets—lines of business, divisions, even whole firms, small or large—in order to fill its performance gap and attain its strategic objectives.

Pursuing each strategic option, though, presents its own advantages, challenges, and risks. The firm's decision criteria for selecting among its strategic options include: the extent of the performance gap that the firm must overcome, the firm's desired growth rate, leadership's sense of urgency and commitment to achieving the objectives, the availability of desired capabilities and in-house resources, a sense of timing about the development of internal resources needed to deliver the desired objectives, and the timing involved in the development of the next generation of products. Other decision criteria could center on the firm's cash flow and profitability, ability to make a financial commitment and/or the availability of outside investors who might back the deal, the rate of external change such as the rate of the evolution of customer and market needs, the rate of obsolescence for the firm's existing products, and the position of competitors. All of these criteria should be carefully considered by the decision makers. The outcome of this analysis will form the strategic framework for the firm to close the gap and attain its vision, its desired growth, and its long term ambitions.

To remain competitive in today's evolving markets, businesses have to work faster, develop better products and services, and offer them at a cheaper cost to customers. The pursuit of horizontal mergers and acquisitions with a competitor provides access to assets, facilities, and production capacity so that the company can meet market demand and reduce the long-term investment risks by way of access to a proven entity. The pursuit can also provide access to cash flows that can fund research and development and help the company gain access to a desirable market share and a customer base. Horizontal deals create efficiencies and bargaining power from synergies that are derived from the alignment and overlap between internal resources and product markets. The firm can lower costs through combining purchasing and procurement, sharing marketing, brand identity, manufacturing capacity, and distribution channels. Examples of horizontal M&A deals abound.

In the same way, a firm can use mergers and acquisitions to pursue a product expansion strategy that will help it gain a competitive advantage. It can expand, change, balance, and fill gaps in its portfolio with compatible brands so that it can gain more prominence and meet the growing market demands and needs of customers. M&As in this respect allow the firm to supplant internal product development, accelerate product development cycle times, and complement internal growth initiative efforts by acquiring new patents, products, product lines, or service offerings. For example, pharmaceutical firms experience a very robust M&A deal environment in search of access to a broad portfolio of products and a robust product pipeline, access to secure sources of cash flows for funding R&D and marketing, and access to new technologies and skilled people. Healthcare spending is the third largest component of the U.S. Gross Domestic Product (GDP) behind government spending and real estate. Investors are attracted to the healthcare industry based on its promise of strong, long term performance. The industry is growing at double digits annually, and by 2011 healthcare spending is expected to top 3 trillion dollars[1]. This strong growth is fueled by the aging baby boomers, longer expected life spans, and overall wellness trends in the population. These factors are accompanied by expected rises in the cost of health care, such as in the cost of prescription drugs, medical devices, and medical services. New breakthrough technologies, such as automated compound creation, testing, and analysis, have transformed the Windustry. Yet drug development is fraught with uncertainty, requiring huge initial investments and long research and developmental timelines. In the U.S., drug makers on average spend over 15% of their sales on research and development[2]. New drug development may face delays, may not always receive FDA approval, or may not attain the

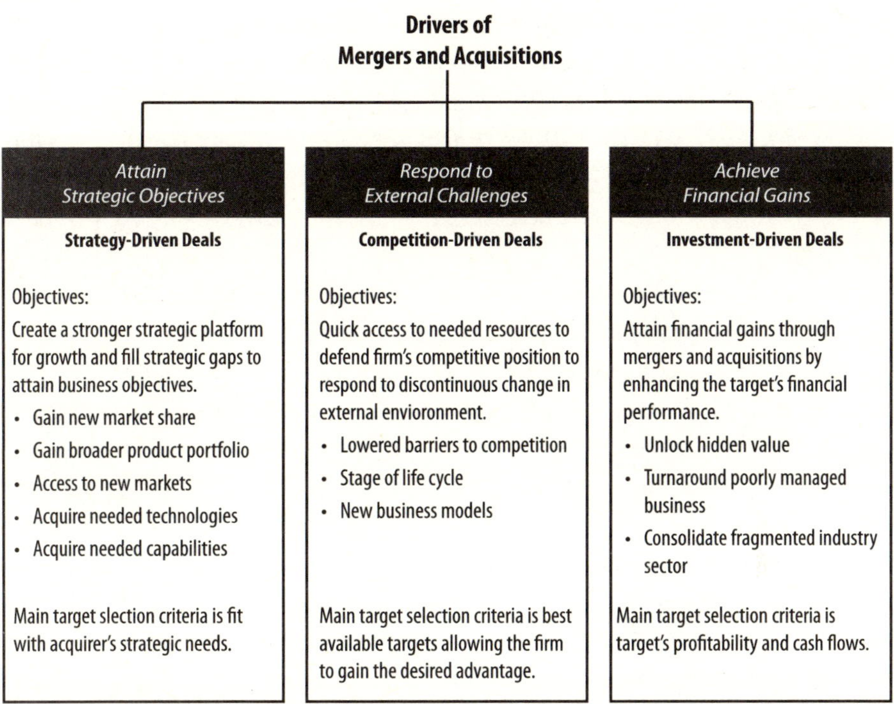

Figure 3. M&A Drivers
The drivers of mergers and acquisitions fall broadly into three categories. Many large deals
may represent a combination of drivers due to their size and complexity.

expected market success. Additionally, the industry is under price pressures from large buyers. These challenges place pharmaceutical firms in a race to gain approval and to fund a rich product pipeline seeking new discoveries as old patents expire. The strength of a pharmaceutical company, therefore, depends on the quality of its product pipeline and portfolio of exiting drugs rather than the firm's sheer size. Thus, M&A deals provide these firms with access to new product pipelines, stable sources of cash flow to offset patent losses from major drugs, and a broader portfolio of drugs that allow large pharmaceutical firms to offer the large drug procurers a single source for their needs and thus better pricing. The M&A deal allows for a combination of R&D programs to enhance innovation in search of drugs with high potential. However, buyer beware: mergers and acquisitions also carry risks since the acquired promising pipelines can always face product launch delays as well. Some forecasts indicate that perhaps a few mega-firms may eventually control most of the pharmaceutical market. Currently, half the total global drug sales is derived from the ten largest firms.[3] Globally, major industry M&A deals include the Anglo-U.S. deal between Glaxo-Wellcome and Smithkline Beecham (2000), Pfizer Inc. with Warner Lambert (2000) and with Pharmacia (2003) and two European firms Sanofi-Synthelabo and Aventis, which together created the industry's third largest player in the world.

Acquisitions allow a firm to grow revenue by entering new, growing, and profitable market segments and geographies for its current products and services. The attractiveness of the market, the intensity of competition, and the ability to create value for new customers provide the drive to enter the new markets. Acquisitions can be quite valuable for this in that they provide a firm with access to various distribution channels as well as sales and marketing know-how to facilitate the entrance into new geographic markets. It should be remembered, though, that moving into a new market may require the firm to adapt its products and services to the needs of a new customer base. Acquirers that can coordinate efficiently between various geographic entities to enhance their utilization of production capacity and resources in a value-added manner can capture synergies in the form of lower costs and increased sales.

In search of new markets, global competition is intensifying, and business is likewise becoming increasingly global. International deals allow the firm to globalize and gain a foothold in a new market and a growing economy. Companies may globalize to utilize a low-cost and skilled labor pool, to avoid tariffs by using local production capability in free-trading blocks, to gain access to raw materials, or to shift their production from one region to another as economic, social, and environmental forces change. Trading blocs and trade pacts, such as the European Union (EU), North American Free Trade Agreement (NAFTA), Association of South East Asian Nations (ASEAN), Asia-Pacific Economic Cooperation (APEC), and Latin American Common Market (MERCUSOR), create blocks of countries for political and trade cooperation.[4] Acquisitions, then, can allow the firm to produce within these blocks in order to avoid trade barriers and to enjoy the relatively free flow of goods and services among those countries. Globalization will likely continue to be an influential trend in mergers and acquisitions; thus, firms will continue to take advantage of opportunities presented by the worldwide coordination of their value chain. Industries as diverse as the automotive, telecommunication, software, technology manufacturing, pharmaceutical, aerospace, heavy equipment, entertainment, and the garment industry all sell their products across national markets. Expertise and service-oriented industries, such as banking, tourism, and business consulting take advantage of these cross-border opportunities.

The automobile industry is facing continued strong global competition due to lower trade barriers. The industry is also affected by the Internet, rising gasoline prices, and higher commodity prices. Foreign auto makers, such as Korean auto manufacturers, are gaining market share in the United States and other foreign firms have opened manufacturing facilities in the United States, taking market share away from the traditional "big three." Product life cycles are getting shorter in response to consumer demands and to the application of technologies that have eased and shortened automobile design timelines. Auto manufacturers depend increasingly on their suppliers to conduct design, development, and engineering, and auto parts are being simplified to ease assembly. IT systems closely monitor sales levels and inventories in collaboration with dealers. U.S. auto manufacturers, faced with excess global manufacturing capacity, have searched for growth and profitability beyond their home countries, which has resulted in numerous cross-border consolidations. Ford Motor Company acquired Jaguar Cars Ltd., Volvo AB, Land Rover Ltd. and Aston Martin Lagonda Ltd. while General Motors Corporation acquired Saab AB and Daewoo Corporation. Meanwhile Daimler-Benz AG acquired the Chrysler Corporation and Renault S.A. acquired Nissan Motor Company.

In a like way, the mature chemicals industry continues to undergo globalization seeking access to new markets and customers. Meanwhile, companies continue to consolidate and restructure with regulatory requirements getting more stringent. Their customers include among others auto manufacturers, housing industry, and consumers. The fragmented chemicals industry has seen significant consolidation over the past decades. Consolidation allows firms to reduce selling, overhead and operating costs and enhance their buying power. Companies divest of non-core businesses to pay down debt and enhance focus and investment on lines of business they are committed to. The M&A activity has slowed in the new millennium but continues at a healthy pace and is likely to continue in the future. The basic chemicals industry continues to globalize as the Asian and Latin

American economies develop. As manufacturers seek to take advantage of lower costs, factories are increasingly being located in developing countries and global trade in basic chemicals is rising. In the United States, basic chemical companies are consolidating to gain efficiencies across the value chain. The Internet is increasing the B2B e-commerce in the chemicals industry through online auctions sites and web based price lists and product information. Chemical companies are also connecting directly to their customers' enterprise resource planning systems to facilitate product ordering. Examples include the acquisition of Union Carbide by Dow Chemical Company (2001) and merger between Shell and BASF plastic businesses (2000).

M&A deals give the acquirers access to proven and promising technologies and applications that can help them meet the demands of market and product change. Technological innovations that boost worker productivity are constantly being introduced and have to be adopted by businesses so that they maintain their competitiveness. The Internet has profoundly affected the buying habits of consumers and businesses. This sort of development can be seen in the pharmaceutical industry, which uses information technology to screen ideas, model molecules, and develop new cures. Health care providers utilize technology to better meet patient needs. Airlines take advantage of technology to integrate flight connections and enhance customer-sharing with their partners. High-technology firms use the power of information technology and the internet to develop innovative products. High-tech firms need to constantly innovate in such ways in order to keep up with the rapid evolution of new technologies, and when faced with these challenges, many high-tech firms have used M&A deals to satisfy their needs.

Over the past half century, the world has witnessed its highest levels of economic growth and prosperity primarily through the rise of information technology and the Internet. New technologies have historically played a significant role in the growth of industry. The cost of technology has continually declined, while technology obsolescence has driven the need for constant upgrading and has also spurred a significant investment of capital to accomplish those upgrades. M&A deals allow a firm to gain access to technology innovations, such as automation and robotics, which result in greater efficiencies and increased productivity. Information technologies, along the same lines, allow firms to make more timely decisions regarding operations, markets, and customers, and increased access to the Internet and related technologies allows consumers to make more online purchases. This enlarged access results in supply chain efficiencies, lower transaction costs, lower inventory levels, and the collection of information by which to gauge consumer preferences. Technology and the promise of the Internet have created new opportunities across industries. For example, over the past few years, home entertainment customers have seen remarkable changes in digital technology and in the way they access movies and music. Spending on Digital Video Discs (DVD) has grown rapidly while theater attendance has declined as movies increasingly are watched at home. DVDs are quickly replacing any spending on videocassettes as well. Music is increasingly listened to in digital formats and is being downloaded from the Internet, which has caused an associated decline in the purchase of prerecorded music on CDs. In terms of mergers and acquisitions, the home entertainment and music industry has been quite active over the past several years. High security valuations have allowed major deals to occur just after the millennium. The publishers of books, magazines, and newspapers operate in a fragmented industry. Similarly, technology is transforming their industry as the Internet and other new technologies are providing the publishers with new forms of content distribution. Publishers need greater size and market share to gain access to greater advertising revenues, and thus they merge and acquire in order to increase their size and gain market share.

Mergers and acquisitions can build a solid foundation for future growth, fill gaps in internal capabilities, and enhance a firm's core capabilities through the introduction of needed expertise, specific skills, and know-how. Through a smart deal, the acquirer can enrich its internal competencies and gain access to a proven history of innovation and product development, attain high quality performers, and accelerate its learning curve. On the other hand, the acquirer could run the risk of losing such advantages, however, as competitors often attempt to lure away key employees during times of uncertainty when there is heightened concern about the changes resulting from mergers and acquisitions. It is for this reason that an M&A must be conducted in such a way so that these risks are minimized and integration speed and efficiency are maximized.

Finally, a firm could move towards the latter through conducting vertical mergers and acquisitions, which would allow it to move downstream or upstream, thereby gaining access to sources of supply or desired customers in a profitable business area. Vertical integration in this manner may improve the firm's flexibility so that it can compete with more nimble newcomers.

MAINTAIN THE FIRM'S COMPETITIVENESS IN THE FACE OF EXTERNAL CHANGES

Driven by a need to maintain a strong industry position in the face of "discontinuous" changes in the external business environment, a firm may find that its best competitive option is to respond primarily through mergers and acquisitions. External events act as triggers that drive mergers and acquisitions and expedite a firm's need for access to resources so that it may adjust to the rapid changes altering the business environment. Such disequilibrium poses a challenge to the *status quo*, at times to the point where a firm will no longer be capable of responding successfully with its internal resources, however well-honed they may be. Relying on incremental changes in these situations may not suffice or be a guarantee of future success. Industry equilibrium can be upset by a number of factors, including drastic changes in regulations, changes in industry growth rates, and new transformational business models.

Regulations are applied to protect an industry's competitive balance. Increases in deregulation, which have been led by the U.S. and are now a global trend, have been a major driver of mergers and acquisitions both in the U.S. and abroad. Historically, the trend towards deregulation has developed slowly, except when there has been a crisis in a sector of the economy or when there are potential risks for failure to major corporations. Deregulation in an industry is generally followed by an increase in M&A activity as competitors rush to take advantage of opportunities and secure a position for themselves. Competitors, at such times, may be allowed to capture a greater market share and enter new markets, or they may be impelled to offer new products and services as a result of the deregulation. In the U.S., the deregulation of a number of industries, including airlines, financial services, energy companies, and the telecommunication field, has changed the competitive landscape in those industries. These kind of shifts often result in numerous mergers and acquisitions.

Airline companies in the United States were regulated in 1938, and the Civil Aeronautics Board was formed to oversee them. With the Airline

Deregulation Act of 1978, 40 years after the initial regulation, the airlines were given gradual economic deregulation. The Civil Aeronautics Board was abolished and the Department of Transportation took over any remaining responsibilities for the airlines. A wave of mergers and acquisitions followed the deregulation, completely changing the shape of the industry. Within a decade, the few remaining major airlines were operating a "hub and spoke" model, with large aircraft flying between the hubs and regional and commuter airlines flying to and from the smaller final destinations. In 2000, the largest airlines in the United States, as measured by market share, operated more than 90% of the airline traffic and generated over 80% of the airline industry's revenue[5]. Recent airline mergers and acquisitions were driven by economies of scale, access to new airport gates, access to trained personnel, and attainment of a proven customer base. Global deregulation of the airlines is a driver of M&A activity in airlines outside the United States.

The Telecommunication Act of 1996 was intended to enhance competition in local markets by allowing local phone providers to enter long distance services and build telephone equipment. The act also allows a variety of other companies, such as cable companies, to provide local telephone services. In a reversal that occurred following the break-up of the Bell System, the act led to significant M&A activity and reconsolidation in the telecommunications industry. The remaining Baby Bells are Verizon (merger of GTE Group and Bell Atlantic Corporation), SBC Corporation, Bell South Corporation, and Qwest Communications (merged with U.S. West). In the United States, the highly competitive telecommunications industry, including voice telephony and long-distance businesses, are mature. Continued deregulation in the wire-line telecommunications, substitution of wire-line by wireless phones, availability of high-speed internet over cable, and the prospects of cable telephony make this industry very active. M&A deals in this industry have pursued new product development efforts to offer a broader array of new services to attain revenue growth (including wireless, DSL, and ISP services), adoption of new technologies, and provide advantages of size. Following the very active M&A deals of 1999 and 2000, M&A activity has slowed but continues as the industry continues to consolidate. Companies are also divesting of non-core assets to pay down debt.

The stock market crash of 1929 led to the Glass-Steagall Act of 1933 and the Banking Act of 1935. Rigid boundaries were created between commercial and investment banks. Banks were in the loan and credit business; Savings and Loans collected savings and provided mortgages; Investment Banks underwrote securities; and Insurance Companies managed risk. In 1956, the Bank Holding Company Act required bank holding companies to sell most of their non-banking operations and banks were not allowed to acquire other banks outside of their home states. In 1999, 70 years after the crash and the great depression, the Glass-Steagall Act was repealed. The Gramm-Leach-Bliley Act of 1999 allows financial institutions to engage in commercial and investment banking, sell and underwrite insurance, and engage in real estate brokerage and development. This change in legislation led to a flurry of M&A activity. The deregulation allowed the firms to consolidate; however, there have been concerns circling around independent analysis and special customer treatment in investment and commercial bank combinations. Examples include merger of JP Morgan Chase & Co. (formed from the mergers of Chemical Bank, Chase Manhattan Bank, and JP Morgan) and Bank One Corporation and the deal between Citicorp and Travelers Group.

Another challenge is tied to the industry life cycle. In growing and fragmented industries, firms must respond to the evolution and proliferation of new offerings, technologies, and innovations while still meeting customer demands for high standards. In maturing industries, firms need to attain growth and maintain their competitiveness in the face of dwindling growth opportunities and saturated demand. Mergers and acquisitions are for these and other reasons an important instrument for gaining a greater market share at various stages of an industry life cycle.[6] As an industry matures, products or services that are offered by various competitors lose their differentiation, and the profitability of many of the involved companies can languish as a result. With the exception of one or two industry leaders, the remainder of the competitors may possibly lose their differentiation and be forced to compete primarily over price. Firms will typically respond to such situations by seeking size and scale through mergers and acquisitions so that they may remain viable players, gain market share, enhance cash flows, and reduce costs. Industry consolidation can also be driven by the proliferation of new competing technologies as well as by changes in customer buying patterns. At this point, there is significant competition to select the best available M&A partners. The weaker brands and their resources get acquired by stronger firms, sometimes at significantly reduced prices. Other industry competitors will often react to an M&A deal by forming deals of their own in order to match the industry leader's new scale and scope; or they may react by strengthening their capabilities upstream or downstream in order to match the leader's bargaining position. Firms that find themselves on the sidelines during such a period of consolidation are faced with the overwhelming pressure to take part in the action to remain competitive with the larger players consolidating through M&A deals.

Industries undergo consolidation to increase market share, gain economies, and increase their offerings. Consolidation synergies may be expected from combining and rationalizing capacity, overhead, and brands, resulting in enhanced future revenues and cash flows. Careful due diligence is necessary here to avoid a target that lacks well-organized processes, owns outdated or poorly maintained assets, and has a rapidly declining customer base. It should always be kept in mind in this respect that having to upgrade the target's operational and technological base may be a costly and prohibitive proposition. Management that is distracted by the process of integrating with its acquired businesses may begin to lose sight of its competitor's moves, or because of its larger size, it may become less flexible in responding to those moves in a timely fashion.

Ninety years after the break-up of Standard Oil, the global oil and gas industry reconsolidated in the U.S. and elsewhere to a few very large players giving rise to "supermajor" oil companies—publicly traded global integrated oil and gas companies that explore, find, develop, transport, refine, and market crude oil and gas. Mergers and acquisitions created global behemoths such as ExxonMobil corp., Royal Dutch/Shell Group, BP plc, Total Fina Elf S.A., and ChevronTexaco Corp. In 2002, Phillips Petroleum added Conoco Inc. having acquired Tosco Corporation in 2001 to become the largest refiner in the United States. The industry is mature and its products are generally commodities with little product differentiation. Industry barriers to entry are high due to significant capital requirements. Billions of dollars in synergies from these deals were realized by streamlining exploration and production sectors, by enhancing efficiencies in refining and marketing operations, and through corporate rightsizing. In the upstream industry, those who explore, develop, and produce reserves, are looking to maximize their returns on each barrel that they produce by reducing costs. With most accessible reserves already tapped, chances of finding new reserves are diminishing and the costs and risks associated with replacing depleted reserves grow higher. The drivers of mergers and acquisitions in this industry are the need to search for replacing depleting reserves, achieving economies of scale, and applying new technologies. There is also a need to address the rising cost and risk of finding new reserves in difficult to reach locations, such as the deep waters of the Gulf of Mexico, West Africa, and Brazil. In the downstream arena, where petroleum products are refined and marketed, consolidations provide advantages of size, access to new distribution channels, reduced overheads, lowered inventory carrying costs, and enhanced capacity utilization. Refineries that are more favorably located, such as those in coastal areas, will likely be the long term survivors. To increase efficiencies, refiners apply the latest technologies to existing refineries versus constructing new facilities. As a result, capacities and utilization of existing facilities will continue to increase. Clearly, as a result of the slow down in new facilities construction, environmental concerns and safety concerns related to an aging infrastructure are driving increased industry regulations.

Consolidation is taking place in the media and entertainment businesses as well. Movies are the main staple of entertainment industry along with television and music business. In the media and entertainment industries, deregulations, the search for economies of scale, access to new talent and innovation, and portfolio changes have resulted in numerous mergers and acquisitions. Consolidations allow for the enhanced promotion of programs, and the ability to distribute content, and leveraging creativity along with greater size allows the companies to manage the costs and risks of developing new movies. Examples of M&A deals include Viacom's merger with Paramount; Disney with ABC; and GE with NBC. Vivendi acquired Seagrams and, through the Seagrams acquisition, it also obtained Universal music and film while AOL acquired Time Warner Inc. The European M&A market was likewise very active in this industry. Some of the deals were not successful. Vivendi Universal SA auctioned itself off and the bulk of its film and entertainment businesses went to GE's NBC unit. Time Warner returned to its old name when it dropped AOL from its brand. Other companies in the industry have sold non-core assets to pay down debt and focus their businesses. Cable is gaining a larger portion of television viewership and is experiencing increased spending on advertising. Comcast sold its shares in QVC Inc. to Liberty Media Corp. in 2003 and dropped its offer to acquire Disney which would have been a powerful convergence of content and distribution. Industry trends include high definition television broadcasts, Internet service through cable and satellite, on-demand interactivity, and cable internet telephony.

Despite deregulation, the financial industry in the United States is still relatively fragmented, but it has evolved and consolidated. Segments such as credit cards, corporate lending, and mortgage market tend to be more concentrated with a few players controlling most of the market share. Financial institutions will continue to consolidate to gain market share and size and deliver efficient, high-quality customer services, develop new e-commerce capabilities, offer a broader array of products and services such as brokerage, insurance, and credit cards, enter new geographic markers, and gain efficiencies in order to remain competitive on a global scale to fend off global competitors. Investments in technology, such as electronic banking over the internet and ATM machines, has significantly reduced the cost of operations. Elimination of duplicate infrastructure and consolidation of back-office operations lead to lower operating costs. For example NationsBanc acquired Bank of America forming Bank of America Corp. which then acquired FleetBoston Financial Corporation and credit card issuer MBNA Corporation.

The wireless phone sector experienced rapid product adoption; however, as the industry matures and growth of new subscribers slows, wireless providers are battling for market share. Companies seek to provide a broader geographic coverage and gain economies of scale as they compete on price and services. The industry has experienced consolidations and partnerships in an attempt to share costs and reduce the risk of new investments. However, the integration of wireless providers is challenged by operational differences, such as the various technology bases employed by the companies. The largest wireless players in the United States include Verizon, Cingular (acquired AT&T Wireless), and Sprint FON Group (acquired Nextel Communications Inc.), and T-Mobile USA. Wireless phones are also replacing some of the wire-line phones. Wireless services in this way are striving to make the cell phone the only needed communication device through voice, data, voicemail, e-mail, and other digital media.

Adopting innovative business models becomes an important way to deal with competitor moves as it can open up new competitive spaces. When a competitor develops a successful new business model, other firms are forced to respond rapidly with new models of their own. The firm with the more innovative offering could become the primary provider by offering a broader and more appealing product line. The need for a quick response may make an M&A deal a primary means of competition. Acquirers wishing to adopt and imitate a firm's innovative model may try to take control of it as an acquisition target, in which case the acquirer would be paying for the target's innovation and its proven business model. In 1998 AT&T Wireless, which owned a national wireless network launched a new business model in the cellular industry: a nationwide flat-rate pricing model. This model required other service providers to develop their own nationwide wireless networks in order to match AT&T's flat-rate model, and with the resulting consolidation in the wireless industry, telephone roaming charges have nearly disappeared.

ESTABLISH THE TARGET'S PROFITABILITY AND CASH FLOWS

The objective of an investment-driven acquirer is to achieve long-term financial gains through mergers and acquisitions by enhancing the target's financial performance and market value. Investor acquirers need to understand the industry and the sources of value creation for their acquisitions. In order to capture an attractive deal, they need to evaluate the favorable M&A opportunities through an exhaustive screening process, and then move quickly to make an attractive deal happen. Most investment-driven acquirers use cash flows as the key criteria for selecting targets as they are seeking long term profitability.

An acquirer may search for a target with hidden value in terms of legal loopholes, tax advantages, or carry-over operational losses that might be attractive to an acquirer who can unlock this untapped value. The target may also present itself as a poorly managed turnaround opportunity in a distressed business, and so it may have a higher breakup or liquidation value. Investment-driven acquirers may also roll up businesses in a fragmented industry in order to consolidate specific market segments that have solid growth potential and room for future expansion. The acquirer may conduct a leveraged buyout and take a public firm private; it might acquire just a division, or the entire company. After the acquisition, it may divest itself of the target's underperforming assets and then use the proceeds from the divestitures to pay down debt and capture cash flows from the remaining higher-value assets.

Many investor-acquirers have their own equity at stake as well, which will give them a greater incentive to act rapidly in order to recover their investment or pay back debt. After the close of the deal, they might act with a sense of urgency to create real operational improvements and invest in enhancement of brand equity while reducing costs. In conducting the acquisition, some acquirers may decide to retain the current management if it appears to be a good fit. They might still permit the management to retain a certain autonomy and offer them financial incentives to run the business, while holding them accountable for achieving stretch results. They may lavishly reward those who exceed their performance goals, but they should also be quick to replace a poorly performing management team. In today's markets, a savvy corporate leader will pursue various approaches to enhancing shareholder value for their firms, and investor-acquirers must compete for market value against these savvy firms and businesses.

Advantages and Challenges of Size

Business combinations can create advantages that are attributable to the size of the combined entity. Through mergers and acquisitions, a combination will be stronger and will increase its resources through leveraging its capacity for growth and competition. It may even, in the end, gain an industry-leading position. Companies with a large size and a leading market position are the only players with the hope of remaining a long term viable industry player as they enjoy many advantages over their smaller rivals.

Lower risks

Large firms are thought to offer lower risks of failure based on their more stable earnings and cash flows, and so they enjoy a premium due to their size over their smaller rivals. Larger firms can get access to sources of financing at a lower cost so that they are able to invest in future growth opportunities. An investor would typically expect to receive and be satisfied with a lower rate of return when investing in a larger business. Larger firms also attract more alliances and partnerships that can help them diversify and lower the risks of their major investments.

Enhanced cash flows

Large firms have higher cash flows to spend on research and development, which enables them to finance a richer and more promising product development pipeline and accelerate completion of current initiatives, while placing more marketing energy behind promising products. Stronger cash flows can also cushion the firm against unforeseen product development problems.

Attainment of synergies

The consolidation of operations, the elimination of duplicate facilities and functions, and a more effective use of work force and resources all work together to increase efficiency. The firm can integrate many of its databases in order to streamline data capture and dissemination. Consolidation allows for the trading of larger volumes, amortizing over a larger number of units, and achieving lower per-unit fixed-costs. Large firms can realize synergies by coordinating and leveraging various elements of their business.

Development opportunities

Size brings a larger budget that allows for broader capability development and for the sharing of best practices. In these cases, a broader pool of employee talent is available to fill positions and attain better results.

Bargaining power

Larger firms are in a stronger bargaining position to deal with suppliers, distributors, and customers, and are less vulnerable to their pricing power. Larger firms have greater lobbying power with the regulators and legislatures. Indeed, very large global companies have enough influence even to affect national trade policies.

Ability to compete

A large firm is in a stronger position to take advantage of new opportunities and to respond to competitor moves. Size affords the firm greater reach to enter new lines of business, to offer a broader and more diversified portfolio of complementary offerings, and a more prominent market presence. A large firm can enter promising growth markets in new geographic locations, or it can move across borders into global markets as a platform for future growth. Greater scale in the end allows for stronger distribution capabilities.

Challenges of size

A large size also presents some new challenges. Maintaining a fast growth rate is more challenging for a large firm in that it would need to find and take advantage of a substantial amount of promising opportunities in a timely manner. Other challenges posed by size involve an increased complexity and a difficulty in maintaining links between disparate parts of its business. A larger size may reduce a firm's flexibility and its ability to absorb change on a large scale as well as management's ability to create change. The increased size of the firm can result in the creation of a complex bureaucracy, an overabundance of rules and procedures, slow decision making, and delayed responses to the changing demands in the marketplace and nimble competitors.

SUCCESS FACTOR #9

SEEK OUT ATTRACTIVE TARGETS IN ALIGNMENT WITH THE DEAL RATIONALE

Striking an M&A deal, though, does not promise continued growth as any acquirer that can raise the necessary funds to finance a deal can make an acquisition. The decision to pursue mergers and acquisitions should therefore be based on realistic assumptions and expectations about market potential, customer opportunities, competitive threats, and the rate at which the acquirer can expect to realize value from the deal. Mergers and acquisitions that are a good fit with the firm's objectives and strategic needs have a better chance of fulfilling its growth objectives. Real value creation is founded on just such a good fit between the acquirer's strategic criteria and the target's characteristics. The key question facing the acquirer is then: what criteria would make an acquisition target a good fit and how it would contribute to closing the acquirer's strategic gap? The fit criteria and parameters for recognizing attractive deals are in alignment with the firm's vision, its growth objectives, and its strategic framework. The fit criteria must also take into account the value creation potential as well as the commercial, operational, and cultural impact of the deal on the acquirer's long term performance.

Deals that are focused and fit the acquirer's strategic framework in this manner can help the acquirer grow more rapidly. Deals that incorporate entire firms and enter the acquirer into new business arenas, however, carry more risks. Targets are seldom an absolutely perfect fit that will neatly fulfill all of the acquirer's needs, especially when the acquirer is buying an entire firm. The target will come with its own financial, operational, product, market, and cultural strengths and weaknesses. To define the fit criteria, the acquirer should examine its own assumptions about the acquisition and conduct a detailed analysis of the key competitive characteristics of the target firm. A lack of fit between the target and the acquirer destroys value for the acquirer. Additionally, it should be noted that it takes time to integrate technologies, tie together processes, and develop the needed skills for the sales force. [7,8] Thus, the acquirer's overall prospects depend not only on its ability to recognize a good fit, but also on its ability to take advantage of the opportunities that the deal presents and effectively implement a growth plan that will create shareholder value.

DEFINE SCREENING CRITERIA FOR IDENTIFYING A GOOD FIT

The criteria that should guide the screening process should be specific, well-documented, and consistently understood by those involved in the search process. The criteria should be realistic, based upon the availability or attractiveness of comparable targets in the marketplace. Prior to the commencement of the search, management must define which criteria are to be the deal killers. Critical concerns at this point can be addressed through innovative solutions while still recognizing that additional costs and management time may be incurred for integration. These additional costs should be included in the deal pricing. The acquirer should also look at its own resources, its cash outlay, and finally its readiness and willingness to take on debt or additional risks.

Target Screening Criteria

The screening criteria for a good fit can be assessed on three levels:
- How well does the target fit the acquirer's strategic agenda?
- How would the combination create synergies?
- How easy would the integration effort be?

Strategic Fit Screening Criteria
At the highest level, the fit between the acquirer and the target is based on strategic criteria. A good fit will accelerate the achievement of strategic goals and growth initiatives by providing strengths to counter-act the acquirer's needs and weaknesses and

close its strategic gap. The greater the acquirer's familiarity with the target's business—attractiveness of its industry , industry sector value drivers, and its growth potential— its ability to recognize a good fit will be further enhanced. Some of the criteria for identifying a target that is a good strategic fit include:

- Attractiveness of the industry and its dynamics.

- The size of the acquisition in terms of industry position, market share, and revenues.

- Future growth potential and the strength of the R&D pipeline.

- The alignment of corporate strategies and shared assumptions about future trends for the business, industry, and applications of technology.

- Target's financial strength, profitability, cash flows, cost structure, and ownership structure.

- Geographic scope and geographic market presence, the location of facilities, and channels of distribution.

- Target's track record of expansion into global markets.

- Brand reputation and portfolio of innovative product and service offerings, complementary brands, product advantages over competitors, and customer base loyalty.

- Asking price for the deal and potential regulatory and anti-trust barriers to a deal.

Synergy Screening Criteria

Synergies are the outcome of the fit between the target and the acquirer. Synergy criteria indicate the degree to which the fit between skills, assets, processes, and technologies contribute to the creation of synergies and value for the combined entity. An acquirer must estimate the magnitude of the short-term and long-term synergy benefits expected from the deal and project a timeline by which the expected benefits may be realized. Benchmarking the target's performance against industry norms can help the acquirer quantify the magnitude and timing of any expected short-term and long-term benefits. Synergies will appear in the form of lower costs, higher growth, and lower investment needs. Synergy fit criteria may include opportunities for benefit realization from:

- Shared strategies and business direction.

- Economies of scale from business overlaps such as administration and shared services as well as enhanced utilization of production capacity.

- The attractiveness and compatibility of assets, vicinity of geographic locations, and fit with processes, distribution networks, and technologies.

- Enhanced bargaining power.

- Cross-selling and expansion opportunities.

- Financial advantages such as tax advantages or carryover losses.

- Access to a trained and skilled workforce with specialist and needed competencies.

- Intangible assets.

Integration Screening Criteria

A successful integration allows for the realization of value from synergies at the expected magnitude and within the expected timeframe. Integration screening criteria will focus on the degree of integration and assimilation that may be required by the deal rationale and its resulting complexity. The integration of the two entities is facilitated when the target has certain characteristics:

- A track record with successful strategy implementation.

- Readiness for change and a low degree of resistance after the deal closes.

- Previous experience with mergers and acquisitions and major transformational change.

- Compatibility of cultural characteristics such as a similarity in management styles, operating philosophies, and operating practices.

- The motivation and quality of the target's management.

- Retention of valued employees.

COMPILE A CANDIDATE LIST

A candidate list can be generated internally or from external references, for example from investment bankers, lawyers, commercial bankers, business brokers, and other industry experts. The ongoing bottom-up strategic planning processes, involving managers from various levels, may identify a list of M&A candidates. A firm's dedicated mergers and acquisitions team may find an attractive M&A prospect when scanning the environment for new deal opportunities. A large firm undergoing industry consolidation and seeking the number-one global position in a product line may only have a handful of major global competitors, and so may start with a short list of interesting industry candidates known to management. If so, the list of potential candidates can be narrowed down relatively quickly. Occasionally, a candidate will standout because of specific strengths that are coveted by its immediate competitors, or due to the acquirer's asymmetric knowledge about the target. For a medium-sized firm wishing to augment its growth through acquisitions or for an investor acquirer looking to roll up companies in a fragmented industry, the number of targets is much broader with hundreds of potential candidates. For a small firm, the question of what to buy is much more complex and emotional since the owners, relatively speaking, have a greater stake in the outcome.

The process sometimes begins with an interested candidate that may step forward. Each year, large firms through direct or indirect means receive numerous offers to purchase companies that are ready at once to sell out. Businesses may sell divisions or lines that they no longer consider core; they may divest assets after an acquisition due to regulatory requirements; or they may be forced to divest themselves of assets because of commercial distress. An acquirer can solicit interested sellers who may be on the sidelines through direct solicitation or through third-party contacts.

SCREEN THE CANDIDATES

The screening process should allow for the close examination of the target's business and operating characteristics. A target that appears to be a good fit in the early investigations may appear less attractive after a more detailed examination. Thus, screening candidates is a multi-level iterative process. Once the selection criteria are determined, a methodical screening process ensues with the goal of narrowing down a long list of potential acquisition candidates to a few attractive targets.

Most screening models use two or three levels of screening as a way to get to the short list of candidates. Starting with a set of broad criteria that are consistently applied, screeners are able to narrow the candidate list by applying, in successive fashion, finer criteria, creating a more detailed examination. At each iteration, an acquirer can eliminate unattractive candidates that fail to meet the key screening criteria. A high-level screening process is basically a go/no-go assessment. The application of upper and lower limits to quantitative criteria would accelerate screening. The candidate must meet the high-level strategic criteria, or it will fall out of further consideration. An intermediate-level screening process utilizes more refined and more detailed criteria that are company specific and are based on the acquirer's business needs and priorities. At this stage, an acquirer is on the look out for any potential deal killers. For each candidate under serious consideration, a high level profile is developed. The initial high-level profile of the target is broad and is compiled from information known by acquirer's internal sources, publicly available data, and industry experts. As the candidate progresses through the screening process, the profile will become more detailed. The short list of candidates consists of the few targets that appear to have the best fit with the acquirer and are analyzed in order to determine their suitability; the suitable candidates are then finally approached to determine their availability. The screening process must also highlight any areas identified where there is an apparent lack of fit between the two firms as well as any potential risks associated with making the deal. Shortlist candidates need to be closely scrutinized through a variety of quantitative and qualitative criteria. The members of this list will be evaluated on their own merits, based on their performance against industry standards and against one another using various benchmarks and performance ratios. These are the finalists that the acquirer will actively approach and pursue. A large portion of the candidates are eliminated before they ever reach the negotiation stage. It is important during the screening process to maintain a good record of companies under consideration and to document any reason why candidates are removed from further consideration.

A systematic screening process does not necessarily imply a bureaucratic process. Companies do not always start their search for a merger or acquisition through systematic strategic development, the definition of search criteria, and candidate screening. A deal may in fact be entirely opportunistic from the perspective of a firm that is ready to sell out. An opportunistic approach, however, does not preclude the need to utilize a set of screening criteria. The acquirer will still need to determine whether or not the target would be a good fit, would create value, could be integrated, or could help the acquirer fulfill its financial and strategic objectives. The screening process requires an initial cash outlay, and it can become costly considering staff time, fees for external sources, and access to databases. This becomes a concern particularly for smaller firms with limited resources. However, the benefits of following a structured screening process, greatly outweigh any of these potential costs by significantly lowering the deal risks and providing for higher rewards in the form of long-term value creation.

A cross-functional team consisting of bright, experienced, and committed experts and leaders should undertake the screening process. The team should understand the significance of the search that they are conducting and its impact on the firm's long-term value creation. The cross-functional team should include a diversity of views and should be guided by a team leader who is inclusive and possesses strong problem solving skills. Selecting a good acquisition candidate also requires a diversity of views as well as an open environment for discussion and the exchange of ideas.

Candidate screening, though, may become biased at times and can pose challenges to the acquirer. Group-think can prevent screening team members from giving their unbiased opinions about an acquisition candidate, helping to avoid conflict with influential team members. An acquisition candidate supported by a strong leader enjoys a "halo effect" and may become highly regarded consistently throughout the selection criteria whether or not the rating is appropriate or realistic. Subordinates may view the deal as inevitable because of the opinions or preferences expressed by their leader, and thus others may fail to explore adequately the underlying issues. They may in this sense ignore the downsides of the deal or may over-emphasize the positives. Upper management often expects the support of middle management in the implementation of decisions even when middle management disagrees with the decision itself. Although management may seek input prior to making a decision, once the decision is made, management expects everyone to fall in line and carry out the decision. Integration of the deal can become more difficult when some managers are not onboard with the deal. It is for these reasons that candidate screening requires an open and careful environment where new ideas are put forth and discussed based on their individual merits and in relation to other possible acquisition candidates, and not on biases or gut feelings.

NOTES

[1] See *http://www.cms.hhs.gov/media/press/release.asp*

[2] Refer to Standard and Poor's Industry Surveys for overview of industry activity and business drivers.

[3] Source IMS, a provider of business intelligence on the healthcare and pharmaceutical industries at www.imshealth.com

[4] APEC's 21 member economies are Australia, Brunei Darussalam, Canada, Chile, People's Republic of China, Hong Kong, China, Indonesia, Japan, Republic of Korea, Malaysia, Mexico, New Zealand, Papua New Guinea, Peru, The Republic of the Philippines, The Russian Federation, Singapore, Chinese Taipei, Thailand, The United States of America, and Viet Nam. See www.apec.org. European Union member states are Austria, Belgium, Cyprus, Czech Republic, Denmark, Estonia, Finland, France, Germany, Greece, Hungary, Ireland, Italy, Latvia, Lithuania, Luxembourg, Malta, Poland, Portugal, Slovakia, Slovenia, Spain, Sweden, The Netherlands, and United Kingdom. ASEAN member countries are Brunei Darussalam, Cambodia, Indonesia, Laos, Malaysia, Myanmar, Philippines, Singapore, Thailand, and Vietnam. See www.aseansec.org. NAFTA members are The United States, Canada, and Mexico. MERCUSOR members include Argentina, Brazil, Paraguay, and Uruguay.

[5] See S&P Industry Surveys.

[6] See Michael Porter for a complete discussion of industry life cycle.

[7] See William Joyce, et al. in References. The Evergreen Study identified the 4+2 rule. Four primary management practices were identified as: 1) Strategy: Devise and maintain clearly stated, focused strategy. 2) Execution: Develop and maintain flawless operational execution. 3) Culture: Develop and maintain a performance-oriented culture. 4) Structure: Build and maintain a fast, flexible, flat organization. The four secondary management practices were identified as: 1) Talent: Hold on to talented employees and find more. 2) Leadership: Keep leaders and directors committed to the business. 3) Innovation: Make innovations that are industry transforming. 4) Mergers and partnerships: Make growth happen with mergers and partnerships.

[8] See Reference: Ansingler, Patricia L. etal. Coopers and Lybrand Trendsetter Barometer was summarized in *Quality* (Apr 1996).

CHAPTER 4

DETERMINING THE DEAL VALUE

Success Factors
- Consider the limitations of valuation methodologies
- Pay the right price

The value of the firm that is the target of an M&A deal is affected by a number of variables. Some of these variables are unique to the deal, such as the level and timing of expected synergies, which will create a specific financial advantage for the acquirer based on the degree of fit between the two businesses. Broad variables that can affect the target's value may include the quality, condition, and desirability of factors that affect the target's current and projected future cash flows such as: the quality of the target's strategy and business model and its alignment with evolving customer trends; the quality and health of its R&D pipeline; the degree of risk involved with the target's projects; the condition and desirability of the target's assets and facilities; the desirability of its geographic business locations; the potential of the firm's intangible assets such as the quality of its management, the desirability of the firm's intellectual capital, and its patents that may point to further untapped opportunities; industry growth potential, future trends, and the intensity of competition; and the projected macroeconomic outlook.

Despite all of the sophisticated models used for evaluating businesses, valuation is not a science; it is a complex and uncertain affair that depends on an understanding of and an appreciation for the underlying value drivers in a business. The quantification of value drivers, especially qualitative drivers, is complicated and subjective. The final valuation depends on a set of assumptions that can be affected by individual errors and biases. The accuracy of the assumptions made and the level of understanding of the models and methodologies used to arrive at the valuation, will affect the ability of the acquirer to reap value for its shareholders. It is up to the senior leadership to reject overly optimistic projections of target's value and walk away from giving their shareholder wealth away to the target's owners.

This chapter will review the potential shortcomings and drawbacks associated with two common valuation methodologies and factors that may affect deal pricing regardless of deal value.

SUCCESS FACTOR #10

CONSIDER THE LIMITATIONS OF VALUATION METHODOLOGIES

There are numerous valuation methods. Two common methods of firm valuation are **discounted cash flow** valuation and **relative** valuation.

DISCOUNTED CASH FLOW VALUATION METHODOLOGY

A company's fundamental value can be seen as the net present value of its forecasted future string of cash flows.[1] Discounted cash flow (DCF) analysis translates the string of future cash flows into a single value at the present time. DCF analysis is a dynamic process based on few constants and a number of variables that can raise or lower the resulting valuation. Key elements of a discounted cash flow analysis are quality assumptions, future projections of key variables, discount rate determination, and residual value calculation. These four elements together determine the soundness of the DCF valuation outcome. If time and resources permit, the acquirer should value the target based on a range of perspectives and using different methodologies such as relative valuation and payback period calculations, in order to give the analysis a broader perspective.

VALIDATE THE UNDERLYING ASSUMPTIONS.

The soundness of the valuation analysis depends heavily on, and is only as good as, the criteria and the assumptions that are used in the valuation modeling, the degree of objectivity of the analysis, and the quality and the reliability of information used in the analysis.

The target's value is determined from future expectations of performance by estimating the growth rate of cash flows, including the effect of synergies, and the period during which the growth rate is expected to continue. The events that affect the future performance of the target firm are uncertain and difficult to predict rationally or forecast accurately. Yet, the acquirer must make forecasts about the period of exceptional stable growth of the target's revenues and earnings by estimating the future size of the markets being served, the industry outlook and the intensity of competitive activity, the demand for target's products and its market share, its unit costs and operating income, and capital investment requirements to attain the expected growth, the effect of deal synergies on these variables, as well as systemic variables such as future interest rates, currency fluctuations, and their associated timing and their probability of occurrence in order to arrive at a range of performance expectations. In evaluating a firm's earnings, the analysis should focus on changes that are permanent and recurring. One-time events such as the sale of assets or inventory revaluation will therefore not have a long-term effect on the firm's earnings and its valuation.

Attaining long-term growth will require investments in growth projects. The ability to create new value will depend on the quality of investments made by the firm and not on the sheer level of investments. Portions of the firm's earnings are paid out as dividends, and the remainder is kept in the firm as retained earnings on the balance sheet. The firm can invest these retained earnings plus cash raised from debt as well as capital raised from equity markets into new sources of growth such as the following: research, new product development, new equipment, new plant capacity, promising technologies, strengthened distribution channels, sales force development, enhanced marketing capabilities, people competency development, and enhanced management know-how.

The industry's competitive intensity along with the availability of quality business opportunities affect the firm's ability to grow and create shareholder value. A clear vision and strategy, a strong management team, the effective use of available resources, and the ability to implement growth projects successfully are all leading indicators of the firm's future ability to create value. Financial indicators such as the firm's profitability and earnings are lagging indicators of the firm's value realization. Knowledge about the industry and the target company results in estimates concerning its future performance that are more realistic and more reliable forecasts for the development of *pro forma* financial statements.

The excessive reliance on historical data or recent operating data may not provide a complete picture of the target's future value creation potential—specially for early life cycle and high growth firms. A target's historical performance is useful for assessing the firm's past performance and highlighting important historical trends as it is for benchmarking against other industry players. A study of the target's annual reports for the past five years combined with recent quarterly reports, the price and activity of the security over the past two to five years, and the firm's relative performance compared with other firms in its industry for the past three to five years should be undertaken

Placing all the trust in black box solutions in the form of complex quantitative modeling and computational techniques for deal valuation can give management and analysts a false sense of security. The complexity of the modeling technique can be confused with a higher certainty and a greater clarity than is actually in existence. Considering time limitations then, it is critical that decision makers allocate some of their time to a thorough discussion about the underlying valuation assumptions and methods used to arrive at a credible valuation. Assumptions can be, of course, affected by biases, which may cause individuals to arrive at different conclusions by analyzing the same dataset. The discussions should consider: whether the base case used for the analysis is representative of the firm's business fundamentals and its long term stability; if the estimates for value drivers and other variables are too conservative or too aggressive; what uncertainties there are associated with these estimates. The discussion requires the focused attention of the executive team so that they can validate the assumptions made and prepare for the negotiation process. The discussion should include the methods used for data collection, data analysis, data interpretation, and the degree of confidence that there is in the credibility of the data and the data sources. A deliberate, disciplined, and detailed due diligence process should examine the assumptions made in the deal valuation and the business case.

DISCOUNT EACH STREAM OF CASH FLOW BASED ON ITS UNIQUE MERITS

The cost of capital is the risk-adjusted rate of return that the market expects to get from investing in a project. Risky investments are less attractive than safe investments, thus investors will demand a higher rate of return for the added risk that they assume. Economic profits represent additional returns over and above the firm's normal returns, which is its cost of capital. The firm's investments in new business opportunities will only create real value when they generate returns that are in excess of its cost of capital. Just as the company's cost of capital is tied to the firm's risk, each new investment initiative carries its own risk-and-return profile. Since the acquirer and the target have different risk profiles and different business models, the target's cost of capital is the appropriate discount rate for discounting the target's future string of cash flows, which it derives from its current assets and projects as well as its future investments, each based on their own merit and their own level of risk. The discount rate is calculated based on the market value, and not on the book value of the projects. Growth in cash flows is compounded year-upon-year, and the sources for financing do not affect firm cash flows.

EXAMINE THE FIRM'S LONG-TERM OPPORTUNITIES

In present value calculations, residual value represents a large portion of the business value. Residual value is uncertain because it will occur at some time in the future; it is based on expectations of performance from future products and services. The firm's growth will not go on *ad infinitum*, and at some future time, the firm will reach *homeostasis*. After reaching *homeostasis*, the firm will have a different expected growth rate than it had during a period of exceptional growth; therefore an appropriate discount rate must be applied to the residual value calculations.

In order to determine the sustainability of the firm's advantage and to estimate the length of time that the firm can sustain abnormal returns, the analysis should examine the firm's competitive environment as well as the available future investment opportunities. The firm functions in a dynamic and competitive marketplace where its every action causes a competitive reaction.[2] The actual time frame during which the firm can maintain a high rate of growth and can generate abnormal returns is limited. The strength of the competition limits the firm's ability to generate abnormal returns, and it impacts how quickly the abnormal returns will fade. When a firm identifies opportunities for capturing abnormal returns, its competitors and other potential market entrants will soon recognize the opportunity and move in to take a piece of the profits. Competitors relentlessly challenge the firm's markets and products by introducing substitute products and copying its strategy and operating practices, by imitating its selling and marketing methods, and by luring away its best talent. Regulatory impediments that favor the firm, such as a patent protection for a new pharmaceutical drug, will help the firm enjoy a more sustained period of abnormal performance. However, most obstructions can be surmounted or will disappear over time. As competitors enter the field, the returns diminish until incremental investment opportunities are no longer compelling. As industries advance in the stages of their life cycle, the firm's ability to grow is limited. It should be kept in mind that eventually the firm will simply run out of opportunities that can result in abnormal returns.

Depending on the life cycle stage, the firm's cash flow is usually forecasted over a planning horizon of five to ten years, beyond which the firm is considered to reach *homeostasis* and is assigned a residual value. The analysis should consider the appropriate period of time during which the firm can demonstrate abnormal returns prior to reaching *homeostasis*. For example, smaller firms demonstrating high rates of growth will have more room for growth compared to large firms. Firms with a high rate of product obsolescence, such as high-tech businesses, may only create cash flow for two to three years before the product is replaced with a new one. Pharmaceutical drugs have a limited patent life. A natural resource asset, such as an oil well, may generate cash flows for 15 to 20 years in the future, but once depleted, the resource will have little residual value. The characteristics of the firm's performance after *homeostasis*, such as in terms of its cash flows, its rate of reinvestment, and the cost of capital will also need to be decided.

Residual value can be calculated as a multiple of future cash flows and then discounted to the present, or it can be calculated based on assumptions of future growth rate and discount rate. The analysis at *homeostasis* uses marginal tax rates and accounts for long-term re-investment requirements and long term performance and growth expectations at the industry average due to erosion of competitive advantage.

RELATIVE VALUATION METHODOLOGY

Similar businesses, or assets with parallel fundamentals, are priced similarly in the marketplace through an approach known as relative valuation. This methodology assumes that the marketplace is efficient in that all of the available information is broadly known and is correctly reflected in the price of the security or asset. The approach used in relative valuation is fairly quick and simple. Surrogates in states comparable to that of the target firm can be used to define the value of the target prior to an in-depth analysis of its fundamentals. This methodology is most useful for acquirers who are knowledgeable and familiar with the target firm's industry.

In the case of publicly traded companies, the firm's security price can be figured as the product of the value reflecting the firm's financial performance (such as earnings, book value, sales, or dividends) and a valuation multiple (such as price-earnings ratio, price-book-value ratio, price-to-sales ratio, or price-to-dividends ratio). Other financial measures include revenues, EBITDA,[3] and EBIT.

The valuation multiple times the current or future financial performance represents a price that the investor is willing to pay to own the firm's security. Valuation multiples demonstrate the relative worth and relative performance of a security compared to other firms in its peer group. A multiple is an indication of the market expectations of the company's performance, its ability to generate positive earnings, and its growth potential. A high multiple demonstrates high expectations and a strong confidence in the current management's ability to sustain a trend of attractive earnings growth into the future. If the firm's fundamentals do not change, a stable and mature firm will generally maintain its valuation multiple over time.

CAREFULLY SELECT VALUATION MULTIPLE ESTIMATES

Equity analysts working at major investment houses usually estimate valuation multiples for a variety of publicly traded firms. However, estimated multiples may present certain risks and shortcomings.

How widely is the security held? The more widely a firm's security is tracked, the more reliable is the information available about the firm's valuation multiple. Equity analysts tend to estimate valuation multiples for firms that are widely held, that have large capitalization, and are held by institutional investors (who tend to use large amounts of valuation information). Many medium or small capitalization firms are not closely followed, and so useful and reliable estimates may not be readily available for them.

How up-to-date is the information used? Information used for valuing a firm is time-sensitive. The more up-to-date the firm-specific information is, the more likely that it is reflective of the firm's fundamentals. This is especially true when analyzing young and growing firms whose business and operating status can change dramatically in a short period of time. For large publicly traded firms, the annual reports and the quarterly 10-Q reports contain the most comprehensive set of publicly available information.

How reputable is the equity analyst? The acquirer should also consider the reputation and experience of the equity analyst who follows the security. The acquirer must scrutinize the quality of the analysis as well as the possible motivations of the analyst prior to accepting the analysis results.

CONSIDER VARIATIONS BETWEEN FIRMS

In M&A valuation, two comparable firms should be priced using similar multiples when their fundamentals are similar. Using probability analysis and sensitivities, it is possible to arrive at a probability distribution for valuation multiples with a range of acceptable prices for the target. Examples of comparable-company selection criteria may include:

- Industry and sector

- Public or private company

- Size of the assets

- Firm default risk

- Stage of industry life cycle and expected growth trends and rates

- Firm's financial performance such as profitability, earnings growth rate, and ability to generate cash flows

- Level of reinvestment

- Product-market similarities

- Location of facilities

- Technologies employed

- Synergies generated from the M&A deal

The selection of comparable companies and differences between firms may introduce unwanted biases into the valuation, which can affect the quality of the assessment. Businesses in small industry sectors and niche businesses are more difficult to value due to the smaller sample of comparable companies. The acquirer can adjust for the fundamental differences between businesses by reviewing the financial and operational information. Businesses that deviate from the industry norms can either become a source of advantage or disadvantage for the value of the target. The impact of each deviation from the norm should be evaluated independently, with the analysis based on the overall business value it brings or destroys. Deviations limit the breadth of the comparable businesses that are available, and thus during M&A negotiations, discussions can get bogged down by talk of how various elements of the business should be fairly valued.

For deal pricing, the analysis of recent comparable M&A transactions is used to determine transaction multiples and the level of premium being paid by acquirers for similar deals. The comparable M&A transaction selection criteria may include the size of the deal, how the transaction was paid for (stock, cash, or a combination), and the degree of integration required. The challenge in this is that there may be few comparable transactions available for comparison. Therefore the analysis may have to take into account a long historical view and make corrections for time period dependent variables, or it may need to search a broad geographic area and make corrections for regional differences.

Benchmarking

The purpose of benchmarking is to use standard industry practices as a point of reference from which individual company performances can be measured. Benchmarks are applied in different ways. The overall strengths and weaknesses of strategy, products-markets, profitability, work processes, and costs are frequently benchmarked by using common key indicators. Benchmarking can identify an untapped potential and can test certain perceptions of company performance.

All benchmarking approaches require a high degree of rigor in order to create like comparisons. Information required for benchmarking can be collected through literature searches concerning publicly traded entities. For privately held entities, as a supplement to the search data, direct interviews are an effective tool. Since benchmarking has gained wide acceptance, firms tend to accept requests for direct interviews or site visits, and they usually want to obtain a copy of the report and the comparisons.[5]

BEWARE OF SHORTCOMINGS IN RELATIVE VALUATION

There are certain shortcomings in applying relative valuation. Since future data are hard to forecast, the analysis is usually focused on recent historical information, and the multiple is generally applied to the most recent twelve month performance. It is complicated in this respect to represent all future changes in a firm's performance, such as the changing expectations of growth, by using a single multiple. In addition, finding a representative sample of surrogate companies and transactions that can be used for comparison with the target may be difficult at times. The acquirer needs an in-depth understanding of industry fundamentals, the key drivers of performance, and the impact of external and internal events on the firm's results. One caution here is that an overpriced industry sector will naturally introduce biases into the valuation.

Accounting rules and practices have limitations, and discrepancies in recent firm data can mask the actual firm performance in the base case[4]. In the case of a public firm, its financial performance, along with its ability to generate income from its operations and investments, is extracted from what the firm reports in its quarterly financial *pro forma* reports. A close examination of the firm's financial reporting and its underlying assumptions is necessary to determine how well the firm's accounting earnings reflect the firm's true performance and the health of its operations. The quality of this analysis, it should be said, is only as good as the quality of the information that is available.

Firms may deliberately or unwittingly engage in practices that enhance the appearance of their business performance in the hope of gaining a higher valuation and thereby a higher price for their firm. The target firm's management generally knows more about the firm and its performance than any outsiders do. Thus, it is critical to conduct a thorough due diligence to understand the underlying firm performance.

Valuing Small Private Firms

Small privately-owned or family-owned businesses, which may not be expected to be viable beyond the tenure of current owners, are not considered to be going concerns and command little or no residual value. Small firms are valued based on the total market value of their underlying assets and investments. Relative valuation can then be applied to such small firms through income capitalization. The capitalization rate is a divisor and can be seen as the inverse of the firm's valuation multiple. The primary economic measures in this case can be revenues, earnings, cash flow, dividends, net income, net sales from the firm's most recent 12 months, sales projections over the next 12 months, or sales averaged over a recent multi-year period. Another method used for valuing these small businesses is the gross-revenue-multiplier, through which a multiple is applied to the business's annual gross revenues. The value of other assets of the business, such as land and inventory, are added to this value.

Variability between businesses is typically the result of factors such as the location of the business, the quality and reputation of its owners, the terms of the lease for equipment and facilities, the types and range of services offered to customers, quality of work, the frequency of promotions, and the age and condition of equipment and facilities. Variability in practices may also in this respect include the owner's compensation, depreciation and amortization practices, accounting for maintenance costs, and capital expenditures. An accredited business appraiser in such a case will have to make adjustments to arrive at cash flows comparable to other similar businesses.

SUCCESS FACTOR #11

PAY THE RIGHT PRICE

The objectives of the acquirer and the target will diverge, of course, on the issue of price. Sellers want to get the highest price that they can for the target. Their emotional attachment to their business compounded by years of hard work and dedication to the entity may cause sellers to over-estimate the value of their firm. For the acquirer, the objective is naturally to pay the lowest possible price so that it can accrue value and wealth for its own shareholders and owners and add immediate value to its bottom line. These divergent objectives obviously have to be brought into some sort of agreement if a deal is to go through.

Overpaying for an acquisition gives away value to the target's shareholders that should have accrued for the acquirer's owners. The value that would accrue for the acquirer because of the deal represents the difference between the target's strategic value to the acquirer less the transaction value that the acquirer ends up paying for the deal. To avoid destroying value by overpaying, the target's strategic value should represent the upper threshold of the price that the acquirer is willing to pay for the deal. At this price, 100% of the value of the strategic synergies would go to the target's shareholders, and the acquirer's owners would accrue no value from the deal. However, an overly anxious acquirer may end up paying too much for the target, owing to a number of factors, which may include the wish to secure a friendly deal and keep competitors out. The acquirer may also overpay because other competing suitors are bidding for the target and creating an auction situation. Finally, after all the publicity and expectations, the pressure to close the deal may be too overwhelming even if the deal is overpriced.

The transaction value can include a premium over the target's fundamental value or its fair market value in the form of a higher price-earnings or price-book ratio. Studies show that acquirers on average pay 20% to 40% of the pre-acquisition share price of the target in the form of premium. This is a significant investment that the acquirer will expect to recover through the deal's immediate synergies and through its more robust long-term growth. The combination is expected to create real value, which ultimately will result in higher security prices for the acquirer's investors.

Studies show that the target's share price generally rises as much as 30% or more following an M&A deal announcement in anticipation of the premium that is to be paid by the acquirer. The acquirer's share price at this time stays even or declines since the market assumes that the premium covers any immediate gains from synergies that could accrue to the acquirer. Paying the premium in this respect shifts the capture of value and wealth from acquirer's shareholders to the target's shareholders. If the M&A deal does not succeed in realizing new value and attractive returns in the long run, the acquirer's shareholders are greatly deterred from accepting an M&A deal. Thus shareholder approval is premised on their trust that the management is capable of realizing the promised synergistic value after the deal. Some deals might take place with a low premium or at a discount to the target's market value either because the target firm is in distress, or it is a mature firm with no apparent synergies and so has difficulty attracting buyers, or because it has a weak or uninformed management that is unable to negotiate a good deal.

The comparable transaction price analysis compares the deal premium to a representative sample of comparable base cases. The price is compared to the fluctuations in the target's security value over the previous 12 months in order to accommodate for various cyclical effects and other temporary price fluctuations using the pre-rumor security value for the analysis. The premium paid by other comparable deals may be analyzed using selection criteria including the transaction value, deal type, or general transactions irrespective of the deal size both inside and outside the target's industry. The deal premium can also be compared to the present value of expected future cost savings and other synergies considering their magnitude, their effect on organizational performance, the timing of their realization, their resource requirements, and the capital investment requirements for their implementation.

Some consider the acquirer's price-earnings ratio as the upper multiple of earnings that the acquirer should offer for an M&A deal. Paying a higher multiple of earnings than the acquirer's own will result in a dilution of or a decrease in relative worth of the acquirer's earnings-per-share after the acquisition. The inverse of this is that if the target has a lower price-earnings ratio than the acquirer, there will be an accretion or addition in earnings-per-share for the acquirer's owners after the acquisition compared to the pre-acquisition earnings-per-share. Both the dilution and the accretion of post-acquisition earnings will be short-term phenomena if the combined entity can attain the expected growth rate from the deal and deliver attractive returns to recover its premium.

In a stock swap—using the exchange of securities to do a deal—the exchange ratio between the acquirer's security and the target's security can be fixed to create certainty about the number of the acquirer's shares that will be issued to the target's shareholders at closing of the deal. This fixed ratio will also create certainty about the percentage of the combined entity that the target's shareholders will hold after the deal closes. The actual value received by the target's shareholders and the premium paid by the acquirer, however, will depend upon the market price of the acquirer's shares at the time that the deal is closed. If the value of the acquirer's share increases compared to the target's shares, the premium will grow. The inverse of this can also occur.

In some stock-swap deals, the seller's shareholders hold an advantage, which is gained through their ability to realize capital gains at a deferred time of their own choosing and so potentially reduce their immediate personal tax liabilities.[6] Under these conditions, the seller shareholders should decide whether to keep the acquirer's shares or to divest of them immediately. If the acquirer's future value creation potential does not appear attractive as a result of an overpriced deal, the target's shareholders are more likely to dump the acquirer's shares. Studies show that firms that pay for the deal by swapping stocks tend to over-price a deal, while deals that use cash perform better in the long term. An acquisition target's shareholders may be better off selling their shares after the deal announcement since studies also show that the acquirer's stock value is more likely to remain even or to drop after the merger in a stock-swap deal.

With the use of technology and valuation modeling, merger and acquisition valuation becomes a dynamic process that allows the acquirer to rearrange, expand, and experiment with key assumptions in order to observe their effects on valuation outcomes. Thus, valuation models are useful for deal negotiation and are an invaluable tool throughout the due diligence process. As the acquirer uncovers new information about certain variables, it can examine the effect of this new information on the target's valuation and arrive at a realistic basis for the negotiations. The problems with a deal price stem from the differences between the actual performance of the valuation variables after the deal closes and the assumptions and forecasts made about those variables during the deal valuation. Cash flow models can be very sophisticated yet very misleading if underlying assumptions are not realistic. Understanding the limitations inherent in each valuation methodology, especially the validation of base assumptions used in arriving at the deal value, and understanding the risks unique to the investment while considering differences between the firms will enable the acquirer to realize greater return from its investment and enhance the chances of deal success

NOTES

[1] See Damodaran in References for a complete discussion of firm valuation.

[2] See Michael Porter's Five Forces.

[3] EBITDA (Earnings Before Interest Taxes Depreciation and Amortization) is similar to firm cash flows.

[4] Following are some examples of issues with accounting earnings:
- Accounting earnings are lagging measures of performance and effects of changes in the firm's operating conditions or external changes are not fully reflected in the firm's earnings until a later period.
- Timing of the operating decisions can affect the firm's earnings (e.g. cash flow can be enhanced by delaying payment of account payables).
- Matching expenses to revenues is open to some interpretation.
- Items may be booked incorrectly in categories that do not reflect their true nature. Operating expenses can be capitalized to spread their effect over multiple periods.
- Non-recurring items can be used to boost earnings in a period when earnings are low. Reserves can be developed to smooth out bumps in business activity.
- Changing accounting practices can improve performance.
- R&D expenditures result in lower earnings in the period during which the expenditure occurs and higher earnings in future periods when the investments pay off.
- Embryonic, fast-growth firms and firms in severe distress, may not have any positive earnings.
- Activities that are not reported on the balance sheet can hide expenses and inflate revenues.

[5] Sources of data for benchmarking studies include the RMA Annual Statement Studies, IRS Corporate Ratios, and other industry sources. These reports provide ratios for businesses in various industries by industry sector and size of business.

[6] Payment for the M&A deal can be in the form of cash, debt, stocks, or a

combination and the deal is subject to shareholder approval. A Taxable Deal is from direct sale of stocks or assets of a company where the seller recognizes a gain or a loss. Tax Free Reorganization allows the seller to defer taxes until a later time when the stock is sold. In a tax free transaction, the acquired entity is extinguished and the sellers should retain sufficient interest in the combined entity.

CHAPTER 5

NAVIGATING THE DEAL DISCUSSIONS

Success Factors
- Do your homework with the best available information
- Promote the deal rationale from first contact
- Know the seller's intents
- Pursue tough but fair discussion criteria
- Assess the quality of the target's management

Having arrived at a candidate shortlist, an acquirer can begin approaching the potential target firm's management in order to explore the possibility of forming an M&A deal. The deal discussions are complex, and the acquirer may be faced with a number of obstacles in arriving at a mutually acceptable outcome. Some of these obstacles may include lack of interest by the target about the deal, a scarcity of reliable information for the deal, low trust levels during the deal discussions, and disagreements between the acquirer and the target on how to run the combined business in terms of governance and control. It is incumbent upon the acquirer at this point to craft a strong deal rationale in its proposal and to present a convincing business case that will get the attention of the target's management, owners, and Board of Directors. The acquirer should explore and learn of the intentions and objectives of the seller, what the target's management values in the deal, and the reasons behind the divestiture. Although price and premium are of critical importance here, the acquirer's approach and its knowledge about the target can enhance its position in deal discussions and significantly improve its ability to win over the target in the end by proposing an attractive package consisting of a price and terms that would address the needs of the target without giving away deal value. Having gained commitment to further pursue the deal discussions, the two sides try to reach an agreement with the assistance of their advisers. Successfully navigating the deal discussions in these terms requires a strong deal rationale, access to quality information about the target's history and potential, and, without a doubt, good negotiating skills.

SUCCESS FACTOR #12

DO YOUR HOMEWORK WITH THE BEST AVAILABLE INFORMATION

Information is the most valuable tool for defining the deal value proposition and developing a well-documented business case. In M&A deal discussions, it remains a source of great advantage for the acquirer. The acquirer should gain access to the best information available regarding the target by doing its homework early on in the process. Investigating the target and obtaining good information is in general a costly endeavor, but an upfront investment in information acquisition will pay-off through the overall enhancement of deal decision-making, better negotiations, and lower deal risks since it provides the acquirer with the opportunity to recognize and abandon a bad deal before making significant emotional and financial commitments to it. As the deal progresses, the acquirer will be able to gain more information about the deal parameters and about the target as a whole. On the other side of things, the target will most likely collect its own information about the acquirer after the initial contact is made. Some types of information that the acquirer would need includes:

- The target's financial and operational information.

- Knowledge of the industry trends, value drivers, norms, and rules.

- Knowledge of key competitors, customers needs, and market trends.

- Information about the target's formal organization structure and key players.

The acquirer should also understand the target's ownership structure as well as its major shareholders, who may require separate agreements to support the deal.

For virtually all publicly traded companies, a great wealth of information is easily and readily available in annual reports, 10K and 10Q filings, and proxy statements. Other sources of data collection could include Internet searches and review of materials available in the public domain such as industry publications, magazines, and books. Other publicly available sources include Ward's, Dun & Bradstreet, manufacturing association membership lists, trade journal listings, media reports, and analyst reports. The acquirer can determine the credit health of the target by going to credit-rating agencies such as Standard and Poor's and Moody's.[1] The acquisition of a division or a smaller part of a public company will make access to data more difficult but not impossible. For small firms, particularly privately held companies, publicly available data are relatively scarce, and companies may not be willing to reveal such data.

Expert advice is available externally through business brokers and finders, listing services, lawyers, accountants, trade associations, investment bankers, and commercial bankers. These intermediaries usually require a fee for their services; whether the seller or the buyer pays the fee may be a matter of negotiation. For small acquirers, the fees involved could constitute an important percentage of the deal price, and acquirers are well advised to understand those costs before initiating their search. The acquirer's internal resources such as their research staff, sales managers, and purchasing staff have regular contact with competitors, customers, and suppliers and can prove to be knowledgeable sources of competitor information. Some firms may even utilize a "competitor intelligence" system to gather data about their industry competitors over time.

When the target's information is closely guarded and limited, the results of an analysis can be subject to wide interpretation. The acquirer here can end up using industry averages as surrogates for the target's particulars. If there are too many assumptions being made at this point, the valuation analysis will not be reliable. In such situations, an acquisition should not be pursued unless the target's audited financial statements have been closely examined.

SUCCESS FACTOR #13

PROMOTE THE DEAL RATIONALE FROM FIRST CONTACT

The initial contact with the target management is an important event. The purpose of the initial contact is to determine the target's general interest level in pursuing a strategic relationship between the two companies. A successful and attractive business model will provide the potential target with a number of strategic options to pursue, and thus the target's management may not respond positively to a proposed M&A deal. When the acquirer approaches the target with the suggestion of a deal, the target may reject the proposal outright, consider it initially but pull back, be interested in discussion but not serious about engagement, or may be willing to consider the proposal seriously. At initial contact, key points of discussion between the two parties should revolve around the deal rationale: why the deal makes sense, how it will bring value to both parties, and what makes the acquirer the right choice. The deal rationale should clearly point out the merits and advantages of the deal and build a convincing case.

INTRODUCE THE ACQUIRER AS A VIABLE PARTNER

The acquirer wants to demonstrate that it is a viable entity and would make a good suitor for the target. It should therefore promote the quality of its company, its fit with the target's business, its positive long-term outlook, and its management's personal energy and enthusiasm about the deal. Thus, the acquirer should present a profile of its company that includes the historical, operational, organizational, and technical aspects of its business. The target management will generally be interested in information about the acquirer such as the acquirer's strategic objectives, its future growth expectations, its financial viability and strength, its capital structure, and any recent major investments or past acquisitions. An overview of the firm's operating plan, its capacity utilization, and expansion plans will also be of interest to the target's management. Other information of interest may include:

- A description of markets, market strategy, market position, and a list of products and services offered, pricing strategy, product and service quality as well as the strength of its distribution channels.

- A list of key customers and benefits derived by these customers from the firm's products and services.

- Its internal capabilities such as the strength of the R&D pipeline, previous R&D successes, patents and trademarks, the strength of management team, and strategy execution successes.

At this early stage, the acquirer should not yet discuss price, but instead should focus on the business benefits that both sides will accrue.

ESTABLISH THE DEAL RATIONALE

To reach an agreement about the M&A deal, the acquirer and the target need to come to a meeting of the minds, in both rational and emotional terms. Rational discussions revolve around the fit between the two firms. The acquirer should promote the financial and operational benefits that will accrue for the owners of the target. The deal may enhance the chances for company survival by keeping the company whole and avoiding distress. The deal may also provide strategic advantages in terms of entering emerging growth opportunities, cash flow for the introduction of new products, a renewed strength to face the industry's competitive forces, lower cost structure, broader combined customer relationships, expansion of the distribution networks, and access to greater market share.

The non-financial benefits of the deal may include: identifying a viable long-term partner, a stronger management team to implement the business strategy, and the promotion of socially responsible policies and positive contributions to the community, which could be expanded through the combination of firms. Other benefits of the deal may include greater job security for the remaining employees, the creation of new jobs, opportunities for employee growth and development, increased job responsibilities, and potential career advancement in a larger firm. Those who stay on with the combined business may have the opportunity to gain attractive roles and titles, above-average remuneration, and perhaps even share ownership in the new business. The acquirer can create new positions in this respect to retain those high-quality employees, thereby potentially preventing any unnecessary departure of valued employees. The acquirer can also offer plans to ease the pressure of lay-offs through outplacement programs for departing employees.

The ease with which integration is achieved remains an important concern to both sides. Integration is facilitated when the cultures are compatible, business processes are similar, and operational locations are geographically close. The development of a detailed and thoughtful integration plan should dispel some of the major integration concerns early on in the process.

The acquirer should at this time be prepared to put forward creative solutions for the target's specific needs. Sellers in medium-sized and small businesses may be interested in alternative arrangements such as taking part of the price in the form of an employment contract. Different partners in the business may have different needs, which the acquirer may be able to satisfy and thereby facilitate the deal. A complex deal structure for these reasons may be less attractive to the seller, but a deal structure that clearly addresses the needs of the different constituent groups will generally be more appealing. The credibility of the proposal can be increased and strengthened through the endorsement of major reputable and credible investors, bankers, and recognized insiders.

Every deal will naturally have certain downsides that the acquirer should make a strong effort to disclose. The downsides may include the loss of jobs, facility closures, and other cost reduction initiatives. On the other hand, the downsides of not doing a deal could include the long-term failure of the business, having to break up the company to sell large chunks of assets, and other unwanted outcomes to the owners. The acquirer should differentiate itself as a valuable contribution when it promotes the deal rationale in order to make the competition appear less attractive, in case other potential suitors should enter the fray.

SUCCESS FACTOR #14

KNOW THE SELLER'S INTENTS

In contrast to publicly traded companies, small private firms are more dependent on their current owners and have more limited access to needed resources. Selling a business in which the owners have invested many years of their time and equity is a difficult and emotional decision. Sellers of successful firms take pride in their business accomplishments and know their industry, markets, and customers very well.

The reasons for the sale may vary. The seller may be motivated by wanting to gain access to resources it could not on its own: for example, new growth opportunities, access to international markets, or in the case of a growing company, access to significant capital investments that could supply additional production capacity. On the other hand, there can be other underlying financial and operational issues for the seller that would make it want to divest itself of the business. The seller of a small business may be planning on retirement and may have personal financial goals that he or she wants to get from the sale of the business. Declining earnings and business devaluation may force an owner to sell the business instead of fixing the underlying issues at stake. A declining business value may stem from issues with business operations, the technological obsolescence of the products, or from an owner who becomes distracted from running the day-to-day business. The business may also have succession issues, or it may have lost key management talent. Without a willing acquirer, the seller may have to liquidate the business and sell its assets. In a partnership, there could be conflict and disagreement among the owners regarding the direction of the business, and the business partners may not be able to agree upon a business strategy.

The seller will try to sell the company while its value is high and while it is still demonstrating a positive business performance with the least amount of post-sale liabilities; therefore it may rationalize a business rebound to the acquirer. It may also in this respect take steps to enhance temporarily the value of the business through cost lowering actions, such as reducing advertising, minimizing insurance coverage, delaying payables, eliminating administrative expenses, and canceling the owner's salary and perks. The seller can enhance the condition of its assets and offices in order to create a more attractive image. Some owners may even try to use more aggressive accounting techniques of which the acquirer must be extremely mindful. The acquirer may be overly pessimistic about the target's business potential, especially as it involves itself with a former competitor, and so the acquirer may become biased through an overly critical assessment of the target's potential. It is incumbent then upon the acquirer to undertake a robust due diligence of the target's business with an objective view of the deal benefits and downsides before the close.

SUCCESS FACTOR #15

PURSUE TOUGH BUT FAIR DISCUSSION CRITERIA

General questions to ask before the deal process progresses beyond the initial stage include:

- Does the target meet the fit criteria and should it be pursued further?

- Does evidence suggest that the target is ready to deal?

- What is the appropriate pace for proceeding with deal discussions?

The deal discussion parameters and timetables are dictated by leadership teams from both firms. Discussions can last weeks or months. Major shareholders or partners will have an impact on the deal discussions. Each side must know what their counterparts value in the deal. For deal discussions to be successful, the two sides need to find areas of common interest, and each side should feel that it has gained something of value. Both sides will have a price range in mind, and deals will go through if the two price ranges overlap. Price is a contentious issue though, and the focus of the initial deal discussions should be on the deal value instead. The value of an offer may be enhanced through appealing terms that the other side covets, such as attractive positions for the target's management in the new organization.

Sellers should approach the deal discussions with a realistic idea about the value of their business. A seller that is not knowledgeable about the value of its business will place itself at a disadvantage during the deal discussions. For a small business, the seller can determine the value of the business by employing an outside appraiser. The value of the target business includes a wide range of value drivers including the "hard assets" of equipment, buildings, land, facilities, and inventory, and the "soft assets" of good managers, quality employees, as well as "intangibles" such as patents, trademarks, copyrights, and customer lists.

GAIN ADVANTAGE IN DEAL DISCUSSIONS

During the M&A process, each side will strive to gain the upper hand in the deal discussions, and as a result, will want to secure more of the deal value for themselves. What follows are some circumstances that can be exploited for one's advantage in M&A deal discussions.

Time can be a strong factor in deal discussions. An impending deadline can place very high pressure on either side, and it may increase their flexibility to reach an agreement. Under time pressure, there is greater willingness to make concessions, and having a knowledge of the opponents pending deadline is an opening by which to extract concessions for the side that is not under such time constraints. To take advantage of time pressures, each side will keep some aspects of their position hidden until the last minute, hoping that through the approaching deadline, it can force the other side to give up something of value. When information about the deal is leaked to the media, for example, it creates certain time pressures for the deal discussions. The company that knows its business performance will fall short of expectations is under pressure to make a deal before its quarterly reports are released. A firm may be in a cash crunch or have succession issues that likewise place it under time pressure. Regulatory requirements and timelines, similar to a tender offer, can create various deadlines as well. The target or other suitors can use delay tactics such as the threat of litigation to create additional time pressures for the acquirer. The passage of time, on the other hand, can help each side get more comfortable with each other's positions, thereby, making them more likely to accept the other's conditions. Patience in deal discussions, for these reasons, can be in the end a great virtue.

Knowledge gathered about the opposite side's weaknesses, its alternatives, and needs will enhance one's ability to exact concessions and demand more favorable terms that will allow for the capture of more value. When a negotiating side is not prepared to walk away from the deal discussions, it is more likely that its side will give up value. A firm whose survival depends on making the deal can end up parting with all the value that could otherwise have been gained. Having an alternative allows one to walk away from an unfavorable deal. The acquirer may have other candidates on its shortlist, and the target may have other suitors who can create an auction situation or may identify a white knight willing to offer the target more attractive terms.

Demanding more favorable terms and being unwilling to budge creates a win-lose situation. Bluffing about one's position may cause the other side to call the bluff; therefore, such a move carries with it the danger that the bluffer may become stuck in a defenseless position in addition to destroying trust. Given that trust remains a key to successful deal making, these strategies can often break down deal discussions.

BUILD TRUST AND RAPPORT

A positive and friendly initial contact, which leads to the seller receptiveness is the first hurdle in deal making. The acquirer should come across as respectful and committed to the target's organization, while remaining mindful of the anxieties that this relationship could create for the target's management. The acquirer should treat the target management as equals and avoid letting egos take over the M&A discussions. For a successful M&A deal, the senior executives of the two organizations will have to work through many difficult decisions together. It is important in this respect to ensure that deal discussions proceed ethically and respectfully. A mutually respectful and productive relationship also keeps the door open should the acquirer want the target's management to stay on after the deal, putting the target's CEO and management team at ease about their future.

It is important to note as well that business relations will go on whether or not the two sides reach an agreement. Early M&A discussions may not lead immediately to a deal; therefore staying in touch with the target and nurturing the relationship may lead to a deal later on through gained trust and rapport. Each company may look at other potential suitors, or they may identify other previously unexplored strategic alternatives that might enhance shareholder value. The two sides may yet return to the negotiating table if presented with a compelling case.

Management chemistry can also greatly affect deal discussions. Good chemistry between two CEO's is not a necessary condition for a deal to go through, but it can certainly facilitate the deal progress. A battle of egos between senior people can most assuredly break a deal. The initial contact can be conducted through a senior executive and trusted advisers, ensuring that decision makers get unfiltered information. When the leaders of the two entities have a common vision about the future of their industry, their companies, and how their companies could fit together, they have a key focal point for deal discussions.

The acquirer can create an atmosphere of trust when it delivers on its promises and demonstrates genuine attempts to reach a win-win solution. The following are some good considerations to keep in mind when negotiating an M&A deal:

- Raise concerns and issues early in the deal discussion process in order to give both sides time to resolve issues through compromise. It is always more beneficial to raise these issues and negotiate solutions before a deadline looms.

- During the deal discussions, be respectful and listen carefully to the opposing side's point of view to gain insights about what they value or fear losing in the deal.

- Stay current on events and news reported in the media or by industry sources about both sides.

- Put forward positions that can be consistently supported with facts and reasoning.

The time and effort invested in deal discussions should be considered sunk costs. Each M&A deal should be evaluated on its own merits and not in terms of the emotional investment of the deal makers who are doing a deal.

Certain agreements can ensure the quality and commitment of both sides to the deal. The acquirer can ask for guarantees from the seller in the form of contingent payouts.[2] A no solicitation clause limits the ability of the target to attract alternative offers or white knights.[3] A termination fee can be used to ensure that both sides are committed to the deal and that the offer is not frivolous.[4]

Throughout the deal discussions, the acquirer and the target need to maintain confidentiality about the pending deal from outsiders as well as their own employees until they are ready to make an announcement. Information about the deal may invite competitors to the table. Typically, sellers avoid the release of any financial information unless they perceive that the acquirer is ready to engage in serious deal making and is willing to sign a confidentiality agreement. If they hear about the deal prematurely, star employees may decide to jump ship. Confidentiality may be especially key for sellers of private businesses whose family members may be on the payroll, who may have an emotional attachment to the company and might want to disrupt the deal.

COMMUNICATE THE DEAL BENEFITS TO ALL STAKEHOLDERS

Once the deal is announced, the acquiring senior management must convince all stakeholders that the M&A deal is a sound undertaking that is worthy of pursuit and worth the investment of their time and energy to make it succeed. This post-announcement communication can include the following:

- The background of the deal and industry and company drivers that created the need for the M&A deal.

- The strategic, operational, and financial rationale of the deal in terms of business success, opportunities for people, advantages for customers, expected synergies, and long-term value creation for shareholders and other stakeholders.[5]

- The direction of the combined entity and the continuity and consistency of operations and offerings.

- Governance and organization structure in the new entity.

- High-level integration plans, synergy targets, implementation timelines, and any potential barriers to successful integration.

- Challenges for the combined entity such as job losses and customer impact as well as key decisions that have already been made.

Timely communication builds trust and enhances employee commitment to the deal's success.

SUCCESS FACTOR #16

ASSESS THE QUALITY OF THE TARGET'S MANAGEMENT

The target management may be motivated by a position in the new company where members can continue to contribute and be valued. An acquirer who intends to retain the target's management is interested primarily in the quality of management talent. Though this is a difficult task, it is imperative that the acquirer undertake a thorough assessment of the quality, stability, and commitment of the target's management team. This will include information about the CEO and other senior managers, their roles and backgrounds, its formal organizational structure, and its decision making style. The acquirer should determine if the target's management is willing to work with the acquiring management, if it is committed to the long-term success of the business, their motivations, their ideas for improving the business, their decision-making ability under difficult conditions, and finally the chemistry they have with the acquirer's senior management.

For the acquisition of a large firm in a merger of equals, managers of the target are in general closely involved in many of the key decisions including governance, power sharing, control, organizational structure, and succession plans; they can be very sensitive even if the deal makes strategic sense. Many deals never make it beyond the initial discussions due to differences on these issues. The outcomes of these decisions have implications in terms of prestige and power; therefore they are closely watched and scrutinized by those who are weighing the winners and losers. Some of the potentially contentious issues that both sides should reach agreement on before any announcement include:

- The name to be given to the combined entity, the new logo, and what will become of previous entities.

- The ownership structure of the new entity and the commercial relationships with major owners and partners.

- The makeup of the Board of Directors in the new entity.

- Who will fill the key positions in the new management team: the role of the Chairman and CEO, the role of other key management team members, and issues of succession.

- Rewards and compensations for the departing senior management.

- The location of the headquarters and the need for relocation of management team members.

Any agreements are documented in a letter of intent and will finally become part of the "memorandum of agreement" that both key parties sign.

DEFINE THE FORM AND FUNCTIONS OF THE NEW ENTITY.

The new entity must be organized so that it can deliver long-term value for its owners. The two sides will have to agree on a number of concepts. At the highest level, the question of autonomy and integration needs to be resolved.

- How much autonomy would the target have in directing and managing its day-to-day business?

- What degree of resource sharing will be needed, and how will the activities that cross the two entities' boundaries be coordinated?

- What elements of the organization will be integrated and assimilated between the two entities?

The outcome of deciding these questions will be the new form of the combined organization. Considering the size of the new entity, the organization model should address the need for flexibility, agility, and a responsiveness to internal and external change drivers. It should likewise address the need to enhance customer focus in order to respond to transformations in the marketplace, the evolution of customer needs, the fit of the technology drivers, and the emergence of new nimble and global competitors.

The organization structure design includes the formal organization structure, the layers of management, the means for a lateral coordination of activities, and key process flows. The new organization structure should be fit-for-purpose and allow for the realization of the M&A vision and strategy, while enabling the achievement of the desired synergies as well as its expected performance results. The new organizational model should enable the effective sharing and coordination of knowledge, skills, and competencies in the new combined entity along with an effective communication with internal and external stakeholders.

Other considerations for the combined entity include the complexity of the work being performed, the need for formalized processes and procedures, and the degree of the centralization of decision-making. Organizations in this sense should not be viewed as static monoliths, but rather as living, adapting, and evolving organisms. Each organization structure offers certain benefits and shortcomings, and so management will invariably make some trade-offs as it selects an organization model. The organization design can take many forms. What follows are some examples of common organization models.

Function-based organization structure focuses on the specialization of functions such as marketing, finance, and operations. In this model, groups of specialists are organized in the same function under one management. Each function provides economies of scale, and functional management is streamlined. The functional model facilitates knowledge sharing within the group, though it is more difficult to share knowledge between functions. This model is more suitable for an established and mature industry environment where changes are incremental since this model may reduce flexibility as well as the adaptability to external environmental changes because decision making is slowed by the need for horizontal coordination across functions.

Product-based organization brings multiple functions into focus on a product-line. As a result, the company can enhance product quality and offer more product features. Product decisions are made locally and thus are accelerated. Each product-line organization, however, will duplicate functional resources, which results in increased costs. Clients purchasing multiple product lines from the firm may get confused and experience inconveniences in that they will have to work with multiple product-based organizations equipped with potentially different pricing and service strategies.

Geography-based organization brings together all the needed resources to adapt to and serve a geographic market's needs in order to understand more fully their local markets and serve them in a cost effective way. Since resources are spread around the globe in various locations, functional excellence may suffer. With differences in customer preferences among locations, there could be a proliferation of products, and hence a complicated and costly new product development process.

Process-based organizations are structured to enable key customer facing processes. Centered on the results, process-base increases the responsiveness to changing customer preferences, applies multiple functions to each step of the process, and reduces the duplication of work as resources are focused on work that would add value to the customer. Functional proficiency will have to be maintained here since individuals may be focused on multiple tasks at each step.

A **matrix organization** brings together a number of vertical organizations in order to deliver a horizontal focus. Managers responsible for the vertical organizations will usually have conflicts with managers responsible for horizontal results pertaining to priorities and resource needs, which can slow down decision making. A **virtual organization** brings together a network of collaborative resources to take advantage of a new emerging opportunity.

There are few absolutes in organization design models, and the combined entity may adopt a combination of these models to fit its new mission and strategy. After selecting the organization model, there should be agreements on staffing and succession plans for the new entity to put an end to any jockeying and to enhance the focus on understanding due diligence results, integration planning, and ultimately taking care of customers.

CASE STUDY
AMGEN AND IMMUNEX DEAL DISCUSSIONS

On December 17, 2001, Amgen Inc., the world's biggest biotechnology company based in Thousand Oaks, California, announced an agreement to buy Immunex Corp., the third largest biotechnology company. Amgen would buy the Seattle, Washington, company for over $16 billion in cash and stocks. Both Amgen and Immunex, like others in their industry, had been on the lookout for strategic moves that would strengthen their companies. The discussions that led to the Amgen-Immunex deal provide a good example of the complexity of M&A deal making and the deal-making timeframes.

M&A deals, partnerships, and alliances, are common in the fragmented biotechnology industry as a way to overcome the industry's uncertainties and its long product development timelines. Smaller biotechnology companies that have obtained FDA approval for their products tend to become attractive M&A targets for larger biotechnology players or pharmaceutical companies. These acquisitions create a broader portfolio of products, give access to streams of revenue that fund new product development pipelines and to cutting-edge technologies, and offer employees with biotechnology know-how. Biotechnology firms that gain critical mass through mergers and acquisitions can rival their pharmaceutical competitors, can market their own products, and are afforded better terms in future partnership negotiations with larger pharmaceutical firms.

The initial contact between the CEOs from Amgen and Immunex occurred at an industry conference early in 2000.[6] Though the two firms did not get into serious discussions regarding an M&A deal, they stayed in touch over the following year. At the time, Amgen was undergoing its own restructuring and revitalization and was about to release two new products. In early 2001, almost a year later, Immunex worked with an investment-banking adviser to identify an appropriate strategic path; one option open was to undertake M&A deals. In mid 2001, Amgen made its first serious attempts to attract Immunex to an M&A deal. Meanwhile, Immunex was in negotiations with another third party regarding an M&A deal, but negotiations with the third party were later suspended. By the fall of 2001, Amgen and Immunex began serious discussions about an M&A deal of their own. The decision by Amgen to acquire Immunex came at a complex juncture—Amgen was getting ready to launch two major new products, and Immunex needed to ramp-up its production of a popular drug by overcoming production constraints and regaining lost market confidence, all of which eventually added to the challenges of integration after the deal closed.

In October 2001, Amgen made a stock swap offer to Immunex's Board of Directors. Wyeth, a major pharmaceutical company that owned 41% of Immunex shares, would not approve the deal since Wyeth did not consider the valuation high enough. To gain Wyeth's approval, Amgen entered into direct negotiations with Wyeth so that it could structure acceptable terms and conditions. If the Amgen-Immunex deal were to go through, Wyeth would become a major shareholder of Amgen securities; deal negotiations needed therefore to include a discussion of Wyeth's future role.

Negotiations went on from October till December. During this period a number of issues were discussed and resolved:

- Amgen raised its offer to include a higher deal premium and payment in the form of combination of cash and stock. Fifteen percent of the purchase price would end up being paid in cash.

- Amgen and Wyeth developed a plan for future co-marketing of products.

- Amgen signed a confidentiality and standstill agreements with both Immunex and Wyeth. A standstill agreement restrains a company from buying shares in another company for a specified period of time.

- Amgen drew up agreements with both Immunex and Wyeth, making Amgen the sole negotiating party for the deal.

- The details of executive roles, succession plans, retention, and severance policies for both firm's employees were decided.

- Amgen conducted an initial due diligence of Immunex and discussed integration planning and people issues.

- The three companies kept their Boards of Directors abreast of the developments.

On December 13, 2001, a CNBC item ended speculation and broke the rumors about a potential merger between Amgen and Immunex. The CNBC disclosure provided a sense of urgency that pushed the parties to finalize the negotiations. Amgen and Wyeth executives worked intensely around the clock to work out an agreement on price, future relationships, termination fees, and people issues. On December 17, the three parties and the Boards of Directors finally reached and signed an agreement, officially announcing their deal.

From the point of their first contact, it took the two companies nearly two years to reach a final agreement. The negotiations were complex; they involved a major shareholder who had to be satisfied with the initial terms of the agreement and then had to be brought on board by supporting the plans for integration. Following this deal, Amgen has grown explosively, significantly expanding its production capacity, its marketing capability, and its geographic coverage. Its revenues increased over 300% between 2001 and 2005.

NOTES

[1] Companies with good ratings can raise funds at a lower interest rate.

[2] These are portions of payment of the price by the acquirer to the seller that are contingent upon the business delivering certain results after the deal closes.

[3] In complex deals that the acquirer needs time to conduct an initial due diligence and with regulatory requirements that must be met, the acquirer may ask for an exclusive right to negotiate with the target for a specified period. The exclusive right gives the acquirer the needed time and keeps other potential acquirers at bay.

[4] The termination fee requires either party to pay the other side a penalty if they should decide to break off the deal. In mega-deals, this fee can run into the hundreds of millions of dollars. The high fee helps offset the degree of disruption that the M&A deal causes both organizations, and any doubts about the firms and their management teams, following the dissolution of the deal.

[5] Stakeholders in communication include employees, customers, suppliers, financial institutions, stock market analysts, local communities, regulators, governmental entities, shareholders, labor unions, community and political leaders, and media.

[6] The case study is primarily based on the Joint Proxy Statement/Prospectus dated March 22, 2002, between Amgen Inc. and Immunex Corporation in section named "Background to the Merger" pages I-19 to I-26. Joint proxy statements can be obtained online from www.sec.gov.

CHAPTER 6

DEFINING THE SYNERGY LOGIC

Success Factors
- Verify that synergies will result in real value
- Develop a clear M&A business case
- Align the two businesses based on sources of value

Synergy is derived from the Greek root "synergos" meaning working together or cooperation. "Synergism" is defined by Webster as the interaction of discrete agents such that the total effect is greater than the sum of the individual effects, which is sometimes referred to as the two-plus-two-equals-five effect. Synergy realization is the main rationale and key justification for mergers and acquisitions. The collaboration between, or the consolidation of, the resources and processes of two distinct business entities that are a good fit is expected to result in new value in the form of growth, higher margins, and more attractive returns to the owners beyond what each parent firm would have created as a standalone entity. Synergy benefits from a deal would be valued differently and accrue at disparate levels for diverse acquirers based on the degree of strategic fit between the businesses. The value of the combined entity is the sum total of the value of each standalone firm prior to the acquisition plus the expected value from the synergistic effect of the combination. The realization of synergy values through enhanced cash flows and an improved return on investment depends on the firm's ability to implement the synergy opportunities in a timely manner.

This chapter will review the drivers and types of synergies that can accrue for an acquirer engaged in an M&A deal. It will take up a discussion of associated costs and risks involved in synergies that need to be reflected in the deal business case and become part of the deal negotiations. Finally, the chapter will move on to cover the effects that the sources of synergism have on the alignment and the extent of the integration necessary for value realization from the combined business.

SUCCESS FACTOR #17

VERIFY THAT SYNERGIES WILL RESULT IN REAL VALUE

After the firm has made an assessment of its strengths and weaknesses as well as its external opportunities and threats, it seeks to fill any gaps in its resources and capabilities and to overcome its weaknesses and propagate its strengths through mergers and acquisitions. The acquirer's competitive strategy and its growth objectives drive the rationale of the M&A deal and the criteria for identifying the good fit.

The recipient of the bulk of the value that is expected to be created from the resulting synergies will depend on whether or not the sources of value reside with the acquirer or with the target. When the target holds sources that are of interest to the acquirer (innovation, marketing talent, people skills, managerial know-how, market position, coveted production processes, distribution networks, product and service quality, etc.), the value will accrue for the target's shareholders in the form of a high deal premium. In this case, there is usually more than one interested acquirer who can bid up the price of the deal. Conversely, when the acquirer transfers its valuable resources and know-how to the target as a result of a deal, the shareholders of the acquirer should stand to gain from the synergies.

When the acquisition involves a firm of comparable size to the acquirer, the magnitude of the expected synergies can be significant and broad-based, and they can have an immediate effect on the acquirer's business results. When the acquisition involves a smaller company, the magnitude of the synergies and their immediate effect on the acquirer's business may be small, but they should still enable the combined entity to accomplish goals that were previously inaccessible to each firm—goals neither entity could achieve on its own in a reasonable timeframe.

IDENTIFY DEAL SYNERGY OPPORTUNITIES

Synergy identification in M&A deals is an iterative process. The acquirer initially screens the target at a high level for synergy opportunities by estimating the positive impact it can have on the target's value drivers. The overall deal value may be based on a long list of synergy opportunities. Each synergy opportunity should be validated through data collection, analysis, and expert advice. It should be examined on its own merits and on its relationship to other synergy opportunities in order to avoid any double counting of benefits derived from the same source. It should be clear how each synergy opportunity fits with the deal rationale and how it will create immediate or long-term value for the combined entity.

Identifying all of the possible synergy opportunities requires creative thinking. Opportunities are identified through financial analysis, work process reviews, and through the study of numerous interfaces between the two entities. Synergy benefits can be volume-related, quick wins, or one-time events, or they can recur in future periods. Quick wins are synergies that are realized rapidly and without significant initial investment or other associated costs. Some synergies, such as inventory reductions, are one-time cash opportunities that result in increased working capital. The acquirer therefore can create synergy value through a number of drivers:

Control: The acquirer can accrue value by providing a clear direction and better management of the target's resources. Market analysts may be assigning a low valuation to the target's management or to its business direction, and the acquirer who demonstrates the ability to use the target's resources most effectively and enhance innovation can gain value from its efforts.

Consolidation: Acquirers can reinforce the base of their business through the horizontal acquisition of similar businesses. Synergies in this case stem from the consolidation or redeployment of assets in terms of administration, operations, and the supply chain. Leveraging the resources of the two entities results in economies of scale and scope. It can also enhance margins and lower per-unit costs through higher efficiencies and greater resource utilization. Horizontal acquisitions are expected to provide immediate cost savings, and therefore they have become synonymous with cost reduction. However, they also provide revenue enhancement and growth opportunities by way of providing access to new customers and new markets. The realization of synergies in this case is again contingent upon the successful integration of the two entities.

Network: The coordination and sharing of selected aspects of the two firms result in network synergies. Network synergies can be taken advantage of if the acquirer has sufficient knowledge of the target's business and a good understanding of the value drivers that would be enhanced through sharing. The successful realization of the benefits of sharing requires clear performance targets and customer focus. The coordination and sharing of business strategies, policies, procedures, core competencies, key knowledgeable experts, shared services, technologies, along with the end-to-end linking of business and operational processes may also create value. Value can in this way be created by organizing teams of experienced and knowledgeable employees from both organizations, who can work together to solve the biggest problems. In cross-border deals, the two firms can come together on issues related to selling, customer service, and elements of their supply chain networks on a global scale. Sharing can enhance the combined firm's bargaining power in dealing with suppliers and customers. Sharing technology platforms can likewise enhance the functionality of the systems that support supply chain management, customer management, and risk management. Value can also be created by joint business and financial planning and execution. The combined entity in these situations is in a stronger position for future alliances, partnerships, and other types of joint ventures that will create additional network synergies.

Financial: The combination of financial resources and the increased stability in the new entity, both owing to its enhanced size, lower the risks associated with the business and, as a result, they improve the access to financing and lower the capital costs for projects and ventures. The target may provide greater access to cash flows that the acquirer needs to fund research and accelerate its product development. The target in this respect may also provide access to certain operating losses that might provide valuable tax advantages for the acquirer.

THE STRATEGIC VALUE of the deal is calculated from the target's expected stand-alone future cash flows plus the additional cash flows resulting from the impact of cost savings and revenue enhancement synergies after the deal. Synergy quantification here requires metrics of synergy attributes that are aligned with the deal value levers and a methodology for calculating the benefits. Understanding the sensitivity of key variables concerning internal and external drivers will enhance the overall understanding of the synergy opportunities and their impact. The quantification of synergies should be based on estimates and assumptions that are conservative, realistic, and consistent. The expected timing for the realization of synergies along with the ease at which they can be implemented should also be assessed. Synergies will accrue to the bottom line in three general forms:

- **Lower costs:** Cost reductions show immediate benefits, and their results are tangible, measurable, and traceable to the bottom line. Management can act to achieve cost reductions quickly since these reductions maintain the same level of sales and revenue with less of an input of resources. The consolidation and rationalization of the resources of the two entities allows for the elimination of redundancies and overlap in areas including: facilities, physical assets, overheads, research and development organizations, shared services, production capacity, supply chain networks, product promotion, customer care activities, and the streamlining of brands.

- **Higher revenues:** The rationale behind revenue enhancement is tied to the attainment of growth and an increase in sales by way of the combination. Growth and revenue-enhancement synergies require taking a long-term view as they are more difficult to substantiate and so pose greater risks. Revenue enhancements in this sense can be more difficult to isolate and reflect accurately in the firm's cash flows: factors external to the firm, such as changes in the economic cycle or currency fluctuations, can affect the firm's results and dilute the effects of revenue-enhancement efforts. Competitors will also react in such a way as to protect their own market position and customer base by overcoming any disadvantages created for them by the deal. Thus, competitors will attempt to shorten the period of extraordinary performance that is available to the combined entity. The assumptions used in developing a revenue-enhancement rationale should be thoroughly reviewed, understood, and documented in the business case. Revenue enhancements simply require more than the consolidation of assets to be realized. They require the convergence of the processes as well as the alignment and integration of the networks and their financial resources. In this they also demand the development of a strong strategy, committed leadership, the ability to execute the strategy, and the seamless sharing of know-how between the two entities in order to create a new and more broad-based approach to attracting customers and satisfying their needs. Revenue-enhancement synergies can accrue from a number of sources including:

— Access to a more innovative, knowledgeable, and experienced employee base

— Access to a new business model

— Deeper penetration of existing markets

— The ability to enter new business segments and broader geographic markets to expand brand distribution

— The accelerated development of regional and national accounts through better sources of new business development

Horizontal acquisitions will then provide immediate opportunities for cost savings; however, these savings may become short-lived if they are not properly aligned with growth opportunities.

- **Cost avoidance:** The combined entity can also lower or defer its capital investment requirements or eliminate planned expenses without affecting the expected revenues. For example, the acquirer may utilize the target's production capacity and thus defer the planned construction of its own production facility. In the case of a global merger, the acquirer can use the presence of the target in the international market to launch a new product and thus reduce its promotion costs. The only expenses or capital investments that can be avoided are those that are real and already committed to in budgeting.

SYNERGY REALIZATION COSTS, RISKS, AND DOWNSIDES: "2 + 2 = 3"

Synergy realization may bear additional costs, additional implementation risks, or may affect customer relationships. Integration and

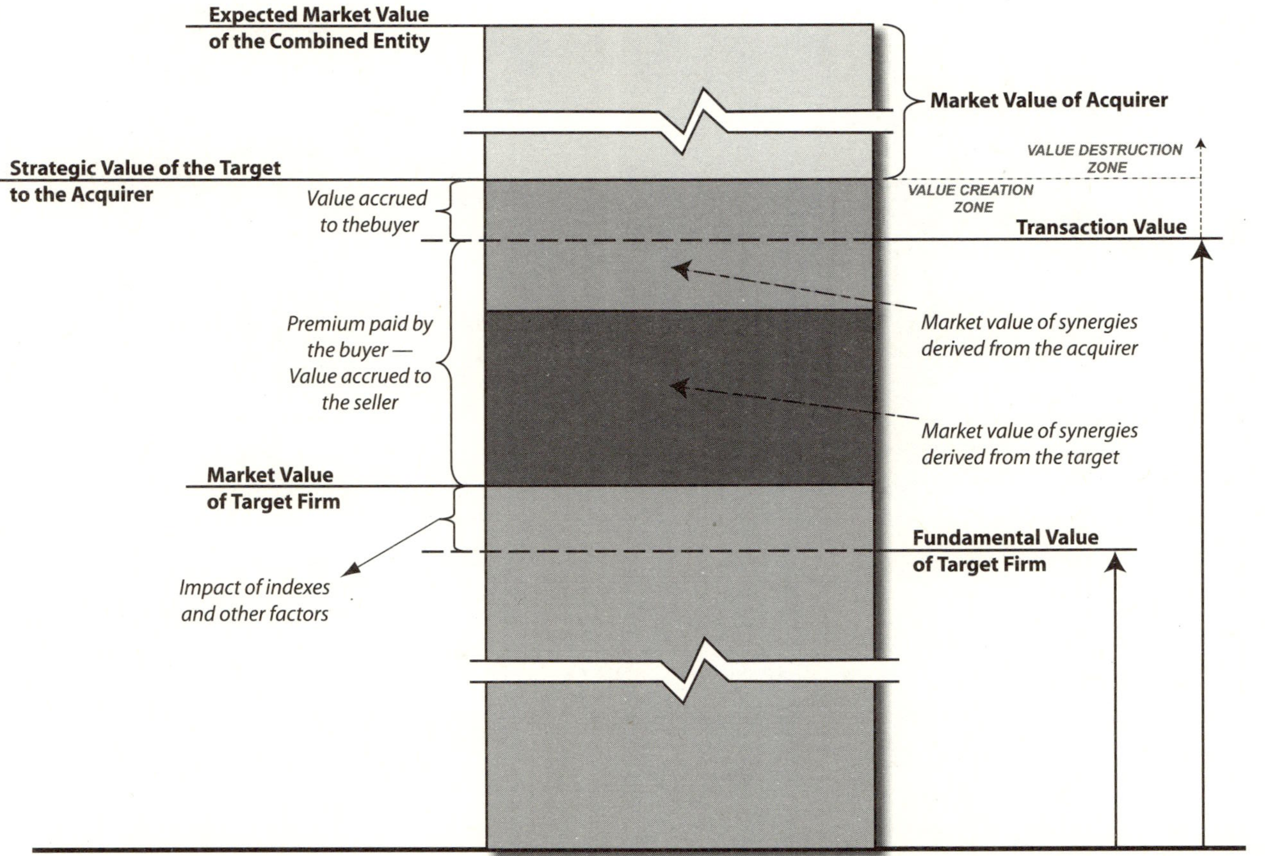

Figure 4. Impact of Synergies on Firm Value

synergy realization may require additional expenditure or investments in technologies and other resources. Although these costs may be overlooked during the deal valuation, they, in effect, increase the deal premium that is paid for the acquisition. Costs associated with synergy realization may include: costs of upgrading of the target's assets, facilities, and equipment in order to bring them up to acquirer's standards; migrating and unifying technology and operational platforms and IT systems between the two entities in order to overcome any incompatibilities; aligning the distribution networks of the two companies; and investments in training along with the development of the sales and marketing staff. All of these potential commitments in cost involve additional time and resources that may in some cases exceed the benefits derived from synergies. Other costs associated with the deal include productivity losses due to cultural clashes and resistance to change, staff costs needed for integration activities, and deal transaction costs. The pursuit of synergies therefore requires periods of dedicated time and attention from management, which likewise carries opportunity costs as management may become distracted from its ongoing business. The business case should, in accordance with these potential costs, present an estimate of resource and cost requirements that will be necessary to realize the expected synergies. The M&A deal, it should be noted here, can actually have the opposite effect of cost avoidance, and so costs and capital expenditures may need to be increased.

Synergy realization is dependent on the acquirer's ability to implement the needed changes. The acquirer has paid a premium for the deal specifically in anticipation of synergy realization. Because synergies are expected to create new value, the failure to realize their expectations will destroy shareholder value and wealth. There are several potential risks and downsides associated with the implementation of synergies and realization of value, and initiatives can often fall short of management expectation. The degree of fit between the businesses may not be sufficient for creating the desired synergy opportunities. Differences among visions and strategies, business objectives, cultures, organizational structures, technology, people skills, and approaches to cost management can all affect the fit between the two entities by complicating their integration and consolidation. The organization's ability to absorb the necessary changes may be exceeded, thus delaying integration and synergy realization. The target's internal capabilities also may not live up to expectations, and it may have inefficient processes, quality problems, high levels of waste and rework, antiquated techniques, and old or poorly maintained assets, all of which will prove to be barriers and complications to efficient implementation.

Forming new customer relationships or restructuring the existing ones may be difficult and risky. Cross selling products and services can increase per-customer sales, but its realization will also require the cross-training of the sales force on the new bundle of products and offerings, which takes up valuable time and money. The sales force must gain the customer's acceptance of these new offerings, and it must learn to deal with the competitive dynamics associated with the new offerings. The target may have customers that demand much, but will not pay for the services they receive. Moving to a common distribution system can be fraught with problems such as different customer return policies, differences in retail outlets, and differing modes of distribution. Additionally, distributors may not have the flexibility to co-distribute the combined entity's products. New business models and new branding strategies naturally entail risks, and so they may not gain customer acceptance as expected.

There is no guarantee that innovation will flourish in the combined entity, or that a new generation of products will result from the combination. When the acquisition is based on people know-how and skills, the combined firm risks losing key employees and customers to competitors after the deal, which would also dilute the value of the deal. The zealous pursuit of synergies, the increased internal focus during integration, an increased business complexity, and a decrease in employee motivation can all affect the firm's ability to implement and provide innovative products and maintain satisfactory customer relationships.

When deal synergies are not realized, considering the time that is invested in them, the firm will be at a disadvantage compared to its competitors who can focus on business as usual because they are not engaged in M&A deals of their own. The potential risks and downsides associated with synergy realization need to be incorporated into the deal valuation so that one can arrive at a range of expected outcomes with varying confidence levels. To enhance the credibility of the expected benefits, knowledgeable internal experts can be called upon to validate the assumptions and conclusions. Should management be pursuing a losing strategy, the analysis and validation of the potential synergies and implementation risks by trusted experts can help convince the decision makers to abandon a bad deal.

Definitions of Value

The value of a publicly held firm is the sum total of the value of its net debt, its common equity, its preferred stocks, and its minority interests. The value of the firm can also be seen as the sum of the market values of each of its lines of business; that is, if each line of business could be sold independently—also known as the firm breakup value. The liquidation value of the firm represents the amount that can be attained through an immediate distress sale of all the assets of the business. The replacement value is the cost of duplicating the assets of a business at today's prices. Tangible assets can generally be valued based on their income-producing potential and their market value.

Fair Market Value

A fair market value is the value at which the business would change hands between a typical buyer and seller. The fair market value is affected by various external factors such as the prevailing economic and industry climate at the time of the valuation; it is therefore valid for a limited time while there are no unforeseen changes in the business environment. The basic assumptions in fair market valuation are that markets are efficient and buyers and sellers have all the necessary information to make an informed decision in a cash deal.

Fundamental Value

The fundamental value is based on the firm's ability to generate stable long-term cash flows and its expected growth rate. The market value of a business could be different from its fundamental value due to market factors such as the effect of indexes and cyclical effects, which may result in overly optimistic expectations of growth for an industry sector. Along the same lines, all market securities may benefit from a strong positive macro-economic outlook.

Strategic Value

A strategic acquirer, who perceives unique synergies in the target, may be willing to conduct a transaction at a price in excess of both the fundamental and the fair market values of similar businesses. The acquirer uses its knowledge of the target business fundamentals and its judgment about its own ability to affect the fundamentals based upon a fit between the two businesses to arrive at a strategic value for the target firm; thus it may be willing to pay a premium for the acquisition. Other acquirers, perceiving their own unique fit with the target, may also bid for the acquisition.

Transaction Value

The transaction value is the final price paid by a buyer for an acquisition that may include a premium. Deals involving comparable targets should attract similar transaction values. The value of a deal is based on the price that the buyer can offer to pay and what the seller will accept. Price plays a pivotal role in M&A deals; however, the terms of the deal can help finalize an agreement. Price is what the acquirer pays for the deal, and value may or may not accrue to the acquirer based on the quality of its assumptions, its due diligence, and its ability to implement changes.

SUCCESS FACTOR #18

DEVELOP A CLEAR M&A BUSINESS CASE

The business case is key for the deal maker in that it fulfills a number of important needs. Each synergy opportunity, and the judgment and approach used to determine its value, should be documented in detail in the business case. The business case should record the following: how value is expected to be created, the financial and operational assumptions, the methodology used in quantification, data sources, data reliability, risks and uncertainties associated with the quantitative analysis, intangible benefits, scenarios considered, probabilities associated with key variables, and the possible range of outcomes. The business case will also outline implementation accountabilities and timelines as it creates continuity and context for the movement from the deal phase into integration. Finally, the business case is used as a roadmap to train the integration teams looking toward synergy realization.

Business case development starts at the deal inception and will evolve as more information become available. The M&A deal logic defines the framework for the deal business case, and its contents are filled in as the acquirer assesses the financial and business performance of the target. The difficulties in attaining reliable and quality information should raise warning signs about the deal's future performance. The acquirer should look for inconsistencies or unfavorable trends in the target's performance as a warning sign calling for deeper analysis during the due diligence process.

During the due diligence period, a detailed review of expected synergies and their impact on cash flows as well as an assessment of the fit assumptions and a determination of the soundness of business fundamentals are all necessary to ensure that the synergy effects are real and can be realized at the expected magnitude. This review should also ultimately show whether the synergies will have a direct impact on the combined entity's bottom line.

The business case supports integration by serving both as a memory of the deal process and also as a decision making tool. It helps to maintain continuity between the due diligence phase and the integration phase. This is particularly important since individuals who have been involved with due diligence and who are most knowledgeable about the deal may not be directly involved with the integration activities. The business case can be used to educate the integration teams and create a common understanding of the deal rationale, the integration requirements and priorities, and the accountabilities for implementation. The business case in this sense can be for management an illuminated dashboard of key indicators on which to track implementation and synergy realization during the integration phase.

SUCCESS FACTOR #19

ALIGN THE TWO BUSINESSES BASED ON SOURCES OF VALUE

The degree of integration between the two entities depends on the deal logic and the sources of value creation. Likewise, the degree to which the locus of value creation resides either within the acquirer or the target, will determine the degree of integration that will be necessary to realize the deal value. The acquirer may keep its acquisition as a separate entity, share some aspects of its business, or integrate the target. The organization's ability to absorb the resulting changes will determine whether or not long term value may be realized in a timely fashion.

SEPARATION

The decision to keep the target separate depends on the source of value that resides within the target and the fundamental characteristics that have made it valuable to the acquirer. Separation keeps the target's organizational boundary intact as it limits the acquirer's involvement in the target's business and minimizes cultural clashes and other conflicts. The target's existing management team is retained to run the business and maintain its current strategy, its customer base, culture, the organizational structure, systems, and processes. The reason for maintaining the separation is to reduce disruptions to the target's business that may affect customer relationships and cash flows or cause departures of valued employees. If the acquirer is moving into a new business or into new product-market arenas where it lacks the knowledge and experience for developing and selling new products into these markets, it becomes dependent on the target's resources to carry out this business. It should therefore, in such a case, keep the target as a separate entity at least in the short term. If the acquirer is gaining a "crown jewel" that is well established, has high growth rates, is highly profitable, and generates strong cash flows, or has special capabilities and a strong management, it will keep the target separate in order to maintain the customer base and cash flows and to retain the valued employees who have valuable skills and are the main source of value in the acquisition.

In the separation model, the acquirer's management must allow the target's management to run their business and be held accountable for it by avoiding any meddling in the target's business, which can reduce conflicts. Over time, the separation may be changed to one of sharing as the relationship between the business and the acquirer evolves. The delay experienced in sharing and integration may be needed to preserve the customer base, to understand their needs, and to develop new relationships with the customers.

SHARING

The acquirer may promote sharing between the two organizations in order to create value from leverage and collaboration between the employees, work processes, and systems of the two entities.

Sharing can take several forms. The acquirer may set strategic direction and impose financial performance requirements on the target while allowing the target to manage its own day-to-day business activities. The acquirer may provide cash flows and help lower the target's financing costs in order to support the achievement of its business objectives. The difference between the acquirer's requirements and the target's previous approach to business may be significant. When the acquirer emphasizes financial results, it may create a short-term focus; whereas, setting a strategic direction provides a long-term focus for the business. The downside here is that the target's management team may not easily conform to or may even resist the acquirer's expectations. The acquirer may keep the target's management so long as they meet its performance expectations, or it may replace them—perhaps with some members of acquirer's own management team—if they fail to live up to expectations. The acquirer should therefore get to know the talented employees in the target's business and promote them to leadership ranks within the target's organization or transfer some of them to its own organization.

The acquirer may undertake a partial integration of the target. Those functions that are considered to be sources of value are allowed to remain autonomous as a way of encouraging them to flourish with their existing cultures relatively undisturbed. Other functions, such as shared services, may be assimilated into the acquirer's organization. The target's systems and processes may also get tied to the acquirer's, including value chain activities where the target may be weak. The acquirer may also restructure the target's organization by imposing its own centralized management structure and aligning the target's organization with its own lines of business.

When the acquirer has specialized expertise that would help the target gain a competitive advantage, the acquirer can embed some of its own specialized functional experts in the target's organization where they can share their know-how and communicate knowledge, standards, and best practices with the target employees quickly in order to accelerate competency development. This embedding process causes relatively little disturbance to the target. However, to be successful, the sponsorship and support of target's management is needed. Target management may feel that their turf is being invaded by outsiders and, as a result, may not properly push for the need for sharing. Target employees also may perceive the sharing as an imposition, and it is not uncommon to find certain levels of resistance to this sharing. Differences in business models may too limit the realization of the sharing advantages.

Sharing may cause cultural clashes, and if so, it will entail additional costs and loss of value. Sharing is enhanced by forming teams consisting of the acquirer's and target's people, which will work on resolving real issues. The teams should be jointly sponsored by the acquirer and target management, and sponsors should be regularly updated on the progress being made. The role of the sponsors is to remove barriers to sharing, set priorities and milestones, and encourage learning in all parts of the organization.

INTEGRATION

The more that the locus of value resides with the acquirer, the more control the acquirer will assert over its acquisition. At the extreme instance, if the value resides mostly in the acquirer's business, then the acquirer may conduct an asset purchase, in which case the acquirer may not add any people to its operations; hence, people issues do not surface. For example, Target Corporation bought thirty-five Montgomery Ward & Co. Inc. department stores in California. The Montgomery Ward brand or business model were not of interest to Target, but this acquisition gave Target access to hard-to-find prime real estate locations. Target then remodeled the acquired stores and reopened them as Target stores

Full integration combines the functions and divisions of the two entities under one management team and under one organizational structure. In functions or units where the acquirer has strong capabilities and thus can add value to the target, quick integration makes sense. The integration of functions or divisions that perform similar work between the acquirer and target provides the benefits of size and scale. Greater value and advantage is created through control of the target's business activities and resources by combining them with the acquirer's own business activities. The two companies can in this way share capacity, facilities, administration, operations, sales and marketing resources, and distribution channels. Integration allows the firm to make gains in market share, cost advantages, and productivity as well as allowing the firm to have a stronger asset base with which to differentiate itself from its competitors. Synergy benefits result from savings that are extracted from the elimination of functional redundancies, such as in purchasing, sales, and marketing, and from the elimination of duplication in overheads. The integration of two business units can also involve lay-offs and job eliminations, but management should strive to retain key valued personnel.

Integration is of course a complex undertaking, since the strategy, the organization and management structures, systems, processes, and the cultures of the two entities must be combined. It requires the highest degree of planning prior to the deal closing. People who perform similar work in the two organizations generally use different terminology, different work processes, and different levels of authority and management styles while employing different operating philosophies within different cultures. When the two groups get together, the work content may not change, but there are numerous communication and procedural differences that may create barriers to collaboration. In addition, people may take pride in the way that they have done their work in the past, and so they may perceive that there is no need for change.

Management must commit the necessary time, costs, and people so that the teams can accelerate the tempo of integration and realize value in a timely manner. Management's role in integration is to coordinate the integration activities and enforce sharing to realize synergies. There are costs associated with the integration as companies learn more about one another and as they monitor implementation activities and invest in new compatible technologies. The use of cross-functional integration teams can help buffer the impact of the acquisition on the target and the acquirer.

CASE STUDIES
SOURCES OF VALUE IN MERGERS AND ACQUISITIONS

The merger of Pfizer Inc. and Warner-Lambert Corporation provides an example of a target having something that the acquirer values. The high costs of development and marketing of pharmaceutical drugs have driven numerous large and small mergers in the industry in order to satisfy the need for a steady flow of cash that can fund the drug development pipelines. In February 2000, Pfizer closed its merger with Warner-Lambert, which resulted in the creation of the second largest pharmaceutical company in the world at that time. Pfizer won the Warner-Lambert merger in a bruising battle with American Home Products (AHP), now Wyeth, through tender offers and litigation. Pfizer paid over $116 billion for the deal, 15% higher than AHP's offer, plus it paid a $1.8 billion break-up fee to its rival suitor. The consolidation synergies were from operations, marketing, and sales forces rightsizing with Pfizer expecting to realize $1.6 billion in cost savings over three years. Why did Pfizer make such an enthusiastic offer and fight such a bruising battle to get the deal through? The reason is the advantages that Pfizer perceived from the deal, which included greater size, access to cash flows, advanced technologies, expanded sales force, and lower costs.

Pfizer was experiencing difficulties with its own product pipeline, and the merger would give Pfizer access to cash flows generated by Warner-Lambert that it could use to rejuvenate it. At the time, some of the products that Pfizer hoped would become blockbuster revenue generators were showing weaker than expected results such as its impotence drug, Viagra. The development of some other drugs in its pipeline was also being delayed. These factors affected Pfizer's ability to generate the needed cash at the anticipated level to continue funding its R&D pipeline. The merger between the two pharmaceutical companies would also create the advantages of size for Pfizer. Greater size would provide access to better financing terms and a stronger position for alliances and licensing agreements with other pharmaceutical and biotech companies.

It was extremely important, then, that there was great potential and promise in Warner-Lambert's drug development pipeline. A big prize in Warner-Lambert's R&D was the Agouron Pharmaceuticals biotechnology group, a Warner-Lambert acquisition in 1999. Agouron's drug pipeline contained many promising drugs, and it had emerged as a leader in computer-aided drug design. The technology allowed Agouron to develop a three dimensional view of disease-causing protein molecules that allowed researchers to discover more effective cures with fewer unwanted side effects.

Pfizer also did not want to lose the value it derived from its existing alliance with Warner Lambert. If Warner-Lambert was acquired by another company, the alliance between Pfizer and Warner-Lambert could be in jeopardy. The two companies jointly developed and marketed a cholesterol-lowering drug Lipitor, which was performing very well and was a significant source of cash flow for Pfizer.

Pfizer also brought its own value to the deal with its own powerful sales and marketing expertise. Pfizer has been known in the industry for its sales and marketing prowess and its ability to maximize the value attained from a drug. The combined company would have a sales force of 8,000 salespersons all of whom would quickly be trained to cross-sell drugs from both companies.

Thus, Pfizer was willing to pay a higher premium for the deal—value that would be accrued for Warner-Lambert's shareholders—because it needed just such a deal to attain its long term strategy.

FROM SOME OF the acquisitions made by Cisco Systems Inc., we see examples where both sides in an acquisition bring something of value to the table. Cisco Systems made mergers and acquisitions a key instrument of its growth in the nineties. For Cisco Systems, a fast-growing high-technology company, the demand for its products outpaced what could be realistically developed and sold through the growth of its internal resources.

Many of Cisco's acquisitions were of companies that lacked a definitive internal infrastructure, and instead could provide an existing product or a potential product, which could be marketed 12 to 18 months later. Typically, Cisco would assimilate its acquisitions and provide the necessary value chain to develop, manufacture, distribute, market, and sell the products of its acquired companies. This provided significant synergies between Cisco and its acquisitions at the same time that it avoided any duplication of effort by the target firms who lacked a value chain themselves.

Although Cisco paid a premium for its acquisitions, its shareholders were handsomely rewarded in the nineties and were able to capture significant value owing to the industry's fast growth rate and to the greater share of the market that Cisco would capture by providing end-to-end offerings instead of pinpoint solutions for its customers.

CHAPTER 7

UNCOVERING DEAL RISKS

Success Factors
- Conduct a timely and effective due diligence
- Evaluate and assess cultural dissimilarities
- Utilize the power of information technology to accelerate the due diligence process
- Know the added risks of cross-border mergers and acquisitions

Having compiled a due diligence team, the acquirer undertakes site visits and information gathering to determine the strength and stability of the target's business. At a high level, the strategic fit between the two companies may appear enticing, and the deal may promise attractive cost savings and synergies. Yet, there may be underlying issues regarding the target or the assumptions made about the deal benefits. If the acquirer is unable to realize the benefits, it will not succeed at the deal. However, management encouraged by the promise of the deal may overlook issues with the merger. In the haste to close the deal, the acquirer may lose focus on intelligence gathering when distracted by staffing or integration issues, or the acquirer may decide that further investigation is not warranted because more insights would not be gained by expending additional resources on the effort. It may do so only to find certain surprises after the close of the deal that will jeopardize value realization. Such a loss of focus can prove to be a significant lapse

Complexity and uncertainty are inherent in M&A deals, and business leaders undertaking M&A deals typically are aware that they are exposing their companies to new risks that can affect the combined entity's long-term performance. The deal risks should be explored and addressed appropriately through a disciplined due diligence[1] process conducted by teams staffed with the appropriate set of skilled members who can identify and bring to the surface business issues by way of a careful investigation of the commercial, legal, regulatory, technological, and human resource aspects of the target's business. The objective of due diligence is to identify any barriers or irregularities that could impact the value of or the smooth operations of the combined entity; it should ensure that the information and the critical assumptions used in making the deal decisions are complete and accurate—that there are no surprises for the buyer after the deal closes. The inevitability of the close of the deal should never be simply assumed.

This chapter will explore the M&A due diligence process with special emphasis on particular issues that may arise from cultural dissimilarities between two entities and those pertaining to companies undertaking global M&A deals.

SUCCESS FACTOR #20

CONDUCT A TIMELY AND EFFECTIVE DUE DILIGENCE

Due diligence should be treated as an ongoing process, and it is started as soon as a target is identified and a business case is begun. Every stage of the M&A process should include due diligence activities, continuing until closing with some aspects potentially extending beyond the close of the deal. The due diligence assessments generally take place in two main phases. The first phase occurs prior to the M&A agreement. After the initial contact, the two sides most often sign a confidentiality agreement that allows the acquirer to undertake a high-level review of the target's financial statements, its financial reporting, and its legal and regulatory performance as well as to visit the operations to assess its people and assets and to review sales, marketing, and distribution practices. After the two sides sign an M&A agreement, the second phase of due diligence continues with an in-depth analysis of the target's business using internal and external sources, which cover two critical perspectives. The first is an assessment of the fundamental integrity and stability of the target's underlying business and the veracity of warranties and representations made in the M&A agreement. Such representations and warranties are intended to cause the target management to disclose information that is important to the acquirer and substantive to the deal. Examples of assessments that the acquirer may undertake include:

- A recognition of risks that can affect the target's viability as a going concern, its growth potential, and the soundness of its new investment opportunities.

- A comprehensive review of the financial affairs of the target business and the strength of its balance sheet.

- A detailed investigation of the legal obligations and regulatory compliance of the target, including pending litigation and environmental issues.

- An evaluation of the target's functional activities, the quality of its operations, and its key business standards, guidelines, and methods.

- An appraisal of the target's ability to meet customer needs and the potential for new markets and new customers.

- An analysis of human resource policies and practices.

The second perspective of due diligence is an assessment of the fit between the target's and the acquirer's businesses and also the risks and potential barriers to the creation of the desired synergistic value. The due diligence assessments should be aligned with the goals and objectives of the M&A deal and include aspects of the business that have a high impact on integration and synergy realization. The evaluation of the business fit includes:

- A review of the deal synergies in terms of viability and size as well as the ability of the acquirer to realize those synergies in a timely manner.

- An assessment of integration risks, the ease of its implementation, and the effect of integration on the target's business processes.

- An assessment of the impact of technology integration on the M&A success.

- An evaluation of the size, distribution, quality, skill level of the workforce, as well as its utilization, motivation, commitment, and history of innovation.

The question of integrity, stability, and fit are relative. The primary objective of due diligence here is to ensure that each aspect of the target's business is assessed from both the perspective of disclosure and the perspective of fit so that the risks associated with the M&A decision are thoroughly understood.

Since private firms are not covered under the corporate governance and stock exchange requirements, the Sarbanes-Oxley Act of 2002[2] will affect M&A deals where a publicly traded firm acquires a privately held firm. Thus acquirers have to follow a more stringent due diligence of the financial reporting and disclosure controls and procedures of the private target firm so that they can certify their results after the deal closes. The private target's management practices, internal controls, and financial accounting practices need to be assessed in order to gain a high degree of confidence about meeting the Sarbanes-Oxley Act requirements after the deal is completed.

Acquirers in this respect have to be knowledgeable about the target's business, its customers, and its markets, particularly as they may relate to these issues. However, risks can also stem from the broader economic, political, and sociological trends based on the best available information and the forecasts of economic performance. Regardless of the effort involved in due diligence, though, the timing of the M&A deal may coincide with adverse changes in the external environment which could negatively affect the deal performance.

SUCCESS FACTOR #21

ASSUME NOTHING

Due diligence involves an enormous amount of effort in a limited amount of time. Throughout the M&A process, the acquirer gathers facts and subjects its assumptions to a rigorous examination in order to determine their validity. The acquirer wants to examine as many aspects of the target's business and its various initiatives as possible within the limited timeframe. The progress of the due diligence process should be managed carefully to ensure that the desired activities are taking place and that the important risks are being reviewed.

Due diligence requires financial, legal, tax, and operational know-how as well as accounting, IT, sales, marketing, human resources, insurance, and risk management expertise. Adequate resources are needed for a complete review of the target firm, including being present on location for data collection, requesting documents and manuals, meeting the target's personnel, and seeing the target's sites and facilities first hand.

Facility and site visits provide the acquirer with opportunities to get beyond the policies and procedure manuals and see the organization, its culture and its people, in action. By visiting the sites first hand, the acquirer can assess the condition of facilities and assets, and it can identify potential capital expenditure requirements needed to move the condition of facilities and assets up to the acquirer's standards. This can be a significant issue for manufacturing and asset-intensive industries; unfortunately, it is often overlooked. The degree of automation, facility maintenance and upkeep, capital reinvestment in the past five years, and the application of information technology all can vary significantly between firms within the same industry, so the specifics of these for the deal must be assessed. Benchmarking data, for this and other purposes, are also very useful for making relative comparisons to industry standards and to the performance of other competitors.

Another effective tool for due diligence data collection is the use of direct interviews either through the phone or face-to-face. Current and past customers should be included in the interviews. Additionally, interviews should be conducted with suppliers, current and past executives, key employees, industry experts, investment institutions, lenders, and any individuals involved in litigations with the target company.

During the due diligence process, the acquirer should maintain a posture of respect and understanding towards the target's policies and practices while identifying opportunities and risks. A respectful approach will build trust with the target's employees and will enhance information sharing. Some of the challenges that the acquirer may face in this respect might include a lack of cooperation from the target company managers, who may mistrust the acquirer or who may become frustrated by too many requests for information from the acquirer's employees.

M&A due diligence intelligence gathering can fail to uncover the facts underlying the deal for a variety of reasons. The due diligence period can be a busy and chaotic time. A lack of communication, combined with unclear roles and accountabilities, can cause important information to be overlooked. The acquirer involved in a horizontal acquisition may decide that it already knows the target's business well enough and may fail to provide sufficient time for due diligence activities. Alternatively, the large number and breadth of the tasks that occur during the due diligence period may, without appropriate prioritization, lead to a scattered approach, where the focus is merely on the completion of the tasks rather than on making quality assessments.

DECIDE THE LEVEL OF RISK TO ACCEPT

The collected data from the investigation of the target are analyzed, and findings are summarized and presented to decision-makers. The objective of the acquirer is to cherry-pick the parts of the business that it feels will add value while leaving the liabilities with the seller. If any surprises that would impact the long-term performance of the combined entity have been discovered, management must assess its ability to manage these risks. Such findings may include: environmental liabilities, unaudited financial statements, the poor reliability of financial information, a lack of quality of cash flows and earnings, intellectual property rights, non-funded pension and healthcare plans, condition of assets, tax liability, product liability issues, labor and management contracts, inventory accounting, deteriorating market posture, and strength of the sales and marketing organization. For each potential problem, the acquirer should determine the level of exposure that is acceptable and how that exposure will affect the target's value. If through its investigations the acquirer identifies conditions that can affect its ability to realize the expected value and cannot manage the risks in an effective and value-added manner, it should not accept the risks.

The acquiring management can respond to risks that it has identified in several ways. It can decide to abandon the deal altogether, which may require the payment of a break-up fee. It can decide to close the deal and accept the deal risks. Prior to closing, the acquirer can usually revisit and renegotiate the deal price and the M&A terms in light of issues that it has uncovered to attain a more acceptable deal. The deal can also close under conditions that reject or limit certain liabilities and risks. As the time of the deal closure approaches, the acquirer should continually ask if the deal still makes sense.

The sellers must also be prepared for the intense scrutiny that they will be subjected to during due diligence. For private businesses and small business owners not accustomed to regular public reporting, due diligence presents a new challenge. Entrepreneurs generally have a strong pride in their business and may not be used to outsiders challenging them about the way that they are running their business. Owners planning to sell out must start early and prepare for the sale by viewing their business from the buyer's perspective. They must proactively deal with potential environmental issues, liquidate slow moving inventory, and develop audited financial statements that can stand up to scrutiny.

Risks of acquiring a part of a company

Strategic acquirers or investment-driven acquirers pursuing targeted acquisitions may show an interest in acquiring only a unit or a division of a firm. These targeted acquisitions, also known as carve-outs, are intended to avoid some of the complexities associated with acquiring a whole company. However, the acquirer should be aware of the unique risks associated with acquiring a division.

Divisions being sold may not have been stand-alone units, and so they may not have a separate balance sheet. The acquirer will have to resolve the financial, cash flow, taxation, and accounting issues that may arise from the deal. The acquirer must thoroughly explore how the division depends on the seller's business for R&D, intellectual property rights, brand names, licensing agreements, patents, information technology infrastructure, suppliers, access to customers, order fulfillment, proprietary technologies and processes, and even employee benefits. The acquirer must ensure that the deal includes the needed infrastructure, the people skills, the financial resources, marketing capabilities, and distribution channels, including all necessary contractual guarantees, to enable the division to function and deliver value as expected. The acquirer must review key employees and consider how the transition of key employees between the companies will occur, while noting what incentives are required to lure the best people to cross over in order to ensure that the division is not starved of its key resources.

The future relationship between the acquired business and its old parent must be painstakingly reviewed, understood, and negotiated. The acquirer needs to avoid a future position in which it would have to renegotiate with the target's parent company in order to make strategic decisions. Other potential risks that must be investigated include any liability risks that should be shared between the division and its previous parent such as environmental management, product quality, and unfunded pension and healthcare obligations. Any such complexities associated with acquiring a division of a company require a higher level of scrutiny throughout the due diligence process.

SUCCESS FACTOR #22

EVALUATE AND ASSESS CULTURAL DISSIMILARITIES

The successful accomplishment of any strategic objective is premised on its alignment with the organizational culture and its ability to absorb the resulting changes from implementation. A dissimilarity of cultures between two entities may result in clashes, and thus a cultural fit should be a key consideration in M&A deal planning—one on par with financial, market, and operational fit and synergy considerations. A cultural fit matters in M&A deal planning because cultural change is difficult, time consuming, and costly, and can hamper efforts to integrate the two entities.

CULTURAL ATTRIBUTES

The difficulty of cultural change lies in its deep roots within the fabric of the organization. Organizational culture is complex and multi-layered[3]. Culture is rooted in commonalities in histories and experiences that have been cultivated through a long period of interaction among the company's people and between employees and management. Cultural development has its inception in the vision and values of the original entrepreneurs who founded the company. If the business succeeds, its culture will perpetuate itself overtime.

Culture can be seen in the behaviors that members of a group exhibit as their *modus operandi* or as their shared work styles and norms. Culture affects organizational decision making, risk-taking, and domains, the selection and implementation of business objectives, and the organizational structure and hierarchy. Culture also affects more prosaic aspects of the business such as the layout of stores and warehouses, the furnishings of

to management meetings and discussions about customers. Meanwhile, the acquirer set up a brand new facility to co-house all its acquired companies and to help attain the expected synergies from its acquisitions. It was only after the people were co-located that cultural differences became apparent and the cultural wars started. The CEO left to join a competitor. Other top talent decided to leave as well, which resulted in a delay of the value realization from the deal.

When cultures come face-to-face, one result can be that they may survive side-by-side for a long period of time with minor integration—dissimilar cultures will simply not mix unless efforts are made to integrate them. A few years ago, during interviews with managers of a plant that were used to analyze their manufacturing processes, a certain maintenance manager talked extensively about the "new" merged company as one that had lost its focus on maintenance reliability since the merger. The merger that was being referenced here took place over 5 years before when three different plants, owned by three separate parent companies, were combined into one operating entity. The plant sites were close to one another, and only one was still producing products. The other two sites were used as distribution facilities, and employees and offices were disbursed among those sites. The employees continued to identify with their old parent companies and so resisted change, which was compounded by a tangle of relationships that attempted to connect people who came from each parent company. These networks of individuals acted as exclusive support groups, communicated together, socialized together, and developed a low opinion of people from other parent companies. This complex web of cultures complicated the new plant manager's goal of transforming the business. Five years after the deal, the lack of cultural integration was still apparent, and some individuals were unwilling to make the transition.

Alternately, when two dissimilar cultures come together, one culture may have stronger survival instincts, which help it to prevail and overshadow the other. In an oil and gas deal that was conceived of as a "merger of equals," the ideas was to take the commercial flexibility of Company B and combine it with the operational excellence of Company A. The goal was to utilize the strength of their combined assets in order to create an ultimately superior industry competitor. Instead of that neatly occurring, the cultures clashed even before the deal was closed, and productivity suffered with years of difficulties ensuing. Gradually, Company A's culture came to prevail over Company B's culture. Company A employees got the top jobs while Company B employees stagnated and either left or where forced out. The careers and the hopes of Company B employees were dashed. The significant energy expended on these cultural wars was finally made apparent by a stagnating bottom-line.

Similarly, in a merger of two major consulting firms, dissimilar cultures became a major stumbling block. The *modus operandi* of the two firms was so different, and there was such strong resistance to change from the partners, that the two firms were, for the most part, operating separately despite being side-by-side. Inevitably, the cultures clashed—sometimes in full view of the clients. Before long, the top talent left, and key clients were lost. When employees in a professional firm depart, the clients with whom they have nurtured strong commercial relationships may also be lost. Business in this respect suffered, and it declined even further as more people jumped ship. Ultimately, one culture came to prevail over the other, but the cost paid in lost talent was too high. The business deteriorated and was finally taken over, resulting in the demise of a once successful business. Therefore, it is important to remember that in a business whose only assets are its people and its intellectual capital, cultural differences in a corporate marriage can become the kiss of death.

When faced with a new organizational culture, individuals can experience a loss of identity, which may result in anxieties and fears, leading to a resistance to change. The closing of the deal for instance brings an initial sense of anticipation as the energy level within the organization rises. After a brief period of enthusiasm, positive feelings about the M&A deal can give way to pessimism and despair. Those groups that perceive a loss will likely try to protect their turf and may become entrenched. Once the employees sense a gap between cultures, a merger may seem insurmountably difficult. People in this sense often revert to their familiar cultures by employing stereotypes, sticking with their cohorts, and even by avoiding any socializing with 'others' entirely. Within their cohort group, individuals are able to defend their own culture; in such a safe confine, it may even become acceptable to objectify and demean others on the outside. An attitude of us-versus-them can often take shape in these instances. Water cooler discussions can quickly turn into protests of how "*they* just don't get it" or how business results might be better if things were only done "*our* way". Cultural clashes in such situations can consume organizational energy and time that should be spent on realizing synergies and creating new value.

Employees will compare the two merging entities and will be quick to focus on the differences. The grapevine can become full of these comparisons of culture, standards, guidelines, processes, and procedures of the two entities. People in such situations begin to keep score as announcements for positions are made, as they speculate about which company will come out on top, about the potential shape of new organization and who is taking over whom. The target's employees may begin to wonder if they will have a say in the acquirer's change efforts. Employee perceptions about post-deal outcomes can include concerns about the loss of quality and standards. Each company's reputation is thoroughly scrutinized at this point. Individuals distracted by these concerns, who are without encouraging hope for the future, will lack the ability to make a positive contribution to the urgent needs of the integration at a time when their input and involvement is needed most.

Previous experiences with major transformational change efforts, perhaps long before the current M&A deal, may have created a level of distrust between management and employees. Each employee will bring past experiences and memories to bear as they hear of the merger. Previous patterns of communication, the treatment of laid-off individuals and change survivors, as well as other similar factors can influence how employees who have undergone significant change will react to a deal. Getting to the point where the employees of the merged organizations know and trust each other may take a long time. Eventually, those who survive the cultural clashes should develop ways to work together. The survivors learn a new way of doing things and a new business language. However, for years after the merger, they are usually still more comfortable with the old ways inherited from their respective parent companies.

CULTURAL CONSIDERATION

The effect of culture on M&A integration varies depending on the degree of integration, the size of the target, and the value of people and their competencies with the deal value realization. The impact is most pronounced when two firms have to be integrated or assimilated.

Any time two organizations are partially or fully integrated culture becomes an important issue. Contact between two cultures becomes a source of conflict when integration must occur. If the target is left as a standalone entity, cultural issues are not as much of a major consideration. The degree of complexity increases when people from two separate organizations, with similar types of work, must work side-by-side and adapt their habitual way of doing things to the new environment. Prior to integration, they may have performed similar tasks slightly differently, used different terminology and abbreviations for similar objects while prioritizing, budgeting, and monitoring activities differently. They may also have been motivated and compensated in somewhat different ways. After the deal, they need to learn all of the new policies, procedures, and a new vocabulary in order to collaborate with their new cohorts. To facilitate integration, the acquirer can adopt some of the target's standards and guidelines, or it can impose its own standards and procedures on the target's employees. The ability of people to absorb the necessary changes and their readiness to accept these changes will depend on their respective histories and the effort expended on making the cultural integration possible.

When the two firms are of comparable size, they are generally viewed in terms of a merger of equals. In a merger of equals, the leadership team is composed of executives from both companies, and the rest of the organization and management hierarchy tend to be a blend made up from the two companies. Cultural issues are more significant for both sides in this model. In the acquisition of a large firm, deal synergies will be larger in absolute terms as they require the commitment of significant resources for their realization after the close. In a similar way, integration activities require more effort and are more complex. Cultural differences become more pronounced and can become a key integration issue. There is a need for a higher degree of detailed planning prior to the closing and better program management after the close.

The goal of a merger of equals is to adopt the best practices from each company and combine them into a surefire formula for success. There are varying points of view regarding a merger of equals, but in general merger partners are not equal. Mergers of equals are generally premised on stating that each company has a strength that it brings to the M&A deal, and the implication is that the other company has certain weaknesses and undesirable aspects. Though this may be true, the insinuation naturally can create conflict amongst the employees of the two firms, since no one believes that he or she is not doing a good job or adding real value. Since in a merger of equals the goal is to combine the skills of the two entities, attempts are made to meld the existing organizational structures, to combine standards and guidelines, and to patch together existing processes, all of which can become very time consuming and mired in emotional issues. A merger of equals also does not typically try to create a unique shared culture for the combined entity, but instead pursues an approach that places members of the two entities side-by-side with the hope that a new culture will emerge from working together. This multicultural approach can result in numerous small daily conflicts between the two cultures. Analysis of cultural integration has demonstrated that when two distinct cultures come into contact, they either survive side-by-side without real integration or else the culture with stronger survival instincts will overcome the other. Employees complain that although some positive aspects of the culture may cross over, negative cultural attributes also get passed on to the newly combined organization.

If the two senior leaderships agree simply to adopt the standards and practices of one firm and impose it on the other, they will save time and effort that would otherwise be spent on long and often unproductive discussions revolving around trying to combine the practices of two firms. Either the acquirer's or the target firm's employees get trained on the new policies, processes, and procedures and are expected to follow them. After an initial stage of adjustment and through sufficient training, employees will learn the new ways of doing things and will comply with the new requirements.

A large company acquiring a smaller company will have greater leverage to set the target's business priorities and impose some of its own standards and procedures. A small acquisition, in terms of the size of the acquirer, will naturally have a relatively small impact on the culture of the acquirer. The overall complexity of the integration diminishes when smaller firms or smaller acquisitions are involved. However, without good integration planning and implementation, it is possible for the large firm to smother the small firm's culture and cause quality people to leave.

When competencies being acquired are of a high value to the acquirer, culture should be a key consideration. If the skills and know-how of the target's people and their retention are of great value to the deal, then culture should become a primary consideration in target selection. The frequent, small daily conflicts that occur between the two cultures during the integration phase set back networking, collaboration, and sharing efforts.

The more complex and knowledge-intensive the work, the higher the degree of integration difficulty that will be faced by the two sides. In some cases, the acquirer may be better off leaving the target as a standalone entity rather than risking alienating the people and losing their valued know-how.

ASSESSMENT OF TARGET'S CULTURAL CHARACTERISTICS

An assessment of the cultures in a merger or acquisition should be based on a broad set of cultural characteristics. It is difficult to describe an organization's culture using just a few high-level characteristics. An examination of a broad array of cultural characteristics can help determine the degree of disparity or correspondence between the two groups. Therefore an examination of the cultural characteristics is one of the first steps toward evaluating the challenges of merging the two cultures. Outside experts can help with this process of discovery by incorporating an objective point of view.

After the deal closes, forming teams of natural leaders from both organizations to focus on real work and real issues will help people collaborate, understand, and respect one another's points of view. Such teams must have charters and must pursue value-added work by delivering useful results; they must also be sponsored by top management. The executive leadership team should plan and implement large-group communication meetings as a way to kick-off the integration phase, to disseminate information, and to work toward initiating the integration of the cultures. It will take time for people to understand their new roles and expectations: how their success will be measured and what types of actions are rewarded or sanctioned.

SUCCESS FACTOR #23

UTILIZE THE POWER OF INFORMATION TECHNOLOGY TO ACCELERATE THE DUE DILIGENCE PROCESS

Complete, organized, and accessible high-quality documentation is at the heart of the due diligence process. All activities conducted during due diligence and all findings for this reason must be thoroughly documented. Good documentation will track the observations, conclusions, and concerns of the due diligence teams, and it will include records of data sources and information gathering methods. Due diligence teams constantly need to access and retrieve the gathered information for the following: analysis, review, comparison, cross-checking, summarization for decision-makers, as well as for any future legal challenges. This need for good access to the information gives rise to the need for a good filing process. Hard copies of the material in addition to the actual forms and data collected must be filed and maintained securely in physical data rooms. Difficulties concerning data management, such as tagging and filing the data and inability to find it in a timely manner, slows the process and creates rework, and important information may get lost altogether.

The digitization of data and information technology systems, for example in the form of enterprise content management systems and virtual online data rooms, allows for the better organization of documents and file sharing. These systems provide immediate and secure access to all due diligence documents, and they allow for the review of information and for input by all individuals involved. The ready access to consistent information increases the quality of the due diligence process, enhances communications between team members, reduces rework and duplication, and may finally reduce the duration of the due diligence process.

Limited resources, especially in cross-border deals, make virtual online data rooms an indispensable technology tool in mergers and acquisitions. By placing due diligence information online, the time and costs of travel to review the information is significantly reduced. Costs associated with outside experts can also be economized in this respect since the need for travel is reduced when outside experts can view data from their home offices. Online data rooms also allow for online auctions, a relatively new M&A concept where a company can simultaneously present its data to multiple potential buyers.

SUCCESS FACTOR #24

KNOW THE ADDED RISKS OF CROSS-BORDER MERGERS AND ACQUISITIONS

The complexity of a cross-border deal is significantly greater than the deals struck within the home country. In a cross-border deal, the U.S.

acquirer has to incorporate the challenges posed by a foreign economy into the criteria for valuing a deal, which can include the possibility of under-developed capital markets, unfamiliar regulations, political risks, fluctuating currency exchange rates, and national cultural differences. Companies may also need to learn to manage a global organization with far-flung operations, which will most certainly add complexity to the deal. A few of the general questions that should be answered in global acquisitions include:

- How to conduct an effective due diligence for the international entity.

- How to address differences in standards, regulations, practices, and policies from the home country.

- How to gain sufficient size in order to be a real player in the foreign market.

- How to organize and manage the global entity.

The acquirer should be aware of differences in practices and customs between their home country, such as differences in information availability and the treatment of warranties and representations. Understanding and managing the unique risks of an international M&A deal is critical to its success.

FOREIGN CURRENCY RISKS

Investing in a foreign economy involves the added uncertainties and risks associated with receiving a stream of cash flow in a foreign currency. The acquirer must account for exchange rate risks as well as the potential negative impacts on the return on investment in its valuation. It is not possible to hedge completely against exchange rate risks, despite the hedging by forward contracts in currency markets. Global currency markets have made the flow of capital between countries easy and instantaneous, while still potentially increasing uncertainties about currency fluctuations. In addition, foreign governments may restrict the exchanging of all or of a portion of their currency into U.S. dollars, thereby forcing the subsidiary to spend a portion of its income locally. Prominent examples of foreign currency risks include the crash of the Thai Baht in 1997 and Argentina's Peso in 2000.

In valuing a foreign firm, the acquirer can use one of two methods. On one hand, the acquirer can calculate the discounted cash flow of the target firm in the local currency, using the target's local cost of capital. It can then convert the present value of the cash flow into the acquirer's currency based on the recent currency exchange rates. On the other hand, it can convert the string of future cash flow into U.S. dollars based on an assumed long-term exchange rate and use the target's discount rate for the present value calculations. Guesses about future exchange rates, though, can be very risky, making the deal highly speculative. In addition, the acquirer should account for regional economic cycles, differing tax rates, and differing inflation rates in two countries.

The acquirer may choose to account for cash flows from foreign subsidiaries as separate from its main business so that investors and analysts can observe the impact of currency changes without assuming that there has been a fundamental shift in company's performance. Foreign governments may also demand taxation on the company's global income, may change their regulations regarding an industry, or even may nationalize an industry.

ACCESS TO QUALITY INFORMATION

The due diligence process in cross-border deals can take longer than the same sort of deal would take in the United States primarily due to a lack of readily available information of quality. The lack of experience with the foreign commercial practices and the geographic separation can divert considerable energy away from a detailed due diligence and move it towards attaining confidence around the accuracy of financial statements only. It can be difficult to get timely operational and financial data as well as updated and audited reports from the target in this respect. The reporting standards may also be very different; the information reported may be unreliable; and endemic problems may not be easy to identify. Language too can be a major barrier to understanding the true intentions of the seller and particularly to effective decision-making during M&A negotiations.

CULTURAL DIFFERENCES

Cultural challenges are much greater when acquirers cross national borders. National origins, societal and cultural norms, and the environment in which the organization operates all affect the organizational culture. A respect for superiors, status symbols, managerial perks, management styles, along with a familiarity with foreign languages must be considerations in the M&A deal. The social obligations of a firm as an employer, the legal and policy impediments to workforce rationalization, human resource management, employee work habits, the reaction to organizational change, and concepts such as pay-for-performance may all differ markedly between countries. These differences can limit the ability of management to operate profitably in the foreign environment. Foreign workers may also harbor resentment towards their foreign employer if they perceive that the employer is focused more on its own home country and appears to be uncaring or out of touch with foreign employee needs.

BUSINESS PRACTICES

In a cross border-deal, the acquirer is faced with differences in business practices. The business practices and management styles in the United States are difficult to impose on a global entity. However, business practices that are not considered good practice in the United States are also usually considered problematic in a foreign country.

Local country rules that regulate cross-border mergers will likely vary from country to country. These rules can increase the legal costs and can adversely affect smaller acquirers. Some of these laws are intended to discourage foreign acquisitions and foreign ownership. When an acquirer is considering the country in which to make an acquisition, it should be aware of the limitations that these rules place on labor laws, restructuring, and taxation. Other differences include:

- Legal structures and regulatory requirements

- Accounting practices and financial systems

- Ethical requirements

- Compensation, reward systems, and executive pay

- Corporate governance, stakeholder management, and the role of shareholders

- Pace of decision making

Human resource practices may differ significantly from country to country, such as in terms of executive compensation, rewards, and perks. These differences can become an issue during merger negotiations and integration; the differences may come to cause some resentment among the executives of the two companies, which may, in turn, become a barrier to effective integration. Different countries also have different approaches to regulations regarding collective bargaining, for example giving labor unions different levels of influence in the workplace.

LOCAL PRESENCE

The geographic separation of operational centers, time zone differences, and the lack of a permanent local presence by the acquirer can allow opportunists in the target entity to take advantage of the deal environment and lure away key customers. Acquirers must get to know their foreign operation's markets and customers; they must pay attention to customer issues and develop direct relationships with their new customers.

Cross-border mergers regularly require people to move and accept postings in foreign countries. The many unknowns, such as the differences in cost of living, language barriers, lifestyles, housing, schools, and the separation from family and support networks, can influence the decision of employees to move between the corporate business sites. To encourage employees to accept international assignments, companies often offer attractive perks, cover moving expenses, and pay for the cost of living adjustments and any additional vacation time. Addressing these factors can add substantially to the costs of integration, and this too may slow down the pace of the integration progress. At a minimum, integration becomes more difficult when teams have to operate in a number of global locations and need to travel for significant amounts of time.

CASE STUDY
CONSECO'S BUSINESS FAILURE

Conseco Inc., a Carmel, Indiana, firm, filed for Chapter 11 bankruptcy on December 11, 2002. With $52 billion in assets, Conseco's bankruptcy was the third-largest ever, following only WorldCom and Enron in size.

Conseco, which sells a variety of life and health insurance products aimed at less-sophisticated consumers, is an experienced acquirer that grew in the 1990s through debt-financed acquisitions. Since its start, Conseco had acquired 44 insurance companies in 17 years. In 1998, the company acquired Green Tree Financial Corporation for $6.0 billion in stocks. Green Tree, which was renamed Conseco Finance Corporation, provided high interest mobile-home financing to people with questionable credit and represented a new line of business for Conseco.

On the surface, the merger appeared to be a good fit. The two companies seemed to have similar entrepreneurial cultures, and both companies dealt with the same consumer segments. The acquisition was expected to create synergies through the cross-selling of financial services to the same market segment. Other firms, such as Sears, had tried and failed to realize value from the cross-selling of financial services in terms of insurance, real estate, and investment services; yet Conseco's management believed that the model was both workable and highly desirable.

Even before the M&A deal, Green Tree was already in trouble. Green Tree had grown dramatically by securitizing its loans, which involved packaging the loans it made to its customers and offering them as publicly traded securities. Green Tree would then supposedly use the cash it raised to make additional loans to its customers and would use an aggressive, but acceptable, accounting method for recognizing the profits from the bundled loans by booking its future gains from securitizing[4] in the present. This method boosted the company's short-term performance, but it also exposed Green Tree to the risks presented by high loan default rates and drops in interest rates. Before the merger, such a drop in interest rates caused Green Tree to take a number of write-downs. As a result of this exposure, its access to capital was limited, and it was faced with either having to sell out or raise its own capital and hope for a stock rebound.

Meanwhile, Conseco was looking for a fast-growing firm that would augment its safe but slowly growing insurance businesses. Management spotted Green Tree, though unaware of its recent woes. Conseco became concerned that someone else would snatch up the opportunity presented by Green Tree, so its CEO signed an agreement to pay an 83% premium over Green Tree's prevailing stock price after only a one-week assessment. Further due diligence activities failed to identify the extent of Green Tree's problems. Having overpaid for a declining business performance, the problems became exacerbated when after the acquisition, the hoped-for synergies did not materialize. Although both businesses sold their services to the same market segment, the customers did not take advantage of the new broader financial offering in sufficient numbers for Conseco to realize the network synergies and the expected return on investment. With a slowdown in the economy, the mobile-home loan foreclosures started to increase for Conseco Finance, and Conseco was saddled with growing bad debts in its loans to mobile-home buyers and manufactured housing. Despite hiring a new, high-profile and highly experienced CEO, the company's debt burden coupled with the lackluster performance of the insurance business were overwhelming. Conseco could not make payments on the $6.5 billion in debt that it had accumulated, leading to the declaration of Chapter 11. In March 2003, the assets of Conseco Finance were sold at auction for approximately $1.0 billion, while Conseco reemerged from bankruptcy focused again back upon its core insurance business.

NOTES

[1] Due diligence means adequate and appropriate care and attention as expected and required.

[2] The Sarbanes-Oxley Corporate Responsibility Act improves financial disclosures, increases vigilance of boards and CEO's, ends self-regulation of audit firms through an accounting oversight board, and eliminates conflicts of interest in stock research.

[3] See Edgar Schein in references for a complete discussion of organization culture.

[4] Similar to issuing a bond, securitizing is collecting an upfront lump sum amount from investors in exchange for promise of a future revenue stream.

Part 3

Do the Deal Right

CHAPTER 8

PREPARING FOR INTEGRATION CHALLENGES

Success factors:
- Name an integration manager at the time of the announcement
- Develop detailed integration plans prior to the closing
- Retain the best people by treating them as the company's most valuable assets
- Maintain a strong focus on customers

Gaining insights into integration requirements, complexities, and challenges will facilitate the preparation and detailed planning needed for the integration phase. Sources of insights for the acquirer include the findings from the due diligence activities, key sources of value as outlined in the deal business case, the degree of integration required by the deal rationale, and lessons learned from other M&A deals.

The objective of integration planning is to facilitate and to accelerate the tempo of integration and value realization. Integration plans are aligned with and tailored to the rationale of the M&A deal and its goals, the implications of which should be well understood for the implementation activities to be effective. Integration plans serve as a blueprint for this purpose and are built on the experiences of and collaboration between the acquirer and the target. The acquirer should communicate and work with the target management in planning for the integration requirements. Development of detailed plans, timelines, and roles take time and thus should start early and need to include a prioritization of activities and areas of business that are expected to create the highest value. Integration efforts and resources will be focused on those value added activities while minimizing disruptions to the ongoing business.

This chapter reviews the key elements of successful implementation planning, which include integration program management, understanding and resolving people issues, and customer management and retention.

SUCCESS FACTOR #25

NAME AN INTEGRATION MANAGER AT THE TIME OF THE ANNOUNCEMENT

Naming the integration manager at the time of the announcement allows him/her to play three key roles. The first key role involves working with the due diligence teams in order to understand the integration needs and to develop detailed transition and integration plans. Prior to the closing, the integration manager, working with a cross-functional team, is responsible for developing integration plans in alignment with the deal rationale that will set the course for integration as well as plan and organize the transition and integration activities. The second key role is to maintain a continuity of knowledge and experience between the due diligence phase and the integration phase. This continuity is critical for ensuring that important knowledge gained during due diligence is maintained and translated into actionable steps during the integration phase. The integration manager's third key role is then to implement capable and effective program management during the integration phase that will help realize the deal value as quickly as possible. Integration manager responsibilities during integration phase are to:

- Coordinate the activities of integration teams and manage the integration of their outputs

- Identify barriers to integration tasks and bring them to the leadership team's attention

- Measure the integration implementation progress and report to line management

- Provide regular updates to the senior management

- Define and support key stakeholder communications strategies

- Promote networking across the organization boundaries

- Manage conflicts, facilitate cultural integration, and deal effectively with people issues

- Provide guidance regarding the business and the acquirer's standards, guidelines, processes, procedures, and expectations

- Contribute to the creation of a sense of belonging to help retain valued employees

- Explain synergy logic, timetables, and accountabilities to the integration teams

The senior leadership's role is to set goals for integration and synergy realization that are challenging yet achievable. The integration manager and the integration teams are then responsible for turning those goals into practice by ensuring that integration activities are being undertaken and completed, that synergies are being realized, and that line management can maintain its focus on running the business. In order to accomplish this, the integration manager needs to have a clear understanding of senior leadership expectations.

Given the crucial nature of integration for the ultimate success of the deal, the qualification of the integration manager is very important. The individual who is appointed must be fully committed to the role of integration manager and also to the company for at least three years. He or she should be an experienced and respected leader with a successful track record of managing and implementing large initiatives. It is critical that the integration manager is a good communicator and is able to deal with ambiguities that will come with this complex role.

The integration manager's role ends and integration teams disband once integration ownership can be handed over to the organization.

SUCCESS FACTOR #26

DEVELOP DETAILED INTEGRATION PLANS PRIOR TO THE CLOSING

Detailed integration plans provide direction as to what must be done, who should do each task, and when each task should be accomplished. Planning for integration may start as early as the acquisition target selection and the preliminary assessment of the target's business. Integration needs and the deal's potential complexity will emerge as the acquirer better understands the target's business. The degree of integration complexity will affect the ease of the deal value realization, and therefore it should be considered during deal valuation and negotiation. The strategic drivers of the deal, the fit between two companies, and sources of deal value characterize the objectives, scope, and logic of the integration plans and the appropriate approach for the integration phase. The integration plans outline the integration requirements by function or by key business process and will consider the impact on employees. Some elements of integration plans include:

- The transition and integration program management and governance

- Organizational structure design and staffing

- Orienting the employees and bringing them into the organization

- Human resource process alignment

- Key internal and external stakeholders communication

- Synergy realization and tracking

- Customer satisfaction and retention activities

- Business and operation consolidation activities

- The strategic assessment of the combined business

- Defining a common business plan, operating philosophy, and consistent practices

- Organizational sharing and learning

In order to define the integration needs the effect of the integration on operational, financial, supply chain, product development, other business functions and processes must be assessed. The capabilities and resource levels needed to carry out and support the integration activities will also have to be determined. Integration activities should be prioritized based on the sources of strategic and operational value for the deal and the ease of implementation. The outcome of the integration planning should be a detailed, prioritized, and collaborative blueprint that includes activity lists, roles, and milestones for a fast-tempo integration that will lead to an acceleration of value realization. Tasks and activities outlined in the integration plan are grouped according to function or line organization. No matter how much work goes into the planning process, the final direction will eventually have to stand the test of reality. It must be remembered, though, that not every situation can be projected beforehand, and not every expectation will necessarily come to fruition. There are unforeseen difficulties in integration such as differences in information systems, differences in customer management processes, and varying approaches to customer problem resolution all of which can exacerbate integration difficulties.

As part of the M&A agreement, the two companies agree to certain conditions, which will remain in effect until the deal closes or is terminated. For example, the two sides generally could agree to run their business in the way that they have practiced in the past, to follow the usual course of business, and to continue their relationships with customers, suppliers, and partners in order to maintain the business performance. The two sides also can agree not to take actions that would adversely affect the future of the business: selling assets or parts of the business; entering into new agreements such as leases, licensing agreements, or intellectual property rights; incurring new debt; making capital expenditures beyond a certain cap that would normally be needed to run the business; or any other key actions that would fundamentally alter the business. The two sides agree not to take actions that would interfere with the deal or impact the ability to get regulatory approval for the deal, such as issuing new shares, paying unplanned dividends, acquiring other businesses, or making any other major commitments, agreements, or obligations. The two sides are also legally prohibited from sharing product lines and other competitive information prior to the close. Only a select group of executives are closely involved with the deal prior to the closing; this group typically includes the acquirer's and the target's senior management, its analysts, subject matter experts, and any outside advisers. At closing, funds or securities are exchanged, and the two firms legally become one firm.

The closing should occur by an agreed-to date or immediately after the two sides have satisfied the conditions of the deal, barring any unexpected regulatory requirements. The conditions that have to be satisfied for the closing to occur include: the approval by major partners, shareholders, and stockholders; the absence of any federal or state court judgments; regulatory approval from the SEC and DOJ antitrust divisions that they meet the Hart-Scott-Radino Act requirements; authorization by other appropriate government entities; the listing of acquiring company's shares on appropriate exchanges; that the warranties and representations made in the M&A agreement are accurate and that they will not have an adverse effect on the deal or on the acquirer.

As for large deals, the deal closure can take up to six months or longer, and one should remember that a deal closing is not a given. Each year, hundreds of deals fail to close. The range of issues that can prevent deals from closing is vast: corporate control, antitrust concerns, bankruptcy, buyers or sellers opting out, shareholder objections, as well as personalities and egos can all be factors that delay or halt a deal.

PEOPLE ISSUES IN MERGERS AND ACQUISITIONS

If not dealt with sensibly and expediently, people issues may distract management from pursuing a thorough due diligence process and from completing the integration planning. Such issues will then seriously threaten the deal value realization. The key people issues faced in M&A deals include:

- The impact of uncertainties caused by major changes in employee's performance and productivity.

- The departure of valued employees.

- Gaining an employee commitment to make the overwhelming amount of effort required to carry out the integration activities.

M&A integration success depends on people's ability to work together, resolve issues, and meet customers' needs. People are the most valuable resource of a company, particularly for one involved in an M&A deal and its integration. Yet in many instances, the employee commitment to the success of the M&A deal along with their willingness to make personal sacrifices in terms of time and energy is often already assumed. In order for integration to be successful on these terms, the impact of the deal on the employees must be understood as plans are developed to deal with people issues in an expedient manner.

Senior leadership expect their employees to demonstrate the same level of dedication and commitment to the success of the M&A deal that they do. Thus, the senior leadership should, in clear terms, convey what they want everyone to aspire to, and they should also be prepared to confront resistance, make a case for change, show interest and enthusiasm, and to back up their talk with action.

One common stumbling block is that line managers who are accountable for integration and synergy realization may not be adequately prepared for or knowledgeable enough about the challenges of the M&A integration; hence they might under-estimate the degree of difficulty, complexity, and effort required to combine two separate businesses into one integrated business.

Another issue is that although most people wish to work for a successful company, many employees are not willing or able to commit long hours to the M&A integration efforts. An employee's commitment to the organization is based on the expectations that the organization will take care of the employee as he or she fulfills the duties of the job. However, M&A deals inherently bring uncertainties about the firm fulfilling its commitment to jobs and careers with job losses and career derailments as well as in its demands of significant time and energy from those who remain. When the deal closes and M&A integration begins, changes to the work environment are inevitable.

M&A UNCERTAINTIES CAUSE employee apprehension. Individuals will often perceive changes caused by the M&A deal as a major threat. Even those who sense a need for change will feel anxious, frightened, and worried about the possible disruptions, losses, and risks resulting from the integration. Changes can create stress, consume valuable employee time, and reduce productivity. New and unfamiliar policies, standards, processes, procedures, and technologies combined with different HR policies in terms of compensation, benefits, rewards, and performance measurement can likewise create certain fears for the employees. Uncertainty and the feeling of a lack of control may permeate the work environment as more and more decisions are made that directly affect employees. Valuable time may be lost on inter-group conflict as changes in organizational design play out and as people are selected for the roles in the combined entity.

Job security and career advancement are two of the primary causes of employee fear and apprehension. The deal in this sense may introduce different titles and unfamiliar career tracks, and individuals may see an infusion of new, qualified, and talented, but unfamiliar, people as rivals with whom they are in competition for promotions and top jobs. The new realities of the combined entity may entirely erase the old succession plans and dissipate any hopes of further promotion. When reassigned to a role that is perceived as having less responsibility and less prestige, individuals may begin to experience a loss of esteem and influence. The target employees in particular may perceive themselves as the losers in the M&A deal as their hopes and expectations of career advancement diminish in their eyes.

The disruption of social and group networks due to departures, lay-offs, job eliminations, transfers, relocations, and new reporting relationships with new and unfamiliar supervisors can severely affect established relationships and the predictability of work expectations. Employees may not want to move to a less attractive city, and the loss of established relationships with key employees, friends, and respected colleagues can negatively influence employee morale. With changes in the organizational structure, employees may become concerned about the new leadership and may perceive a decline in the quality of leadership due to issues and conflicts with a new supervisor. Customers and vendors provide a different but equally important support network for employees. Having to interface with and manage new customer relationships will take time to gain a comfort level. Finally, plant and facility closures will affect local communities and local economies, and they will most certainly lead to negative feelings among employees and local communities.

Employees who identify strongly with a certain mission and a corporate identity and who see themselves as contributing to an important goal may feel a particularly strong sense of loss and dissociation. This is compounded when two competitors join forces, causing a sense of trepidation for both employees and customers. The merger of old competitors and rivals may result in employees acting territorially about who bought whom and who owns whom. In a small company, employees rarely appreciate the influence of the large acquirer. Egos and politics can therefore get in the way of implementing new programs. Ultimately, resistance to change, low work morale, lower productivity, and increased turnover rates will likely be seen in the workplace, especially for the employees of the target organization.

According to a study conducted in 2000, one of the top three reasons given by technology workers for changing employers was the changes and uncertainties that stem from organizational restructuring and from mergers and acquisitions[1]. Studies have shown that in many past M&A deals, a large percentage of talented people walk away within the first 12 to 24 months. Studies also show that over half the management of a target firm will depart within five years after an M&A deal. Experience has continually demonstrated that people-retention issues are often insufficiently addressed before integration begins.

What makes an M&A deal so dramatic in this respect is both the pace of change and the uncertainties that come through having interactions with people and organizational cultures with which the employee has no history. Once the magnitude and difficulties of integration work become apparent, a sense of gloom may be cast over the organization. The initial euphoria generated at the announcement here can give way to fear and worry well before the close. As the grinding work of integration gets under way, the people may show signs of frustration, unease, and withdrawal. Integration deadlines and time constraints will further affect people who are already busy fulfilling their daily job expectations. These factors place a high level of stress on employees. It is crucial that during this period that management is visible, that training and development are emphasized, and that a decisive pace of decision-making occurs. Organizational rewards and incentives must be aligned with the new organizational direction; otherwise incentives can work against changes taking root.

SUCCESS FACTOR #27

RETAIN THE BEST PEOPLE BY TREATING THEM AS THE COMPANY'S MOST VALUABLE ASSETS

If valued high-performing people feel that they are being treated poorly, or if they feel as if they are lacking influence, they will likely depart. Valued employees may also decide that they cannot work for an opponent from which they have worked hard in the past to differentiate themselves. The departure of valued employees should be a major concern to the executive team, since loss of their skills and capabilities will affect the M&A success and potentially dilute the deal value. The flight of valued employees is especially threatening and can have a long-lasting impact on the combined entity in deals where the fundamental strategic goal is to gain access to "soft" assets, such as the knowledge and expertise in a consulting business or a growing industry where the rate of innovation is high. The development and implementation of retention plans for valued employees is critical to the success of any M&A deal.

Performance reviews and feedback opportunities need to be conducted on time, and they should include two-way communications. Incentive bonuses should also be paid on time. The implementation of new HR programs, such as those that involve mentoring and tying incentives to business results and individual contribution, can build enthusiasm. Employment contracts, lock-up agreements, and pecuniary incentives such as stock options that are vested over time or retention bonuses that are paid out over time can also be used to keep valued employees from jumping ship.

Valued employees also need to have a sense of purpose. Creating a positive work environment where the employee feels connected to their environment and their workgroup is the first step in retaining key employees. Facilitating the development of new social networks helps employees reconnect to their workgroups and the business quickly. Valued employees need to be engaged in early discussions, so that they realize that they are indeed valued and are needed in the new entity—that all of the hard work will eventually pay off for a better future both for them and for the company as a whole. Opportunities for career advancement and for implementing new ideas can encourage these valued employees to stay. High performing people typically wish to enlarge their circle of responsibility and gain autonomy in their job. Given the chance to take part in redesigning their own jobs and defining their own future, valued employees will be motivated to challenge and stretch their capabilities. High performing employees can also be given greater freedom in these instances to move between groups, to share their practical knowledge, and to gain a broader role in the integration activities. An involvement in key integration activities, the communication of the big picture, updates on integration progress, and the establishment of goals and milestones all will help create an environment of mutual trust and openness.

Employees, whether they choose to stay on or whether they decide to or are asked to leave, must be treated with respect and compassion. Those employees who leave the organization may do so for a variety of reasons, and management may sign non-compete agreements with those who end up leaving. Employees being transitioned out of the business can be placed in temporary positions in order to fill resource gaps and allow for sufficient resources during the integration phase. The acquirer can also make an effort to fill available jobs in the new entity with in-house employees first prior to looking outside because they are more knowledgeable and informed about the company.

CUSTOMER RETENTION AND M&A DEALS: KEEPING A CLOSE EYE ON THE CUSTOMER

Through an M&A deal, an acquirer attempts to address the strengths and shortcomings of its offerings in order to better meet customer needs, to strengthen its base business, and to gain a competitive advantage. Losing customers during the M&A process would defeat the purpose of undergoing the difficult M&A deal. A loss of customer relationships during the M&A deal will result in the dilution of long-term deal value. Changes and uncertainties that can result from the M&A process can affect customer retention and satisfaction.

During the M&A process, a firm can become too internally focused, which will affect how it interfaces with its customers. Busy with the tasks of integration, businesses may not realize they are adversely affecting their customers; they may begin to overlook the needs of their customers or might be making decisions affecting their customers too slowly. The firm and its management may become too preoccupied and internally focused with issues such as realizing synergies, dealing with people concerns, and cutting costs. The manner in which the larger firm organizes its structure after the M&A deal can also affect how it interfaces with its customers in the future, and so it can potentially dilute the focus on the customer requirements. Customer communications may be overlooked, may be insufficient, may not be timely, or the may not simply address customer concerns.

Consolidation of facilities, sales and marketing organizations, and elements of the supply chain may initially produce temporary irregularities in value delivery processes and procedures. Customers that are inconvenienced during the deal are more likely to look elsewhere to satisfy their needs. Inconveniences may include delays in deliveries, product quality glitches, and transaction errors. An overarching goal of the M&A process must be to reduce customer inconveniences throughout.

Customers may become concerned and anxious about the effects of the deal on their business. Concerns could include the discontinuity of product and service offerings, the closure of a convenient location, the reputation of either partner in the deal, as well as the impact of the deal on price or product and service quality. An acquirer may phase out some of the target's products and replace them with its own products, leaving a perceived gap in its product line. From the perspective of the customer, changes to products or services can affect its ease of purchase, and thus they are not often welcomed. The notion of ease of purchase includes the customer's familiarity with the product or service, their existing purchasing habits, and their expectations about the consistent availability of familiar products. Customers originally select a brand or product and will consistently purchase that product with the expectation that it will be available when they need it. They therefore may not feel so comfortable with the substitutions being introduced, even if the substitute product or service may be comparable. Changes that affect the ease of purchase may also impact the manner in which the supplier stands behind its products and the availability and quality of after-sales service, customer support, and the approach to joint problem solving.

The customer's buying experience also includes the quality of the relationship with the sales force and other customer-oriented representatives with whom they may interact. After the deal closes, the lay-off of sales people who are familiar to the customers may result in feelings of loss. Anxieties that customer-oriented employees experience regarding the pending changes can affect their morale and their productivity, and these worries can trickle down to the customers themselves and affect the quality of relations, especially when such employees get distracted by the integration. Customers may become suspicious of the practices of the new sales force as well as the resulting changes to the familiar culture and practices with the arrival of the new regime. The two companies involved in the deal can have conflicting approaches to meeting their customer expectations. Changes in the pattern of sales calls, follow-ups, the format of documentation, payment terms, and the like can all contribute to customer frustration or alienation. The degree of customer focus in each company can, of course, vary, but attention should remain on the issue as a key challenge for the integration process.

Customers may not associate the increased supplier size as a result of an M&A deal with superior service. Customers seeking intimacy in terms of service and its relationships may feel put off when there is a perceived lack of attention by the seemingly impersonal approach of a large provider. These customers may reject the notion of a larger company that can exert considerable market power, and they may instead prefer a local supplier that appears more responsive to their needs. Customers can also become distrustful of the market power and influence that the firm will be able to gain as a result of a deal. In general, customers are not concerned about the benefits that would accrue for the acquirer as a result of the merger such as the additional market share, the access to new markets, and new customers; they are rather concerned about the resulting market power that the combined entity gains through the acquisition and its impact on the future business.

When a firm is in an M&A deal with a competitor, the customers have probably heard negative comments about the competitors from the people with whom they interact. Customers may be suspicious of either firm's business reputation, and so they may have developed a negative image of the deal partner with whom they will work in the future. Customers too may be concerned about service, pricing, delivery, and the quality being impacted after the deal.

Customers, though, do not always vocalize their concerns. They demonstrate their dissatisfaction through fewer purchases, by delayed purchasing decisions, or by altogether seeking out other purchase sources for their products or services in anticipation of what they see as undesirable changes. Satisfied customers, in contrast, are more likely to be loyal and to be retained during the transition and beyond. Because it is more expensive to find a new customer than to retain an existing one, firms must make every effort to keep their customers satisfied throughout the merger and acquisition process. Customer retention in M&A deals requires detailed planning and may require additional expenditures. Retaining customers starts with a detailed understanding of how customers gain value from a firm's products and services. Thus, the acquirer should understand how the target's customers gain value and what the key attributes of the target firm's customer satisfaction are for them. These attributes must constitute a key criteria for target selection, and so they must be thoroughly analyzed during due diligence.

SUCCESS FACTOR #28

MAINTAIN A STRONG FOCUS ON CUSTOMERS

The acquirer must make customer retention a key priority throughout the deal and integration phases. In order to maintain customer loyalty, the negative impacts on customers must be curtailed and managed throughout the M&A deal process. The acquirer and the target each must contact key customers to ensure that they are aware of the deal and to allay any initial concerns and trepidations. After the close, the acquirer must commit to paying close attention to the customers of both firms; it must address their needs and concerns in a timely manner and ensure that customers are taken care of by maintaining a continuity in customer focus and managing the customer facing processes.

The acquirer should thoroughly understand its new customer needs, issues, and expectations. After the close, the acquirer can learn about its newly acquired customer base by reviewing customer information that has been collected by the target firm. The acquirer should also identify key loyal and profitable customers of both firms and track their satisfaction systematically and regularly.

MAINTAIN FREQUENT AND REGULAR CUSTOMER CONTACT

By closely monitoring customer reactions to the deal, any concerns or negative feelings about the deal can be addressed in a timely manner. Brand reputation must be protected during the deal process through customer communications and a fast response to issues that arise that might potentially threaten brand value. Following up on customer feedback and comments will ensure that issues are addressed to the satisfaction of the customer. Key customers will expect that executive-level focus will be maintained; executives of each firm should to this end conduct regular visits to key accounts and be actively involved in interacting with these customers. Customer satisfaction will be enhanced if customers are contacted directly with a message tailored to their market segment or to their customer grouping. Direct communication provides an opportunity to talk to customers while introducing both firms and receiving customer feedback about any potential concerns. Updating letters to customers and to vendors will keep them abreast of the events. The firm can initiate a targeted marketing campaign in order to generate enthusiasm with the customers and to conduct customer service surveys that can help determine its impact.

ADDRESS CUSTOMER CONCERNS

Customers seek continuity and certainty with respect to their suppliers. Clear plans for product continuity and future support should be drawn up and communicated to customers as early as possible. Employees who interact with customers should be able to explain clearly any changes to products or services in order to put customers at ease about how their needs will be met.

Acquirers will have to plan for key changes that might affect the customers and any inconveniences that they may experience as a result of the deal. The message to the customers in this respect should be that the company is being open about the potential challenges of the deal. This communication will involve preparing the customer for any potential glitches that may occur during the deal process, detailing how long the transition may take, and informing the customers about who they can contact to resolve issues quickly. The sales force can allay uncertainties and fears by highlighting and explaining the changes that the customer may experience in any customer-facing process such as delivery scheduling, pricing, and payment terms, the timing in which the changes may take place, and how customer needs will be satisfied. The sales force must also initiate the problem solving process with customers in terms of how best to prepare for the changes. Employees who interact with customers must explain the M&A deal outcomes in terms of customer benefits and in terms of how the combination will directly deliver additional customer value such as lower prices, higher quality, and enhanced delivery.

If a customer decides to leave, that customer should be immediately contacted by management so that they can try to understand the reasons for any dissatisfaction and departures. If the firm is delivering less than what the customer has come to expect and to depend on, then with quick corrective action it may be able to overcome the customer's dissatisfaction and retain the account. Setting solid expectations and then exceeding them will finally enhance the firm's standing in the eyes of the customers. Another way to keep customers from switching to the competition and to entice them to stay active during the integration period is to consider offering incentives in the way of discounts and other promotions that will reward loyalty. Along with potential discounts, additional financial incentives could be necessary to make up for the any customer inconveniences during the M&A process.

BRING CUSTOMER-INTERFACING EMPLOYEES ONBOARD EARLY

When customer-oriented employees are brought onboard with the M&A deal requirements early, they can focus on retaining existing customers and reducing anxieties during the transition and integration. The sales force representatives, the business development executives, and the customer service employees all must have input into the development of customer-related integration plans. The roles and responsibilities for customer care need to be clearly defined in the integration plans. Employees will need to understand their new roles and will need opportunities to get to know their new co-workers and managers. Rewards and incentives given to the sales force can support customer retention activities throughout the M&A process. Greater training and development of customer-oriented functions is key in preparing for the cross-selling of products and services from the two organizations.

Visible leadership focus on customers is important for customer-oriented groups. To do well in both the short and long-term, cost reduction efforts must be combined with plans that limit the adverse effects on customer service. Employee departures increase the need for stronger and standardized customer-relations processes as well as for implementing quality systems that would reduce the impact of an individual's departure on customer relationships.

CASE STUDY
A MODEL FOR CULTURAL INTEGRATION

In October 2002, the fragmented computer services industry, of which International Business Machines Corporation (IBM) is a flagship firm, was undergoing further consolidation with IBM's acquisition of PricewaterhouseCoopers LLP's consulting business. The growth of computer services companies depends on the availability of quality people, technical know-how, geographic presence, and funding. PwC Consulting amounted to only a fraction of IBM's global leadership position in systems integration. Nonetheless, the expertise of the two companies complemented each other, and the deal was a good fit. PwC's experience in business transformation was combined with IBM's operations and outsourcing expertise, which created a global leader and a full service provider for technology services. The merger created a one-stop shop that could provide consulting in business transformations, operations, IT, and outsourcing in a new global unit created for IBM by combining the PwC employees and about 30,000 of its own. The resulting unit was named Business Consulting Services.

Hewlett-Packard (H-P) had intended to acquire PricewaterhouseCoopers Consulting a year earlier for $18 billion, but H-P had scrapped its plans when its own stock price dipped sharply. After the accounting scandals involving Enron and Arthur Andersen, regulators wanted auditing firms to separate from their consulting arms. PwC attempted to spin off its consulting business through an initial public offering in early 2002, but at the time, the IPO market was soft and so the attempt failed. Owing to concerns about a potential conflict of interest between the consultant activities and the business auditing activities of the firm, PwC Consulting was experiencing a deterioration of its consulting customer base. IBM acquired the 30,000-employee consulting unit for $3.5 billion. The rapid loss of customers created a sense of urgency for IBM to move quickly to integrate the PwC business into its own consulting services following the close of the deal.

The merger discussion between IBM and PwC had started at a May 2002 strategy meeting between senior executives from the two firms. As a result, the two management teams were moving forward with a common mindset about the deal and their future together. Despite the deal's momentum, the deal was not without intrigue. Reportedly, at one point during the negotiations, PwC's representatives in deal negotiations had bluffed by committing themselves to a higher price for the acquisition. However, IBM's knowledge of the regulatory demands on PwC and the slumping IPO market had helped it call their bluff. Three weeks of deal negotiations involved 150 managers from both entities in July 2002. A number of complicating factors were involved in negotiations: (1) PwC consisted of numerous partnerships around the globe that had to be sorted out (2) since PwC was IBM's auditor, SEC had placed a deadline on the deal, and there was a sense of urgency, and (3) IBM could not be seen as overpaying for the deal and giving way to the perception of favoritism to its auditors.

IBM made cultural integration a key part of its merger strategy and of the deal negotiations. IBM believed that there was a good cultural fit between PwC and IBM, and it regarded the people of PwC as a key asset in the potential merger. The management at IBM spent significant time trying to convince the PwC employees to stay after the merger. Although almost twenty percent of PwC's partners were let go in order to eliminate redundancies as PwC was consolidated into IBM, IBM designed a number of incentives to keep the remaining partners and key consultants from departing and thereby taking clients with them. To show their commitment, IBM even adopted some of PwC Consulting's practices. IBM retained the firm's top three partners who would then report directly to the President of IBM services. It then reorganized IBM Services by industry grouping in order to match PwC's existing structure. IBM adopted PwC's employee skills tracking process, and PwC Partners were allowed to retain their titles. Additional structural changes within IBM Services facilitated the integration of the PwC employees who were still tied to PwC human resource processes and titles. Consulting partners also split a multi-million-dollar stock hand-out that was delivered over a period of five years, plus stock options that vested over the same period. In return, top employees were asked to accept a pay cut. After the deal, IBM management maintained a strong focus on the customer and avoided getting embroiled in internal issues. IBM has also invested in people development and in the growth of the combined business. In a deal where people competencies are the key to value realization as in this one, the acquirer must take actions to ensure that the valued talent will not leave and that the value of the deal therefore will not become diluted.

NOTES

[1] See in references article by Cristina McEachern regarding retaining technology workers and John A. Byrne regarding Cisco Systems.

CHAPTER 9

BEYOND THE CLOSE

Success factors:
- Transition to an integrated management team quickly
- Maintain a fast integration tempo
- Communicate the integration priorities
- Define a common operating philosophy and consistent practices
- Realize M&A deal benefits tangibly and in a timely manner
- Tie employee incentives to synergy realization and to the fulfillment of integration requirements
- Develop in-house M&A skills

The integration of two separate entities is a complex task irrespective of the size of the deal. It affects large portions of the firm's employees, requiring their buy-in and commitment for the completion of the integration activities and the realization of synergy benefits. The goal of integration is then the creation of a single entity with a shared strategy and with integrated standards, policies, processes, practices, technologies, and cultures that operate efficiently and remain seamless to customers.

The initial task at hand beyond the close is for the combined entity to transition to a single management team and a unified organization structure, to name all employees to their new jobs, and to familiarize everyone on the new HR policies and programs. Following the transition, a fast tempo of integration requires leadership to provide direction and overcome resistance, middle managers to implement the changes and communicate with their employees, and the integration manager to provide strong integration management. Integration teams will work with the line organization to carry out integration activities and realize the deal synergies.

Communications, which is a key enabler of integration, should be timely and clear. Employees need to be encouraged to get to know one another, and they need to know who to go to for problems and share knowledge to get their work done. The operating philosophy and operating practices of the combined entity needs unification for efficient management of the operations. The realization of the synergy benefits requires the allocation of sufficient resources to the task—design, implementation, training, tracking, and reporting. Senior leadership must both drive the synergy realization and question the underlying information being reported. Success beyond the close requires in this respect a sense of urgency for the effective management of integration programs, a steadfast leadership willing to dedicate their time, the active involvement of everyone by creating a common mindset about the integration logic, and a holistic appreciation of the business needs.

SUCCESS FACTOR #29

TRANSITION TO AN INTEGRATED MANAGEMENT TEAM QUICKLY

When the deal is announced, there are two separate entities with two management hierarchies operating side-by-side. Prior to the closing, key leaders are named to important leadership positions in order to start the transition to a unified management team. Success is in large part based on a well-planned and short transition to a single management hierarchy that will run the combined entity. In the interim, until all layers of the new management are identified and can assume their roles, the continuity of management for business decision making and direction setting is provided by transition teams. Interim transition teams consist of existing management and other respected leaders and implementers who assume day-to-day management responsibilities. Transition team members also provide input into the detailed design of the new organization. The interim transition governance is defined prior to close with clear lines of reporting, team roles and responsibilities, authority limitations, and other important information.

During the transition, the senior leadership's role is to provide direction as to the organizational structure and to clarify the lines of reporting and ensure a sense of urgency. The transition period may last a few weeks, at the end of which the two companies will be under one management hierarchy but still operating in a fragmented manner. The integration manager's role during transition is to support the transition teams, to understand their role, and to facilitate the detailed design of the organizational structure as well as the staff selection. After the transition phase is completed, some transition team members may move to line management roles in the new entity, and some may move to integration teams so that they can support the integration effort.

At this point, communication and orientation sessions that cover the new combined entity's common objectives, the organizational changes that are underway, the integration activities that will take place, the changes to human resource practices, and the new expectations of management for the integration phase and beyond become a very effective way to ease employee anxieties. An awareness of the business priorities and how best to contribute to the success of the company will encourage employees to participate in making the deal a success through their individual and team contributions. During the transition, teams of customer-oriented employees from both firms can maintain a continuity of focus on key customers and brands while the organization is busy with the M&A transition. A fast tempo for transition and integration will also help to diminish any customer disruptions.

Human resource (HR) systems, policies, guidelines, and procedures, which include incentive compensation and benefits packages at executive, management, and employee levels and the alignment of jobs, job titles, and pay grades based on job content have to be aligned and communicated. Support concerning human resource issues through the transition and integration phases here is critical for addressing employee concerns. Additional human resource activities during integration include:

- Consolidating HR organizations, systems, processes, and practices

- Managing employee redundancies, outplacements, relocations, and other moves

- Implementing a strategy for retaining valued employees

- Defining and delivering needed training, education, and development

- Tracking employee satisfaction and retention rates

Differences in HR programs may become contentious in M&A deals, considering the potential costs involved in moving to a unified system. The leadership should resolve these issues quickly and set common standards that can be adhered to.

To enable an efficient staffing of the new organization, a detailed organizational structure and reporting relationships must be defined as quickly as possible. The details of the organizational structure may include: the lateral separation of work units and their domains, the definition of shared services and the types of services provided, the number of layers of management, the desired staffing levels, and the roles and responsibilities for managers and supervisors. The organizational design overlays key business processes, provides functional capabilities to meet business and technological requirements, and allows for enough flexibility to meet customer needs. The approach to implementation taken by the new organizational model will lay out the standards, guidelines, and processes for staff selection, communications, and employee orientation.

RIGHT JOB TO THE RIGHT PERSON

Employees are generally concerned about the fairness in how individuals are matched to available jobs, and they may mistrust management's intentions by constantly scrutinizing the process for signs of favoritism. Employees often fear that the important jobs are going to people in the other company and that new layers of management are being added as a way to promote people from the "other side." The target employees are concerned that they will be perceived as less valuable by the acquiring management. Such perceptions must be confronted in order to avoid giving the impression of favoritism in the selection process and to prevent an adversarial environment from taking root. Management will want to get the new entity off to a good start, and so generally it will take pains to ensure that the new organization is staffed by the best individuals who are selected from a fair available pool of employees from both companies.

A fair process does not necessarily mean a process that is excessively time-consuming and bureaucratic. The selection process usually involves defining positions, interviews, and the layer-by-layer selection of people. Valuable high-performing employees from both organizations can be identified through background reviews and reference checks. There are two differing mindsets regarding the pace of the selection process. One school of thought believes that time taken at this stage to ensure the best organizational design and to select people is time well spent, considering the gravity of the matter at hand. The other school of thought says that it is more important to have an initial organizational structure in place with people named to positions in order to avoid losing valuable time agonizing over the best structure and the perfect selection process. This group believes that a long selection process takes up valuable time, adds to employee anxieties, and distracts the employees from working on key priorities. The early announcement of people's roles will put an end to the jockeying for positions, and it will focus employees on what is in the best interest of the company—the pursuit of a fast tempo integration and synergy realization. In either case, the organizational structure may need to undergo some modifications six months to a year after being devised so that it can incorporate lessons learned during the integration.

Integration activities start after the transition period is completed and may continue for months or even years until the two companies are consolidated and operate as a single entity. While the business continues to run and serve the customers, the task of integration is pursued in parallel.

SUCCESS FACTOR #30

MAINTAIN A FAST INTEGRATION TEMPO

The appropriate pace of integration is the subject of much debate, but many managers who have been through an M&A deal have said that they wish they had done more to accomplish the integration activities faster. In general, the faster the integration tempo, the more value is realized. The keys to accelerating the tempo of the M&A integration are a detailed planning prior to close, a strong integration program management after the close, a sufficient resource commitment, strong leadership, and quality decision making by leaders.

LEADERSHIP MUST LEAD

The M&A integration, and specifically the degree of change associated with it, presents the leadership with new and challenging opportunities. Senior leadership directions during the integration phase ensure that middle managers are not distracted from key business and integration priorities. The challenge here is that everyone is climbing the learning curve as it concerns integration activities and synergy realization simultaneously. Managers at all levels have to enter new and unfamiliar employees from the other organization into a dialogue in order to enable good decision-making and to get work done efficiently. The leadership's responsibility is to promote the benefits of the deal and to face up to the challenges presented by the deal through allocating sufficient personal time and attention to the integration activities and by following through on the integration and synergy realization plans to push them toward their completion.

It is the responsibility of the leadership to address line management concerns early, to get the managers on board, and to listen to their experiences and concerns. Informal leaders, people who are known and respected by the organization, play a critical role at this point in the integration, and they need to be kept informed and involved as their influence can convince others to contribute effectively as well. The leadership's needed skills during integration include early issue identification, issue resolution, effective problem solving, dealing with resistance and managing conflicts, and effective communication skills. Successful integration requires skilled resources from both organizations that can be applied to carrying out the integration activities. The role of the leadership is to tap talent from both entities in order to make integration a success.

The pace of the leadership decision-making then will naturally affect the tempo of the integration. Understanding decision criteria, clarifying the decision process, and making the decisions in a timely manner will all help to speed up the integration. In some cases, a consensus on a decision may need to be sacrificed in favor of forward momentum.

MIDDLE MANAGERS MUST IMPLEMENT

Two common lessons learned from managers at various levels of the organization who have been through an M&A deal are that they wish that they had implemented more sweeping changes and had undertaken integration activities at a faster rate. Most are in this respect surprised by how easily value can be destroyed during the integration. An executive going through a complex integration related, "Some mornings I wake up and wonder why am I doing this? Why am I putting myself through all this stress? Then I have to pull myself up by my bootstraps and remind myself of the importance of what we're doing." The employees, in a similar way, are faced with certain anxieties and stress. They too need to be given a reason to face their day and to work through the challenges that have been placed in their path.

Uncertainties about the future are a key concern for middle management. The lack of information and involvement prior to the close creates concerns about the M&A deal. Before closing, managers who are not part of the due diligence effort often feel as if they are in a holding pattern as they begin to worry about their own roles in the new organization. They fear that the new company is being formed and defined somewhere behind closed doors and that they will be faced with an outcome they may not like. Middle managers face additional organizational and personal challenges, some of which include:

- A lack of awareness about the differences between the two companies' policies, standards, procedures, and expectations

- Having to manage a major change effort

- An unfamiliarity with the details of integration plans

- A lack of commitment to the M&A deal from individuals at various levels of the organization

Concerned with their own careers, managers may get distracted and may not maintain employee communication; they may likewise neglect the behaviors and practices that have come to sustain the employees. Placed under stress, individual managers may resist changes in order to protect their own turf and positions, and thus inadvertently, they can add to the integration complexities. Their attention may shift from the realization of strategic goals to infighting over positions and portfolios. Because they receive limited information prior to close, managers may face pressing questions from employees about the deal that they are unable to answer adequately, and in this way, they may not know how to calm employees fears about the M&A outcomes.

Middle managers can inadvertently create more barriers to change by not providing the tools employees need and by making employees feel more insecure about the future through the airing of their own negative feelings, or by coming across as uncaring about employee fears. Management values often speak louder than words and will be carefully watched by the employees, who will draw their own conclusions about the overall culture of the combined entity based on what they observe in managerial actions. As management immerses itself in the daily challenges of integration, long-term plans and long standing work standards may get ignored; the organization may therefore get distracted, causing potential failures in safety performance, in meeting regulatory requirements, and in satisfying customer requirements. Frustrated with the slow pace of change, some managers may decide to steamroll changes through, which can erode employee trust and damaging morale. In the process, a single-minded focus on cost reduction can also create uneasiness and mistrust for people about the intentions of the acquirer.

Finally, some managers may be concerned that when they look ahead and see the daunting task of integrating two entities—of meshing two diverse cultures and realizing the promised synergies. They may have concerns about the loss of organizational knowledge and functional expertise by way of job losses, early retirements, and employee departures. Some may also worry about having enough competent staff during the integration process who can ensure that the business will continue to run well and will remain customer focused.

The fallout from mistakes made during integration then can have lasting impact on the organization as well as the employees affected by it. Senior leaders must deal with the root causes of organizational issues and effectively remove any barriers to change. Middle management's ability to focus on the business priorities and create opportunities for collaboration by building trust and promoting win-win situations will affect the overall willingness to embrace the future changes and take part in making the M&A deal successful. For middle managers to be successful during the integration phase, they need to focus on directing their employees toward carrying out their work and the integration tasks; they need to communicate with them in order to learn and apply the appropriate change management competencies.

DISCIPLINED PROGRAM MANAGEMENT

A quick implementation of integration plans requires strong program management, focus on integration activities, and a sense of urgency with clear roles and accountabilities for line managers and integration teams. The integration manager is responsible for setting up an effective integration organization that includes integration teams and the establishment of its governance structure. Integration team members, who are named after closing, are made up of high-performing employees from the various levels and functions of both entities. Integration teams aid the line management with integration and synergy realization activities, and they help to avoid the duplication of effort while allowing the line organization to focus on a day-to-day running of the business.

Integration teams are sponsored by senior management and are chartered with the implementation of the integration plans as they act as catalysts of change. Senior leadership and integration team members must act together as role models for the desired new behaviors and norms in the new entity, and they must be quite mindful of their role at all times. The teams need clear objectives, team charters, detailed calendar-driven integration work plans, clearly defined and well-understood roles and responsibilities, and tangible milestones for deliverables. The integration framework and plans help the team members to understand the approach and deliverables for the integration and assimilation activities. The business case likewise remains a tool for the integration teams to use in order to understand the goals of the expected synergy opportunities. Integration teams generally have the ability to expand on the integration plans with their own input and manage their own activities so that they can meet the integration timelines.

During integration, the role of the integration manager is clearly distinct from that of the line management. The integration manager is responsible for maintaining focus on the integration activities, while line management is responsible for business profitability and growth. The integration manager has no responsibilities for running the day-to-day business; yet during the integration period, the day-to-day work may include or may become affected by integration activities and the pursuit of synergy capture. This interdependent relationship creates the need for close cooperation between the line management and the integration manager.

Additional roles of the integration manager include:

- Identifying and resolving people issues.

- Sharing knowledge regarding opportunities and synergies with employees and other parts of the organization.

- Communicating the M&A vision and strategies effectively and helping employees understand their own role in the M&A success.

After the deal closes, and after the transition to the new organization is complete, line managers are often eager to get on with the task of running the business, of managing budgets and staffs, and of working with customers. The line manager's role in this respect is also to sponsor the integration activities in their related organizations; they are ultimately accountable for realizing the synergies and completing the integration activities under their domain as integration teams are their support. Once the majority of integration and synergy realization activities are underway or completed, integrations teams will disband while the line management assumes its responsibility for completing any remaining integration tasks. Line managers need to step back regularly and ask the following questions so that they can evaluate how the integration process is progressing:

- How well are the deal and integration requirements being communicated?

- Are timely decisions being made?

- Are integration and synergy realization roles and accountabilities clear?

Such observations can help line managers make early course corrections where necessary.

The individual and team rewards for the integration team are based on their contribution towards achieving results as they concern the organization's ability to realize its performance goals. Generally some teams may over-deliver, and some teams may under-deliver. Timely and public rewards and recognitions for those who are genuine contributors will enhance motivation, and relating success stories from the frontlines will reinforce the anticipation that the integration will be successful. Integration teams track the attainment of deal synergies and the integration progress on a regular basis by maintaining a scorecard, conducting periodic audits, and by reporting to senior leadership. They also provide feedback and coaching for the line organization while also mediating any conflicts.

The consolidation of the two entities entails aligning key operational and business functions. End-to-end business processes are mapped and aligned as the operations are integrated. Supply chain processes, customer-oriented processes, the research and development pipeline, scheduling and order processing remain some examples of this. Other key consolidation activities may include: combining head offices and other facilities; analyzing infrastructure and deciding what to keep, close, or divest; unifying financial accounting reporting and practices; rationalizing strategic relationships with vendors and distributors; aligning systems and technology platforms including their transition, migration, and convergence; aligning customer-oriented processes; and implementing common sales, marketing, pricing, and positioning strategies. There are numerous complex and emotional decisions tied to these consolidation issues. Management therefore must move beyond the emotional and political barriers in order to make the objective and hard decisions that will aid in the capture of the deal value.

In today's competitive environment, companies are 24/7 operations that cannot afford any discontinuity as they meet customer needs. Events that adversely impact customers should be dealt with expediently. The development of the capabilities and skills of the sales force and any other customer-related personnel to deal with customer issues throughout the transition and integration reduces the adverse impact on the customers. The acquirer should execute plans to ensure product and service continuity and to manage product and service changes. Customer satisfaction and retention should be monitored accordingly throughout the integration phase.

It is not unusual for a new entity to get inundated with numerous integration and change initiatives. Synergy realization, integration activities, meshing together systems and processes, training and developing employees, new cost reduction expectations, and revenue enhancement demands all can take away from precious management time. A common complaint during integration concerns the proliferation of meetings and how they can take too much time away from real work. Some initiatives may be ill-defined or difficult to show results for in this respect. These initiatives can sap resources needed for higher priority activities and synergy realization. Initiatives need clear objectives so that they can be related to an issue that is a priority for integration and synergy realization; they need to have clearly articulated benefits, measures of success, completion dates, milestones, and well-defined resources. Initiatives that do not meet these conditions are best put on hold or eliminated altogether so that the organization efforts can be better allocated to higher priority items.

Organization sharing and the development of lateral networks will also enhance the performance of the acquisition and the ability of the combined entity to create value. The objective of organization sharing is to increase employee commitment and employee understanding of the business objectives and its implementation plans. Sharing can take many forms, such as technology transfer, information sharing, knowledge sharing, experience sharing, relating lessons learned, identifying best practices, and developing communities of practice consisting of subject matter experts. Information sharing helps to fight rumors and mobilizes the employees around the integration objectives. Opportunities in this way can be created for open communications that will build trust through town hall meetings, small group meetings, making leaders visible and approachable, individual coaching, and performance feedback.

Integration teams must partner with the line organization to challenge the *status quo* mindset and overcome any lingering resistance to change. Through their interaction with the organization, integration teams will develop significant knowledge, experience, and insight about the two entities as they interact with people at all levels and at various sites. They must then transfer and share their knowledge, learning, and their implementation approaches with the organization and invite the participation of all employees. Integration teams need to put the new organization values regarding knowledge sharing and learning into visible practice to help set an example for the rest of the organization.

With the new management team in place, a strategic assessment of the potential opportunities and risks involved with the combined businesses can assist managers in understanding their new domains and the main sources of value creation in their new business. The objective of the assessment in this respect is to gain a broader picture of the strengths and opportunities associated with each line of businesses, to create a common strategy for overcoming threats and realizing value from the combination, and to help set consistent business priorities. The strategic assessment here focuses on an understanding of the offerings of the new entity, its business and operational plans, and its customer needs. Some key inquiries posed by the assessment include:

- What are the main sources of value creation for the business?

- What are the key markets that are being served and what opportunities do they offer?

- How does the new product and brand portfolio meet the customer needs?

- Who are our new competitors and what moves are they making as a result of the deal?

- What advantages does the M&A offer the firm in terms of the combined internal capabilities?

- What are the combined performance expectations for the entity over the next five years?

A discussion of the results of the business assessment will help in aligning the new management team's vision of the future and in creating commonly understood and integrated business objectives. It will also present valuable strategies for realizing value from the highest priority opportunities.

SIGNS OF TROUBLE DURING INTEGRATION

There are many barriers to maintaining a fast integration tempo. The organization faces several challenges during the integration phase that may monopolize management time and distract from moving at a rapid pace. Such challenges include interpersonal conflicts, cultural clashes, and dysfunctional financial, operational, and human resource processes. There can also be unforeseen problems with payables and receivables, and employee morale and productivity may sag under the stress of integration. Customer deliveries can also get affected, and synergy realization may begin to slip. Line management must therefore create a balance between an immediate focus on cost reduction and the resources needed for integration and preparing the foundations for growth. They must keep a strong focus on running the business and on customers without getting overly preoccupied with internal issues such as staffing and spending. If problems endure, suppliers will start to lose trust, and frustrated customers will defect, which will begin to destroy shareholder value.

During integration, some warning signs may be subtle in the early stages and easily overlooked. Over time, if left unchecked, these problems may become exacerbated and soon will be apparent to everyone. Based on past experience, the following is a list of signs to keep an eye on:

- Management takes weeks after the close to finalize organization design and staffing.

- The cultures of the two companies differ markedly and cultures clash.

- Differences in operating philosophies create new daily conflicts.

- Budgeting, accounting, and financial systems, practices, and reporting are not quickly and effectively consolidated.

- Financial data are deemed unreliable.

- The leadership team is deadlocked and dysfunctional.

- Leadership team members are frustrated.

- Individual leaders take sides with an us-versus-them approach.

- Key decisions are delayed or not made.

- A shortage of resources slows the integration progress.

- Business and financial results fall short of expectations.

- Businesses and operations run their own fiefdoms while management is distracted with integration issues.

- Hundreds of staff hours are poured into the development of common policies, standards, and procedures but still are not completed or

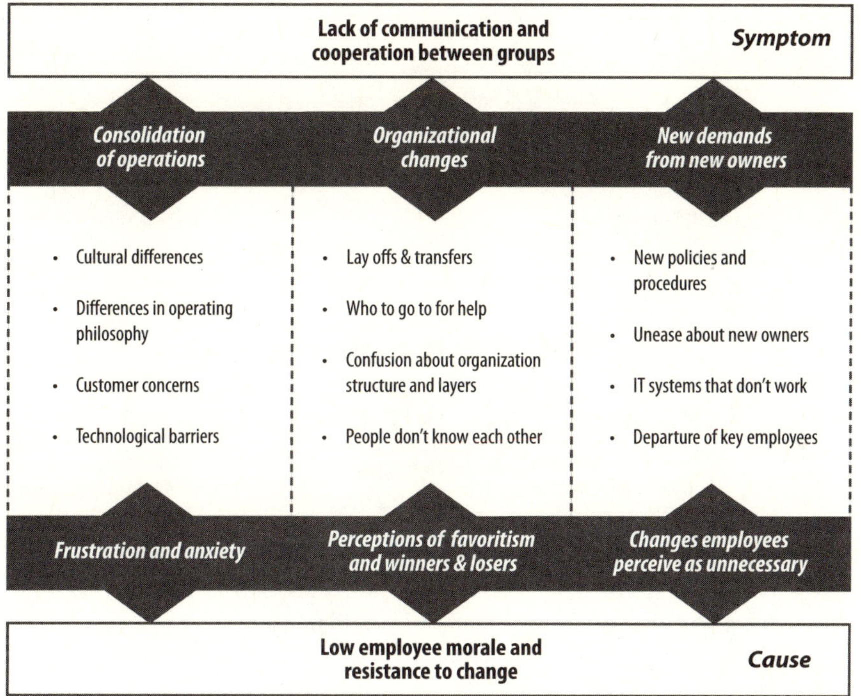

Figure 5. A Root Cause Diagram

implemented.

- Customers defect to competitors.

- Turnover at the executive and management levels reduces leadership continuity.

- The executive team initiates a major transformational effort to fix a broad array of urgent issues.

- The job of integrating the two businesses is still going on months after the close, with no end in sight.

- The business results continue to deteriorate, and targets are missed quarter after quarter.

- Leadership resorts to further cost reductions and job cuts in order to stop the bleeding.

- Newly acquired assets are divested to make-up for revenue shortfalls.

A quick identification of these issues and the resolution and removal of any implementation barriers by an involved leadership will then enhance the chances of integration success.

SUCCESS FACTOR #31

COMMUNICATE THE INTEGRATION PRIORITIES

Communication is one of the most important tools in M&A integration, yet differences in cultures and philosophies can inhibit effective communication. The complex integration of people and cultures requires a deliberate communication strategy, which can provide substantive information that is timely and relevant to stakeholders. Employees must be informed and involved, which may help them to overcome any anxieties and feelings of mistrust caused by the M&A deal. The M&A change is not some distant menace to the employees; it is personal. Stakeholders in an M&A deal include internal audiences at all levels of the organization and external groups, which include: customers, suppliers, vendors, shareholders, the investor community, regulators, and the public, each of which will require different but consistent information. Employees must see and hear from management directly in order to judge management's commitment and sincerity for themselves. Customers also require communication about the changes that will be relevant to them, including any temporary impact that might come about during the transition and integration period. Communication to vendors ensures that their level of service is maintained through the ensuing changes.

MAINTAIN REGULAR AND TIMELY COMMUNICATIONS

Information that is communicated must be timely in order to keep employees abreast of events, changes, and developments, and in order to help them stay informed about their role in making the deal a success. Communications must start early, as soon as the deal closes, and must be followed through on often. Management must provide sufficient lead-time when communicating activities and events to allow time for employees to react and adapt effectively and to demonstrate fairness in procedures. Any major surprises in this manner can create employee anxiety, erode trust, and increase resistance to change. Too much time between communications has a negative effect on an organization that is hungry for direction. Regular communications help people to cope with changes and encourage them to become part of the solution rather than part of the problem.

To be effective, communications have to be tailored to their audience. As for internal communications, its content must be sensitive to the histories and cultures of the two organizations that are coming together. One of the integration team's roles is in this regard to help the leadership set communication guidelines; they can use multiple vehicles for getting the leadership's message out to ensure that the communication reaches its broad and intended audience. The message needs some consistent repetition if it is to be heard completely, which will enhance a common understanding of the issues, the priorities, and the path forward. Individuals and groups at this point need to understand their accountabilities as well as the current status of integration.

It takes time for employees to comprehend what has occurred, where the organization wants to go, what is expected of them, and what they can do to contribute. The communication may include the M&A deal's goals, its future business direction, new business priorities, company financial performance objectives, integration strategies, and critical success factors for attaining the deal value. People in the combined entity need to learn how things work, who to go to for answers to problems, what resources are available to them, and what the expectations are for their roles. They need to learn what the acceptable new company behaviors are, the changes in the reward system, the opportunities for career advancement, and other key HR policies. The communications must also emphasize the need for change. It is important to recognize also that there should exist an appropriate degree of confidentiality so that employees can freely provide feedback and raise personal issue that will make the environment less threatening.

PRESERVE OPEN COMMUNICATIONS

The goal of communications is therefore to create a climate conducive to open dialogue and feedback about issues, expectations, results, behaviors, as well as any barriers to integration. Communications must be clear, open, to the point, and focused on the key messages. Communication that is primarily top-down serves only to relay information such as updating employees on events and activities. Encouraging employees to give their input and to express their own ideas through two-way communications will enhance understanding and trust. Two-way communications along with providing forums for open discussions between management and employees will develop trust and understanding while continuing to facilitate the integration process. During interactions with employees, leadership needs to solicit questions and be prepared to answer them openly and honestly and to follow up on any expressed concerns.

Communication venues may include large meetings where senior executives make presentations, but also should include other more open settings such as town-hall style meetings, small group luncheons, facility walk-arounds, one-on-one discussions, monthly e-mail updates, posters, fact sheets, and/or public announcements. Conducting management by maintaining personal contact with employees and keeping an open door policy will in the end build trust. Cross-functional and group meetings that occur regularly enhance sharing between functions and can help get everyone on board with the same message in an effective way.

Communications in this respect needs to be pushed downwards and should not stop at any level per se. Employees expect to hear about relevant issues and shortcomings because they are on the front lines so to speak. They are familiar with the issues as they have to deal with them everyday, and so they will want to know that management is aware of the challenges ahead and is prepared to deal with those challenges. They, for this reason, will want their concerns and questions answered. Managers may wish to avoid openness because they view it as airing "dirty laundry," but transparency in communication about any hardships and problems certainly can go a long way toward fostering employee loyalty and commitment. Management's role is ultimately to explain why it is important to undertake the challenges of integration, to explain the benefits associated with a successful integration, and to identify the difficulties and challenges faced by the organization because of integration effort.

The overstatement of facts and the exaggeration of promises will therefore destroy trust. Controversial issues must be discussed head-on, and rumors must be expediently addressed. During periods of major change, people are thirsty for information and are willing to accept any type of information no matter how credible. So it is in management's best interest to ensure that the information available is accurate, complete, and timely, and finally, that it is coming from them and not from some less reliable source.

ENCOURAGE NETWORKING

Employees need the opportunity to introduce themselves to other parts of the business and get to know their counterparts. Technology can be a barrier to this if systems are not compatible; for example, employees may not have effective access to even simple e-mail systems for periods of time. Overcoming such technical issues can take months. As a result, groups may end up operating independent of each other simply because they are unable to overcome the barriers to communication. Employees at different levels of the organization must be encouraged to communicate and network with one another so that they can share information and learning. Employees must be encouraged by management to work together and collaborate on common issues. The activities of teams working on different aspects of the integration program will require ongoing coordination, knowledge sharing, and collaboration.

If encouraged to network, employees will learn to work together and communicate together as they get to know one another. As trust builds, employees will work more with their counterparts, and there will be less need to go up the ladder for approval and authorization concerning collaboration and sharing. The business in this respect will begin to figure out how to work together and to resolve issues in a more organic fashion.

COMMUNICATE WITH GLOBAL STAKEHOLDERS

Executives leading global mergers need to be aware of the histories, cultures, language specifics, and political trends in the countries that they operate.[1] They must be aware of the unique issues that can impact the success of the merged companies, including the key investors in each country, the role of unions in the workplace, the extent and effect of regulations, and key global customers. The cultural complexity inherent in global deals means that a message which works in one setting may not work in another. Communication plans in a global deal need to be culturally appropriate, which will bring an added level of complexity to the planning process. Prior to the announcement of major global deals, the senior leadership may need to get in touch with influential national, regional, community, business, and labor union leaders, or any other stakeholders in their global locations. Significant media outlets and influential market analysts in international equity markets may have to be contacted and kept informed as well. Even seemingly trivial issues such as time zone differences for major announcements need to be considered.

SUCCESS FACTOR #32

DEFINE A COMMON OPERATING PHILOSOPHY AND CONSISTENT PRACTICES

A newly merged business is a combination of two sets of company-wide policies, standards, guidelines, processes, and procedures as well as numerous local business and operating practices. Without a common operating philosophy, the organization will have a segmented approach, and as a result, it will be reactive to external changes. The combined entity assumes new business and financial risks and will approach the new customers and other stakeholders with differing experiences and mindsets. The members of the two businesses are typically unfamiliar with each other's *modus operandi*, and so they will approach issues and decisions based on their previous experiences and mindsets. The previous parents may have adopted differing approaches to areas of business that provide competitive advantage, such as in customer service, risk management, safety, environmental performance, regulatory compliance, engineering design, product or service quality, cost management, and the application of technology. Defining a common operating philosophy in this respect will help guide consistent decision-making and will have a lasting impact on the effective allocation of resources and on the implementation of the combined entity's strategy.

The operating philosophy sets broad guidelines and policies for managing the company's operations in alignment with the firm's business strategy, its customer needs, and regulatory requirements. It creates a common mental model of understanding concerning the fundamental business drivers that will, in turn, drive the allocation of resources. The operating philosophy affects how work is managed, how decisions are made, the degree of centralization, risk exposure, the standardization of policies and guidelines, and the formation of company-wide procedures and practices.

Often organizations underestimate the importance of developing a standard operating philosophy and consistent policies for key business practices. Executives will often overlook this issue because they may see it as a mere meddling in details; however, without attention to standardization, the two companies will be operating from different understandings of future trends, assumptions about the business drivers, and expectations about how to succeed in the future. The development of a common operating philosophy requires the involvement and sponsorship of the leadership team, which articulates and validates the business priorities and the key business drivers.

A successful model for defining a shared operating philosophy and common operating practices involves a two-stage effort. In the first stage, the executive team articulates a common set of overriding philosophies that set the direction around key facets of the business. Executive retreats are very useful means to conduct focused sessions that can contribute to this. The outcome of this effort is communicated to the organization at large, and it builds the foundation for a common operating philosophy. This effort generally creates a sense of relief and unity in the organization, and for this reason, it can overcome significant cultural hurdles.

The second stage of the effort is a series of work sessions involving middle managers and technical subject matter experts. The goal of the sessions is to recommend consistent operating practices that are to be implemented across the company by prioritizing among various business imperatives in order to satisfy customer and regulatory requirements. These sessions are intensive and will require good planning and strong facilitation if one is to ensure that the discussions are focused on key operating issues. Once these priorities are established, the operating units can implement the consistent practices. Some policies and guidelines may be new or modified, and so implementation may entail additional costs. Ultimately, the line managers own the implementation of the new policies and practices.

SUCCESS FACTOR #33

REALIZE M&A DEAL BENEFITS TANGIBLY AND IN A TIMELY MANNER

Every deal has its own synergy justification based on the strategic fit between the two entities. A top priority of the integration phase is realizing synergies that will benefit the firm's bottom-line results. Synergy realization requires a strong, uncompromising leadership that is willing to stretch its goals and enforce collaboration across workgroups and functions. Line managers own the realization of synergies in their respective organizations.

Appropriate levels of resources are needed for synergy realization after the close. The integration phase is a period in the life of an organization at which more people in the short term will pay off for the long term. By maintaining adequate staffing levels, integration teams can undertake many of the integration activities and support synergy realization. Synergy realization is in this way contingent on the development of detailed plans, clear accountabilities for realization at the line management level, and prioritization in the way of realizable value and ease of implementation. For each synergy opportunity, the expenditure and capital requirements as well as the associated timelines for completion must be defined. A synergy tracking scorecard that is simple, easily set up, and well-understood can be implemented to allow workgroups to track their own progress and provide regular executive updates. The impact of synergies on the bottom line should be clear and should be measured with a consistent methodology. Leadership must communicate and encourage the achievement of synergies and monitor the progress in a timely manner; it must understand the gaps and implement course corrections.

M&A deals involve the integration of technologies, systems, and processes. The deal can cause the termination of existing alliances, partnerships, and outsourcing contracts if they no longer make good business sense for the new combined entity. For example, IT outsourcing contracts of either company may no longer make sense if both companies move to a common IT platform. Care must be taken, though, when terminating existing contracts. Ending contracts prematurely can cost the firm large penalty payments, and, if handled poorly, it could negatively affect relationship with partners as well as the firm's reputation for future partnerships.

BARRIERS TO REALIZING DEAL SYNERGIES

There are barriers to synergy realization that are prevalent beyond the close. Such barriers may be caused by individual behaviors, or they may result from organizational impediments. In either case, they require strong leadership if they are to be overcome.

In order for synergies to be realized, integration must successfully take place; and when integration does not take place as planned, the chances of realizing synergies are lowered. Integration issues therefore can delay a firm's ability to move forward with its business objectives and concentrate on growth opportunities.

Keep in mind also that there may be overly optimistic and bloated expectations for synergy opportunities. At times, synergies may be poorly defined when based upon one's best guesses, interview questions, or on group discussions. For this reason, they may lack adequate credibility because they were insufficiently analyzed and inadequately scrutinized. The organization, in turn, may not respect the credibility of those individuals who conducted the synergy analysis. Another concern is that expected synergies that might appear to make sense on paper may not materialize in actuality, for example: expected synergies may take a longer time to be realized, the magnitude of the results may be below expectations, the initial capital and expenditures outlays may be greater than expected, or the duration of recurring benefits may be shorter than expected (they may also taper off due to stronger than expected competitive reactions). Due to these various complications, then, the actions required to realize the synergies may not be well understood; thus, apathy may settle in and result in a lack of cooperation on synergy realization.

Another problem is that line managers may not be properly brought onboard, and so they may be handed the list of synergies without a sufficient explanation of their underlying rationale. Managers who lack this in-depth understanding may not feel committed either to implementing the synergies or to reporting on them on a regular basis. Without adequate communication, employees may be unaware of the existence of the synergies and what they can do to help realize them. They may even fail to realize that they are accountable for the delivery of synergy benefits. A real difficulty persists, then, in that regular synergy reporting could be delayed because the workgroups may not either be taking the task seriously enough, or they may not fully understand the underlying drivers and the calculation methodologies. At times, the only person knowledgeable about the synergies is the financial manager, who has no final accountability to realizing them.

Synergy tracking, which may demonstrate that synergies are being realized or even exceeded could increase accountability, but business results still may be lagging and so might fail to reflect the impact of the synergies. The reason here may be that what is being reported might not be completely reliable, or that the synergies being realized do not have the expected impact on bottom line results. The integration teams and line management, who have to deliver the commitments and whose compensation may be on the line, may deliver numbers that will not truly impact the bottom line. On the other hand, a workgroup that too easily and quickly surpasses their synergy targets may become a sign that either their targets were not challenging enough: reported results in this respect may be overly optimistic or the benefits could have been double counted. Taking account of such potential problems, experience shows that synergy realization requires a healthy dose of skepticism.

Synergy realization, though, beyond skepticism also requires some degree of sharing as well as an overcoming of self-interest. Organizational boundaries, lines of reporting, and differing strategic priorities may impede the realization of network synergies.[2] Impediments to organizational sharing also include differing policies, practices, specifications, and requirements for meeting customer needs. Differing operating philosophies, approaches to risk, leadership styles, and rewards all can become major barriers to healthy collaboration that will inhibit sharing. Geographic separation may also affect the level of sharing in operations, as it may tend to reinforce cultural differences and raise new barriers to collaboration.

The benefits of network synergies should both outweigh the costs and the time consumption associated with aligning work groups and creating consistency. Changes necessary for the promotion of sharing may also reduce the flexibility and the customer focus of some work groups, but they may nevertheless create value. It is valuable as well to keep in mind that network synergies may not accrue consistently for all of the work groups, and that while some may have to incur costs, they may not receive a proportionate level of benefits, thus reducing their willingness to sacrifice for the greater whole. Conflicts also arise over who owns the synergy benefits and who is accountable for realizing them and for incurring the costs. These types of issues often come about when a number of business lines share the same facility. Synergies therefore require an agreed-upon formula for their accrual, and the tracking and reporting systems should, in turn, reflect the agreement. For all of these above reasons, business units may tend to resist the collaboration necessary for the realization of synergies; thus any sharing will require solid leadership and enforcement.

Managers may pay lip service to synergy realization without expending the proper effort to implement it as they often resist any changes required for synergy realization due to a fear of a loss of influence or prestige when their domain is affected. Senior managers, for this reason, may not push the issue of synergy realization so that they can avoid affecting personal relationships with their direct reports. Alternately, an over-zealous pursuit of easy cost reductions through laying off staff may result in a lack of requisite experience and resources necessary for working toward realizing the synergies. Management, in this respect, may fall prey to taking a short-term view and overemphasizing immediate synergies instead of looking for opportunities that would provide for long-term advantages. The role of the line management, then, is to understand these barriers and work on removing them, while dealing with any underlying issues that might prevent synergy realization and actively pursuing new and innovative means for identifying additional synergies.

SUCCESS FACTOR #34

TIE EMPLOYEE INCENTIVES TO SYNERGY REALIZATION AND TO THE FULFILLMENT OF INTEGRATION REQUIREMENTS

Rewards play an important role in the integration of the new entity. A good design and implementation of incentive programs that are closely tied to accelerated integration and synergy realization will aid in supporting management's objectives. Rewards in this way can affect a number of organizational aspects:

- The achievement of results.

- The promotion of team work, collaboration, and individual contributions.

- The enhancement of the retention of valued employees.

- The facilitation of cultural integration by aligning goals with rewards.

- The reinforcement of desired values and behaviors.

- The enhancement of a focus on the realization of synergies and the acceleration of their attainment.

Managers need to be rewarded for their successes in the integration effort as well as for the realization of synergies and the achievement of business performance. Moving to a rewards system that emphasizes the achievement of results and that has a larger portion of its total employee remuneration placed in incentive-based compensation, which remains tied to M&A and business results, will promote the deal success. Given sufficient time, the reward system can help to change organizational behaviors and facilitate integration.

A balance of leading and lagging indicators needs to be assembled so that the performance of the organization can be monitored and effective action can be encouraged. Lagging indicators following an M&A deal include financial indicators such as synergy realization goals, business results, and other such indicators as meeting quality goals, regulatory requirements, and customer satisfaction. Some leading measures of M&A success in this regard may include customer retention, customer issue resolution, valued employee retention, human resource strategy implementation, and the completion of integration activities.

Indicators used for the rewards system are weighted in terms of how they align with the business strategy. Giving too much weight to any single indicator, such as financial indicator, can skew the results towards that indicator and can make other indicators seem less important. The introduction of a new rewards system with new weighted indicators will change the rules of the game for the players. This change, though, can cause anxieties and fears, and therefore there may be cause for initial resistance by those being affected. Management at such a time will need to communicate the drivers of change and the impact of the new indicators on employees in order to ensure that the transition to the new model follows a fair process.

It will take time for groups and individuals to understand and trust a new rewards system. The indicators and their relative weight need to be selected carefully in order to ensure that they are controllable by the groups being measured and that they will promote business and integration priorities. The rewards system must be objective as more subjective systems give the impression of favoritism and can be rather counterproductive. The reward system must promote trust and ownership; it must follow a methodology for auditing the results that are being reported to make certain that the results are real and have a direct impact on the bottom line. To this end, the rules pertaining to the rewards system need to be published and communicated as soon as possible.

Results attained for each indicator must be reviewed and communicated regularly to the work groups. An objective observer must monitor and report on progress made towards the desired goals on a monthly or quarterly basis. One must be aware that external factors such as commodity prices and currency fluctuations can end up masking the impact of synergies on the bottom line and can make their financial impact difficult to measure. Management may not be comfortable with an objective system that would take away their influence in distributing rewards. It is not unusual for groups to try to negotiate their results with management when they perceive that their rewards will be affected by adverse events, thus testing the true objectivity of the rewards system.

Employees, in any rewards or remunerative system, should be compensated according to the value that they bring to the organization. Competencies are attributes of people and not of positions, and not all employees deliver the same value to the firm. Talented employees and managers are in high demand, and there is always strong competition to attract and retain the best people in the marketplace. Even though compensation may not be the key motivator for many employees, if people feel that they are being under-compensated, they will likely feel under-appreciated and so may leave for another job. Market surveys in this respect will help management to ensure that they are providing total compensation packages that are on par with their competitors.

M&A Success From Employees' Perspective

The following is a description of a successful deal based on the comments of fifty employees in different industries who participated in various mergers. It is a list of criteria that employees responding to the questionnaire attributed to a successful combined entity:

- Financial prosperity

- The creation of new jobs

- Beating the competitors

- Satisfied people working together with a high morale who feel good about coming to work

- Employees who exhibit pride in the company

- A work environment that is not dominated by conflict

- People knowing where to go in order to get their problems solved

- The elimination of waste as well as the duplication of effort

- Meeting the needs of the customer with fewer customer issues

- Satisfied customers who see the combined firm as one company

- Proactive and open communication within the organization that appears seamless to the customer

- The alignment of objectives and working together versus working in competition

- The alignment between management and staff

- Better communication of management expectations

- A common communication protocol

Employees, in general, finally just want to do their jobs well and want to contribute to a smoothly run company where everyone is giving their 100% effort and being held accountable for both successes and failures.

SUCCESS FACTOR #35

DEVELOP IN-HOUSE M&A SKILLS

Few companies can constantly generate all the resources, innovations, and skills that they require to achieve organic growth. As discussed in detail in this book, M&A deals are a viable option for companies to consider as they look to the future to implement their vision and strategy. Thus, at some point, a firm seeking growth will need to undertake a merger or an acquisition and will need the skills necessary to make the deal successful. Companies that develop their own in-house capabilities to review industry and business trends, to track and identify potential targets, to identify deal synergies, to conduct due diligence activities, to negotiate and close deals, and to integrate their own acquisitions will have an advantage over those firms who do not develop and possess these skills.

The reason for this advantage is that the in-house M&A teams better understand their own firms and its vision and strategy; therefore they can make better and more relevant comparable assessments of other firms in the industry—especially when the target is private and public information about the firm is limited. In-house teams can be looking for acquisition opportunities on an ongoing basis using competitor intelligence gathering to develop and review lists of potential candidates, and thus have a better chance of identifying attractive opportunities and make more focused acquisitions. They would have a more long term view for investments and a more in-depth understanding of the firm's objectives, its assets, and its portfolio of products. In-house teams can also be more efficient in information gathering within the firm, whereas outside advisers have to take up executive time with their queries.

The in-house M&A team may be small and specialize on M&A knowledge, and it may draw from business units and other functions for needed expertise at various stages of the deal life cycle. The team requires skills such as the M&A process, M&A decision making, competitive intelligence gathering, business and financial analysis; it can draw from the organization for specific knowledge of operations, customers, and markets. Outside bankers and advisers can bring opportunities and a broader perspective both inside and outside the industry based on their broad contacts. Outside experts also bring value through their skills with financing deals, legal advice, and other needed specialized skills.

Internal teams are not protected from becoming either overly cautious or overly focused on deal making and potentially falling prey to the pressures of group think. When the CEO is determined to make a deal, he or she may not be willing to listen to contrary advice. Senior management interested in gaining the needed in-house skills should fund it and dedicate top quality people to work on the effort. The M&A team will need seasoned and experienced individuals who would be trusted by the senior leadership and who can have direct contact with the senior leadership and engage in dialogue and discussions with them.

NOTES

[1] See in references Youssef M. Ibrahim regarding communications in Daimler-Chrysler merger deal.

[2] See writings of Ansoff and Porter for an in-depth discussion of network synergies.

Epilogue: Looking Toward the Future of M&As

The issues discussed in this book extend beyond its pages and will extend beyond our current climate. It is important in this area, as in most fields, that we keep an eye on what might be coming around the bend so that we can be best prepared to meet those challenges and changes with a thoughtful and complete approach. If we look toward the future, in a decade from now when the year 2015 arrives, we can probably predict with a high degree of certainty that the pages of the Wall Street Journal and other major business journals will contain numerous stories about mergers and acquisitions. Whether M&A deals will be front page news or whether the deals will be as sensational as those we saw taking place in the nineties, is unknowable, but, it is safe to say that irrespective of what the prevailing economic conditions might be, mergers and acquisitions will continue to take place at the rate of hundreds or even thousands of deals per year. Each industry will have its own drivers for deal making, and it is difficult today to predict what those specific industry drivers will be—or even what new industries might emerge by then. However, it is fair to predict that some of the current trends that we are witnessing will continue on into the future and even accelerate their current pace. Globalization, in this respect, will likely continue to be a major force shaping M&A deals, as growing countries such as China and India continue to develop and Japan and Europe progress in their economic evolution. Through all of this, various opportunities for growth and global challenges will present themselves to business leaders who need to be ready to adapt to changing climates. Thus, companies will find themselves seeking M&A deals across national boundaries in order to respond effectively to global competitive threats or to take advantage of new sources of growth and profitability. Trends toward deregulation that

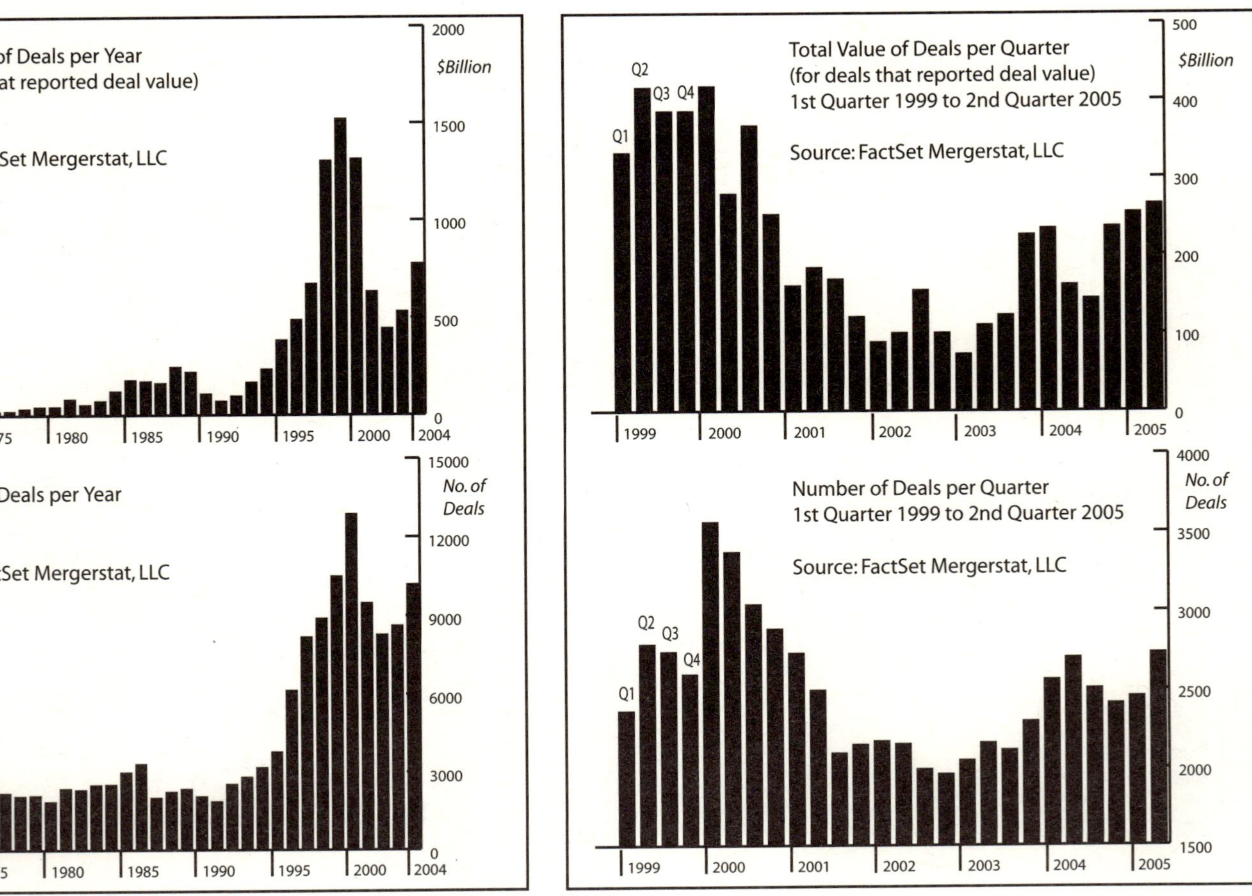

Figure 6. Historical View of M&A Activity

we have seen will also likely continue—in the process changing industry landscapes both in the U.S. and in other parts of the world. Companies will continue to evolve, transform, grow, or decline as new technologies emerge, which surely will continue to happen, and as industries move through the stages of their life cycle. Mergers and acquisitions will therefore be a continued option for providing quick access to needed resources, and companies will continue to vie for market share, new products, and new markets. New information technology will make access to data easier and easier, and there will be certain pressures to respond to these issues in such a way as to retain a competitive edge. In short, projecting trends into the future will almost guarantee that M&A activity will remain a major player in the national and global game.

Some things, though, should remain rather constant and predictable despite some uncertainties about what we will meet in future business markets, and this book therefore equips one with a dependable framework with which to meet future M&A trends and issues. The price and premium of a deal will still have to be justified based on the firm's ability to create new value for the shareholders, and firms will still be in need of the skills listed here in order to implement the deal requirements and to realize the promised value. We can even see evidence of this continued M&A activity by looking backward as well, and what follows is a brief historical context that might clue us in about where things are coming from and going toward. The figures show the number of M&A deals from 1968 to the end of 2004 and the total reported value of the deals over the same period of time.

Although the rate of M&A activity has varied over time, it is interesting to note that the total number of deals has rarely dropped below a couple of thousand per year. Over the decades, the drivers of M&A deals too have varied. In the fifties and sixties, mergers and acquisitions were driven by the formation of conglomerates and the business philosophy of diversification. This trend was later reversed, and companies divested themselves of unrelated businesses and focused on their core capabilities through horizontal deals. In the seventies and eighties, companies shifted their outlook and philosophy towards creating greater shareholder value. This philosophy was driven partly in response to corporate raiders who conducted leveraged buy-outs in order to take advantage of untapped value. The deal decade of nineties, experienced huge horizontal mergers made possible by overvalued equities and a robust economy. Deals in this respect were conducted in search of size and economies of scale in response to global competition, deregulation, and industry consolidation. In the new millennium, firms are faced with new uncertainties, yet the pace of M&A deals is increasing as firms continue to merge and acquire in search of growth and strategic fit at home and abroad. This is not likely to change any time soon, and so it is now more than ever that the business leader, the manager, and the student of business all need to prepare themselves to face what will very likely be a part of their professional futures.

Many of the rules of success that have been outlined in this book, are in this same way likely to continue to apply in the next decade and beyond, providing readers with a way into thinking carefully about M&A issues. Savvy deal makers, if they are to be successful, will continue to follow a disciplined focus on fundamentals in their deal making so that they can realize value for the firm's owners and shareholders. Such value and such business values spoken of here will continue to help drive growth and progress, and any of us in and around the business world who are interested in pursuing these things would do well to pause and consider thoughtfully the role that M&As have played and will continue to play in this changing and progressing world.

REFERENCES AND FURTHER READING

A

Aamodt, Michael J. and Raynes, Bobbie L. 2001. *Human Relations in Business: Developing Interpersonal and Leadership Skills.* Belmont: Wadsworth.

Aaker, David A. 1995. *Developing Business Strategies.* New York: John Wiley & Sons, Inc.

Abrams, Jay B. *How To Value Your Business And Increase Its Potential.* New York: McGraw-Hill, 2005.

Ackerman, L.S. 1982. "An In-depth Look at Managing Complex Change." *Organizational Dynamics.* 11 (1): 46-66.

Adams, Bruce. 2004. "Cultural Issues Determine Mergers' Success." *Hotel and Motel Management.* 219 (Aug): 4-6.

Adler, Herbert S. 1984. "Planning for a Successful Acquisition." *Corporate Accounting.* 2 (Fall): 42.

Allen, J. Genaldi. 2002. "Fraud in Foreign Operations." *The Internal Auditor.* 59 (Aug): 61-65.

Anders, George. 1992. *Merchants of Debt: KKR and the Mortgaging of American Business.* New York: Basic Books.

Andrews, Edmund L. and Bradsher, Keith. 2000. This 1998 Model is Looking More Like a Lemon." *New York Times.* (Nov 26): 3.1.

Andriessen, Daniel. 2004. *Making Sense Of Intellectual Capital: Designing A Method For The Valuation Of Intangibles.* Burlington: Elsevier Butterworth-Heinemann.

Ansoff, H. Igor. 1965. *Corporate Strategy.* New York: McGraw-Hill.

Anslinger, Patricia L. and Copeland, Thomas E. 1996. "Growth Through Acquisitions: A Fresh Look." *Harvard Business Review* (January-February): 55.

Argote, Linda. 1999. *Organizational Learning: Creating, Retaining and Transferring Knowledge.* Boston: Kluwer Academic Publishers.

Arminas, David. 2002. "Bringing It All Back Home" *Supply Management* (Sep 19): 16.

Arndt, Michael. 2002. "3M: A Lab For Growth?; CEO Jim Mcnerney--The First Outsider Boss--Is Overhauling A Company Long Known For Innovation." *Business Week.* (January): 50.

Arnold, Jon. 2003. "Just Like A Kid In A Candy Store Six Months After Swallowing Pwc Consulting, IBM Is Showing Few Signs Of Indigestion. For Bob Vallee, Leader Of The Energy Practice In The Firm's Business Consulting Services Group, Working For IBM Is Like Being A Kid In A Candy Store." *Platt's Energy Business & Technology.* 15 (Mar): 42.

Arredondo, Lani. 2000. *Communicating Effectively.* New York: McGraw-Hill.

Arthur, Diane. 2001. *The Employee Recruitment And Retention Handbook.* New York: AMACOM.

Ashkenas, Ronald N.; DeMonaco, Lawrence J.; Francis, Suzanne C. 1998. "Making the

Deal Real: How GE Capital Integrates Acquisitions." *Harvard Business Review.* (Jan/Feb): 165-78.

Atkinson, Gerald. 1990. *Negotiate the Best Deal: Techniques That Really Work.* Cambridge: Director Books.

Avery, Susan. 2003. "Rockwell Collins Takes Off." *Purchasing.* 132 (Feb 20): 25-28.

B

Bahree, Bhushan. 1999. "Oil Mergers Often Don't Live Up to the Hype: Most Deals Fail to Achieve Sought-After Benefits Amid Low Crude Prices." *Wall Street Journal.* (Jul 23): A10.

Bahree, Bhushan and Barrionuevo, Alexei. 2000. "Shell Oil Discusses Buying Texaco From Big Refining, Marketing Ventures." *Wall Street Journal.* (Dec 19): A.2.

Bailey, Kimball. 2001. "Taking a Byte Out of M&A Failure." *CMA Management.* (May): 16-19.

Bailey, Mark W. 1995. "New-Age Challenges to Acquirers in High Technology." Mergers and Acquisitions. 29 (Mar/Apr): 30.

Baker, George P. and Smith, George David. 1998. *The New Financial Capitalists: Kohlberg Kravis Roberts and the Creation of Corporate Value.* Cambridge: Cambridge University Press.

Baker, Jonathan B. 1999. "Econometric analysis in FTC v. Staples." *Journal of Public Policy & Marketing.* 18 (Spring): 11.

Baker, Wayne E. 1994. *Networking Smart: How to Build Relationships for Personal and Organizational Success.* New York: McGraw-Hill Inc.

Baldock, Robert. 1999. *Destination Z: The History of the Future.* Chichester: John Wiley &Sons.

Ball, Deborah. 2000. "Pair of Italian Banks Tantalize the Matchmakers." *Wall Street Journal.* (Jun 16): A.12.

Ball, Jeffrey. 1999. "Your Career Matters: DaimlerChrysler's Transfer Woes — Workers Resist Moves Abroad — And Here." *Wall Street Journal.* (Aug 24): B.1.

Ball, Jeffrey and Miller, Scott. 2000.. "DaimlerChrysler's Wrong Turns --- Merged Auto Giant Is Less Than Sum of Its Parts; Missteps in U.S. Market." *Wall Street Journal.* (Jul 26): A.18.

Ball, Jeffrey and Miller, Scott. 2000.. "New Chief of Chrysler Unit Begins Job With Pink Slips for Three Top Executives." *Wall Street Journal.* (Nov 21): A.3.

Ball, Jeffrey and Miller, Scott. 2000.. "The Pressure On Daimler Ratchets Up --- It Hires J.P. Morgan to Aid in Suit, Braces For S&P Downgrade." *Wall Street Journal.* (Dec 4): A.19.

Balto, David. 2002. "Uncle Sam Is Calling." *Electronic Engineering Times.* (Apr 22): 33.

Bamford, James and Ernst, David. 2002. "Managing an Alliance Portfolio" *The McKinsey Quarterly* (3): 28.

Band, William. 1991. *Creating Value for Customers: Designing and Implementing a Total Corporate Strategy.* New York: John Wiley & Sons.

Bangsberg, P.T. 1998. "Success Of Mergers, Acquisitions Relies On Considering Employees And Culture." *Journal of Commerce.* (Nov 12): 2.A.

Bantz, Charles R. 1993. *Understanding Organizations: Interpreting Organizational Communication Cultures.* Columbia: University of South Carolina Press.

Barker, Robert. 2002. "No Suckers, Those Smuckers:The Jam-And-Jelly King Has New Products--And a Savvy Deal On Buying Jif and Crisco From P&G. It Could All

Add Up To Long-Term Value For Investors." *Business Week.* (Mar 4): 112.

Barrionuevo, Alexei. 1999. "Equilon, Shifting Its Focus, Is Selling Two Refineries for Atleast $600 Million" *Wall Street Journal.* (Jun 7): C18.

Barrionuevo, Alexei. 2000. "Texaco, Phillips and Unocal Post Surging Profits." *Wall Street Journal.* (Jul 28): A.8.

Barrionuevo, Alexei. 2001. "Texaco Talks on Unwinding Shell Ventures Stall." *Wall Street Journal.* (Jun 18): A.4.

Barron, Kelly. 2001. "Holding the Bag." *Forbes.* (Jul 23): 90.

Bazerman, Max H. and Neale, Margaret A. 1992. *Negotiating Rationally.* New York: The Free Press.

Beach, Lee R. 1997. *The Psychology of Decision Making: People in Organizations.* Thousand Oaks: Sage Publications.

Beaumont, Perry H. 2004. *Financial Engineering Principles : A Unified Theory For Financial Product Analysis And Valuation.* Hoboken: John Wiley.

Beck, R. 1987. "Vision, Values, and Strategies: Changing Attitudes and Culture." *Academy of Management Executive.* 1 (1): 33.

Becker, Brian E.; Huselid, Mark A.; Ulrich, Dave. 2001. *The HR Scorecard: Linking People, Strategy, and Performance.* Boston: Harvard Business School Press.

Bekier, Matthias M. and Shelton, Michael J. 2002. "Keeping Your Sales Force After The Merger." *The McKinsey Quarterly.* (4): 106.

BenDaniel, David J. and Rosenbloom, Arthur H.1998. *International M&A, Joint Ventures, and Beyond.* New York: John Wiley & Sons.

Bennett, Robert H., III; Fadil, Paul A.; Greenwood, Robin T. 1994. "Cultural Alignment In Response To Strategic Organizational Change: New Considerations For A Change Framework." *Journal of Managerial Issues,* . 6 (12-22): 474.

Benning, Greg. 2003. "The Usual Suspects Plague the Middle Market." *Mergers and Acquisitions Journal* 38 (Aug): 10.

Bennis, Warren G. 1989. *On Becoming a Leader.* Reading: Addison-Wesley.

Berman, Dennis K. and Young, Shawn. 2001. "Bells Make a High-Speed Retreat From Broadband --- After Billion-Dollar Build-Up, Expansion Plans Are Put Off." *Wall Street Journal.* (Oct 29): B.1.

Binaco, Anthony. 2001. "Exxon Unleashed: How the World's Most Powerful Corporation Plans to Dominate the New Age of Oil Exploration." Business Week. (Apr 9): 58.

Blair, Margaret M., Ed. 1993. *The Deal Decade : What Takeovers And Leveraged Buyouts Mean For Corporate Governance.* Washington, D.C.: Brookings Institution.

Blair, Margaret M. and Uppal, Girish. 1993. *The Deal Decade Handbook.* Washington, D.C.: Brookings Institution.

Bloxham, Eleanor. 2003. *Economic Value Management: Applications and Techniques.* New York: John Wiley & Sons.

Boast, Molly S. 2001. Acting Director, Bureau of Competition, Federal Trade Commission Before the American Bar Association Antitrust Section; Spring Meeting at Washington, D.C. March 29, 2001.

Bolman, Lee G. and Deal, Terrence E. 1991. *Reframing Organizations: Artistry, Choice, and Leadership.* New York: Jossey-Bass Publishers.

Boudette, Neal E. 2003. "Road Less Traveled --- Peugeot's Formula for Success: Steering Clear of Megamergers; Undistracted by Big Alliances, Car Maker Becomes One of World's Most Profitable; The Big Three's Wrong Turn." *Wall Street Journal.*

(Aug 4): A.1.

Bourgeois, L., and D. Brodwin. 1984. "Strategy Implementation: Five Approaches to an Elusive Phenomenon." *Strategic Management Journal.* 5 (Jul-Sep): 241-264.

Bouwen, Jan E. and Overlaet, Bert. 2001. "Managing Continuity in a Period of Takeover. The Local Management Dealing With the Experience of Being a Target." *Journal of Management Inquiry.* 10 (March): 27-38.

Bowe, Christopher. 1999. "Local Banks Proliferate Despite Wave of Mergers" *Wall Street Journal.* (Sep 1): C.1.

Boyacigiller, Nakiye Avdan; Goodman, Richard Allan; Phillips, Margaret E. Ed. 2003. *Crossing Cultures: Insights from Master Teachers.* New York: Rouledge.

Bradley, M.; Desai, A.; and Kim, E.H. 1988. "Synergistic Gains From Corporate Acquisitions And Their Division Between The Stockholders Of Target And Acquiring Firms." *Journal of Financial Economics.* 21 (May): 3-41.

Bradsher, Keith. 2001. "Daimler Rebuffs Kerkorian's Suit in Chrysler Deal." *New York Times.* (May 10): C.5.

Branham, Leigh. 2001. *Keeping The People Who Keep You In Business: 24 Ways To Hang On To Your Most Valuable Talent.* New York: AMACOM.

Brantley, Mary Ellen and Coleman, Chris. 2001. *Winning The Technology Talent War: A Manager's Guide To Recruiting And Retaining Tech Workers In A Dot-Com World.* New York : McGraw-Hill.

Brealy, Richard A. and Myers, Stewart C. 1991. *Principles of Corporate Finance.* 4th Ed. New York: McGraw Hill Inc.

Brimson, James A. 1986. "How Advanced Manufacturing Technologies Are Reshaping Cost Management." *Management Accounting.* 67 (Mar): 25.

Briner, Russell F. and Fulkerson, Cheryl Linthicum. 2001. "Will Elimination of Pooling Accounting Reduce Mergers and Acquisitions." *Multinational Business Review.* 9 (Spring): 9.

Brooks, Nancy Rivera. 2000. "Critics Line Up Against Chevron-Texaco Merger; Energy: Consolidation In Industry Has Yet To Boost Oil Explorations, Making Many Wary Of Latest Deal." *The Los Angeles Times.* (Oct 17): A.1.

Brouthers, Keith D; Van Hastenburg, Paul; Van den Ven, Joran. 1998. "If Most Mergers Fail Why Are They So Popular?" *Long Range Planning.* 31 (Jun): 347.

Brown, Shona L. and Eisenhardt, Kathleen M. 1998. *Competing on the Edge: Strategy as Structured Chaos.* Boston: Harvard Business School Press.

Brown, Terry; Massoudi, Barry; Rupple, Allen. 1997. "Priming the Performance Pump." *Oil & Gas Investor.* (Second Quarter): 4-9.

Brull, Steven; Anderson, Jenny; Schack, Justin; Gopinath, Deepak. 2003. "The 2002 Deals Of The Year: Mergers & Acquisitions." *Institutional Investor.* 37 (Jan): 36.

Buchanan. Doborah and Connor, Michael. 2001. "Managing Process Risk: Planning for the Booby Traps Ahead." *Strategy & Leadership.* 29 (May/Jun): 23-28.

Bulkeley William M. 2002. "IBM Adds PwC Consulting, With Few Bugs --- Incentives Help Smooth Integration, and the Head of the New Unit Gets Much Credit." *Wall Street Journal.* (Oct 2): B.3.

Bulkeley, William M. and Dunham, Kemba. 2002. "IBM Speeds Move to Consulting With $3.5 Billion Acquisition." *Wall Street Journal.* (Jul 31): A.1.

Burton, Thomas M. 2002. "Probe at Syncor Puts Sale in Peril --- Cardinal Health Uncovered Possibly Illegal Payments By Officials of Target Firm." *Wall Street Journal.* (Nov 7): A.10.

Business Brief. 2002 "Hewlett-Packard Co.: Compaq Computer Acquisition Is Completed After Long Fight." *Wall Street Journal.* (May 6): B.6.

Byham, William C. 1989. *Zapp! The Lightening of Empowerment: How to Improve Productivity, Quality, and Employee Satisfaction.* Pittsburgh: Development Dimensions International Press.

Byrne, John A. and Elgin, Ben. 2002. "Cisco: Behind the Hype" *Business Week.* (Jan 21): 54.

Byrne, John A. and Elgin, Ben. 2002. "Cisco Shopped Till It Nearly Dropped." *Business Week.* (Jan 21): 60.

C

Caisse, Kimberly. 1999. "Cisco's Buying Binge Goes On." *Computer Reseller News.* (Jan 4): 128.

Campa, José Manuel, Hernando, Ignacio. 2002. *Value creation in European M&As.* Madrid: Banco de España.

Cappelli, Peter, Series Adviser. 2002. *Hiring and Keeping the Best People.* Boston: Harvard Business School Press.

Capron, L. and Pistre, N. 2002. "When Do Acquirers Earn Abnormal Returns?" *Strategic Management Journal* 23 (Sep): 781-94.

Carey, Dennis. 2000. "A CEO Roundtable on Making Mergers Succeed." Harvard Business Review. 78 (May/Jun): 145-54.

Carey, Dennis C. and Feigen, Marc C. 1999. "Before Your M&A Deal, Do a Human Capital Audit." *Directors and Boards.* 23 (Spring): 47-49.

Carey, Dennis C.; Aiello, Robert J.; Eccles, Robert G. 2001. *Harvard Business Review on Mergers and Acquisitions.* Boston: Harvard Business School Publication Corp.

Carey, Dennis C.; Ogden, Dayton; Roland, Judith A. 2004. *The Human Side Of M&A: Leveraging The Most Important Factor In Deal Making.* Oxford: Oxford University Press.

Cartwright, S. and Cooper, C.L. 1993. "The Role of Culture Compatibility in Successful Organizational Marriage." *Academy of Management Executive.* 7 (2): 57-70.

Ceniceros, Roberto. 2001. "Baxter Manages a Smooth Transition During Mergers." *Business Insurance.* 35 (Apr 30): 92.

Centers for Medical and Medicaid Services. 2002. "Healthcare Costs Expected to Rise to $2.8 Trillion Over Next 10 Years." *http://www.cms.hhs.gov/media/press/release. asp* (March 12)

Chan, S.; Kensinger J.; Keown, A.; and Martin, J. 1997. "Do Strategic Alliances Create Value?" *Journal of Financial Economics.* 46 (Nov): 199.

Chang, Joseph. 1999. "Scale and Synergy: Worldwide Specialty Chemicals M&A Activity Accelerates." *Chemical Market Reporter.* 255 (Apr 9): FR3-FR6.

Chorafas, Dimitris N. 2004. *Management Risk: The Bottleneck is at the Top of the Bottle.* Houndmills: Palgrave McMillan.

Chowdhury, Subir. 2002. *The Talent Era : Achieving A High Return On Talent.* New York: Financial Times Prentice Hall.

Clark, John J. 1985. *Business Merger and Acquisition Strategies.* Englewood Cliffs: Prentice Hall.

Clark, Kent, and Ofek, Eli. 1994. "Mergers as a Means of Restructuring Distressed Firms: An Empirical Investigation." *Journal of Financial and Quantitative Analysis.* 29 (Dec): 541.

Clark, Peter J. 1991. *Beyond The Deal: Optimizing Merger And Acquisition Value*. New York: Harper Collins Publishers.

Clarke, Christopher J. 1993. *Shareholder Value: Key To Corporate Development*. Oxford: Pergamon Press.

Clemente, Mark N. and Greenspan, David S. 1997. "Keeping Customers Satisfied While The Deal Proceeds." *Mergers and Acquisitions*. 32 (Jul/Aug): 24.

Clendenning, Alan. 2001. "FTC Ends Investigation, Approves PepsiCo-Quaker Merger." *Washington Post*. (August 2): E3.

Cleverley, William O. 2000. "Calculating The True Value Of Healthcare Organizations." *Healthcare Financial Management*. Pg. 4-9

Cohan, Peter S. 2003. *Value Leadership : The 7 Principles That Drive Corporate Value In Any Economy*. San Francisco: Jossey-Bass.

Cohen, Don and Prusak, Laurence. 2001. *In Good Company: How Social Capital Makes Organizations Work*. Boston: Harvard Business School Publishing.

Colella, Peter C., Jr. 1987. "Psychological Aspects of Buying or Selling a Company." *Buyouts & Acquisitions*. (Sep/Oct): 35-38.

Collins, Jim. 2001. *Good to Great: Why Some Companies Make the Leap… and Others Don't*. New York: HarperBusiness.

Conner, Daryl. 1999. "Human Due Diligence." *Executive Excellence*. 16 (Oct): 10.

Connor, Michael. 2001. "M&A Risk Management." *Journal of Business Strategy*. 22 (Jan/Feb): 25.

Conti, Craig and Elek, Steven, III. 2002. "Investing in Healthcare." *Healthcare Financial Management*. 56 (Sep): 94-98.

Copeland, Tom; Koller, Tim; Murrin, Jack. 1990. *Valuation: Measuring and Managing the Value of Companies*. New York: John Wiley & Sons.

Copeland, Tom; Koller, Tim; Murrin, Jack. 2000. *Valuation: Measuring and Managing the Value of Companies*. 3rd Ed. New York: John Wiley and Sons, Inc.,

Cooper, Robert G. 2001. *Winning at New Product: Accelerating the Process from Idea to Launch*. 3rd Ed. New York: Perseus Publishing,

Cooper, Robert G.; Edgett, S.J.; Kleinschmidt. E.J. 1997. *Portfolio Management for New Products*. Hamilton: McMaster University.

Copinath, C. "When acquisitions go awry: Pitfalls in Executing Corporate Strategy." *The Journal of Business Strategy;* 24 (2003): 22

Cowart, Carl M. 1997. "Mellon/Dreyfus: Can success be bought?" *American Bankers Association. ABA Banking Journal*. 89 (Oct): 60.

Cox, T., and Blake, S. 1991. "Managing Cultural Diversity: Implications for Organizational Competitiveness." *Academy of Management Executive*. 5 (3): 45-56.

Craven. Alistair. 2004. "People a priority at HP." *Development and Learning in Organizations*. 18(2):19.

Crawford, David B. 2000. "Levels of Control." The Internal Auditor. 57 (Oct): 42-45

Cross, Richard and Smith, Janet. 1995. *Customer Bonding*. Lincolnwood: NTC Business Books.

Cullinan, Geoffrey; Le Roux, Jean Marc; Weddigen, Rolf-Magnus. 2004. "When to Walk Away from a Deal." *Harvard Business Review*. 82 (April): 92.

Currie, Antony. 2001. "How Chase Fueled a Feud at JP Morgan" *Euromoney*. (Nov): 98-104.

D

Daly, James. 1999. "John Chambers: The Art of the Deal. After Acquiring 40 Companies in 6 Years, CISCO's CEO Knows How to Size Up a Buy." *Business 2.0*. 4 (Oct): 106.

Damodaran, Aswath. 1994. *Damodaran on Value: Security Analysis for Investment and Corporate Finance*. New York: John Wiley & Sons.

Damodaran, Aswath. 1996. *Investment Valuation: Tools & Techniques for Determining the Value of Any Asset*. New York: John Wiley & Sons.

Damodaran, Aswath. 2002. *Investment Valuation – Tools and techniques for Determining the Value of Any Asset*. New York: Wiley and Sons.

D'Aprix, Roger. 1996. *Communicating for Change: Connecting the Workplace and the Marketplace*. San Francisco: Jossey-Bass Publishers.

Darragh, Olive M.; Dodig, Victor G.; O'Hanley, Ronald P. 1997. "Will Success Spoil Investment Management?" The McKinsey Quarterly. (2): 56.

Davidson, Mike. 1996. "Discussion Brief on the Integration of Two Companies." *Davidson Associates*.

Davidson, Sidney, Stickney, Clyde P.; Weil, Roman L. 1988. *Financial Accounting – An Introduction to Concepts, Methods, and Uses*. Fifth Edition. Chicago: The Dryden Press.

Davis, R. B. 1968. "Compatibility in Corporate Marriages." *Harvard Business Review*. 46 (4): 86.

Davis, Bob. 1999. "The Millennium --- Ideas: Think Big --- What is the Greatest Technological Innovation of the Past 1,000 Years? A Hint: It's Not Just the Thought That Counts." *Wall Street Journal*. (Jan 11): R.14.

Davis, Julie L. and Harrison, Suzzane S. 2001. *Edison in the Boardroom: How Leading Companies Realize Value From Intellectual Capital*. New York: John Wiley & Sons.

Davis, S. 1984. *Managing Corporate Culture*. Cambridge, MA:Ballinger.

Davis, Steven I. 2000. *Bank Mergers : Lessons For The Future*. New York: St. Martin's Press.

Deal, T., and A. Kennedy. 1982. *Corporate Cultures*. Reading: Addison Wesley.

Deal, Terrence E. and Kennedy, Allan A. 1999. *The New Corporate Cultures: Revitalizing the Workplace After Downsizing, Mergers, and Reengineering*. Reading: Perseus Books.

Deogun, Nikhil and Lipin, Steven. 2000. "Food Fights? Unilever Bid Could Prompt Merger Binge." *Wall Street Journal*. (May 4): C.1.

Dess, Gregory G.; Picken, Joseph C.; Janney, Jay J. 1998. "Subtracting Value by Adding Business." *Business Horizons*. 41(Jan/Feb): 9-18.

Devlin, Godfrey. 1989. "A Strategy for Shareholder Value." *Accountancy*. 103 (Feb): 89.

Dillavou, Jim. 2002. "The Three Questions to Ask Before Buying a Business." *International Tax Review*. 13 (Nov): 16-18.

DiNapoli, Dominic, Editor. 1999. *Workouts & Turnarounds II : Global Restructuring Strategies For The Next Century : Insights From The Leading Authorities In The Field*. New York: J. Wiley.

Doorley, Thomas L. III and Stivers, Sam R. 1984. "Acquisition Approaches for Financial institutions." *The Bankers Magazine*. 167 (Nov/Dec): 64-69.

Doran, Tom. 2001. "Agents Seek M&A Measures For Success." *National Underwriter*. 105 (Dec 10): 12-15.

Drucker, Peter. 1981. "Five Rules of Successful Acquisitions." *The Wall Street Journal.* (October 15): B.1.

Dutton, Jane E. 1997. *Strategic Agenda Building in Organizations.* Cambridge: Cambridge University Press.

E

Ebeling, William H. and Doorley, Thomas L. 1983. "A Strategic Approach to Acquisitions." *The Journal of Business Strategy.* 3 (Winter): 44-55.

Eisinger, Jesse. 2003. "Ahead of the Tape." *Wall Street Journal.* (Nov 19): C.1.

Egan, Cathleen. 2000. "Coke Gives Outsiders an Unusual Peek at its Plans for Attracting New Business." *Wall Street Journal.* (Dec 18): C.1.

Elgin, Ben; Cady John; Park, Andrew. 2004. "Carly's Challenge." *Business Week.* (Dec 13): 98.

Ellison, Sarah. 2001. "Cadbury Schweppes Works to Tempt More Sweet Tooths – Growth In Home Market Is Tough Egg to Crack, But Emerging Markets Beckon." *Wall Street Journal.* (April 24): B.4.

Ellison, Sarah and Taylor, Ed. 2003. "Henkel's Deal to Acquire Dial Raises Questions About Clorox On News Stake May Be Dumped." *Wall Street Journal.* (Dec 16): B.4.

Etzel, Barbara. 2003. "PwC Consulting's Best Hope: With The IPO Market Dead, And Regulators On Its Back, A $3.5 Billion Sale To IBM Won Out." *The Investment Dealers' Digest.* (Jan 6): 1.

Etzioni, A. 1961. A Comparative Analysis of Complex Organizations. New York: Free Press.

Ewing, Eileen Smith. 1999. "Pooling Ruling Could Dampen the Economy." *Boston Globe.* (Aug 24): D.4.

F

Falis, Neil D. 2004. "How Sarbanes-Oxley Affects Merger Considerations." *Financial Executive.* 20 (June): 44-47.

Farber, Donald C. 1996. *Common Sense Negotiation: The Art of Winning Gracefully.* Seattle: Bay Press.

Farmer, Randye. 1996. "After The Courtship: Managing Merger Transitions." *Banking Management.* 72 (May/Jun): 34.

Feldman, Mark L. and Spratt, Michael F. 1999. *Five Frogs On A Log : A CEO's Field Guide To Accelerating The Transition In Mergers, Acquisitions, And Gut Wrenching Change.* New York: Harper Business.

Ferrara, Donna. 2002. "Mergers and the Claims Made Policy." *Risk Management.* 49 (September): 32-38.

Ferris, Gerald R.; Rosen, Sherman D.; Barnum, Darold T. 1995. *Handbook of Human Resource Management.* Cambridge: Blackwell Publishers.

Ferris, Kenneth R. and Pecherot-Pettit, Barbara S. 2002. *Valuation Avoiding the Winner's Curse.* New York: Prentice Hall.

Finance Division. 1958. *Corporate Mergers and Acquisitions: Basic Financial, Legal, and Policy Aspects.* AMA.

Finkelstein, Brad. 2003. "Investment Group, GE Consumer Finance Will Buy Conseco's Assets." *National Mortgage News.* 27 (Mar 10): 2.

Fitch, Thomas P. 1986. "M&A the Personal Way." *United States Banker.* 97 (Oct): 71.

Fombrun, Charles J. 1983. "Corporate Culture, Environment, and Strategy." *Human Resources Management.* 22 (Spring): 139-152.

Fossum, Cory. 1997. "Do Long-Term Shareholders Benefit From Corporate Acquisitions." *Weekly Corporate Growth Report.* (Mar 17): 8920A.

Foust, Dean; Pascual, Aixa; Pallavi, Gogoi; Kerstetter, Jim. 2002. "M&A: Companies Shopped – Now They've Dropped." *BusinessWeek Online.* (Feb 25).

Freedman, Eric. 1998. "How to keep readers when the deal's done." *Folio: The Magazine for Magazine Management.* 27 (May): 35.

Freier, Jerold L. 1981. "Acquisition Search Programs." *Mergers and Acquisitions.* 16 (Summer): 35-39.

Fuller, Joseph and Jensen, Michael C. 2001. "Manager's Journal: Dare to Keep Your Stock Low." *Wall Street Journal.* (Dec 31): A.8.

Furst, Richard W. and Markland, Robert E. 1969. Evaluating Merger-Acquisition Opportunities – A Risk Incorporation Model. *University of Missouri Business and Government Review.* 10 (Jul-Aug): 21.

G

Gale, Bradley T. 1994. *Managing Customer Value: Creating Quality and Service That Customers Can See.* New York: Maxwell McMillan.

Galpin, Tmothy J., Herndon, Mark. 2000. *The Complete Guide to Mergers and Acquisitions: Process Tools to Support M&A Integration at Every Level.* San Francisco: Jossey-Bass Publishers

Ganchev, Oggie. 2000. "Applying Value Drivers to Hotel Valuation." *Cornell Hotel and Restaurant Administration Quarterly.* 41 (Oct): 78-90.

Gannon, Martin J. 2004. *Understanding Global Cultures: Metaphorical Journeys Through 28 Nations, Cluster of Nations, and Continents.* 3rd Ed. Thousand Oaks: Sage Publications.

Gargiulo, Abert F. and Levine, Steven J. 1982. *The Leveraged Buyout.* AMA Management Briefing.

Garrison, George E. 1994. "Acquisitions: Buyers' Views." *Chemical Business.* 16 (Feb): 5.

Garten, Jeffrey E. 1999. "Mega-Mergers, Mega-Influence." *New York Times.* (Oct 26):27.

Garten, Jeffrey E. 2001. "The GE-Honeywell Fiasco: Where to go From Here." *Business Week.* (07-23): 28.

Gasiorek, Alan D. *Merger & acquisition : Valuation And Structuring.* Norcross: Corporate Development Institute.

Gaugan, Patrick A. 2002. *Mergers, Acquisitions, and Corporate Restructurings.* New York: Wiley.

Gaynor, Gerard H. 2002. *Innovation By Design: What It Takes To Keep Your Company On The Cutting Edge.* New York: AMACOM.

Geis, George T., Geis, George S. 2001. *Digital Deals : Strategies For Selecting And Structuring Partnerships.* New York: McGraw-Hill.

Geisst, Charles R. 2004. *Deals of the Century: Wall Street, Mergers, and the Making of Modern America.* Hoboken: John Wiley & Sons.

Genaldi, Allen J. "Fraud In Foreign Operations." *The Internal Auditor.* (August 2002): 61.

Gerstner, Louis V. Jr. 2002. *Who Says Elephants Can't Dance: Inside IBM's Historic Turnaround.* New York: HarperCollins Publishers.

Gitelson, Gene; Bing, John; Laroche, Lionel. 2001. "How the Cultural Trap Deepens in Cross-Border Deals." *Mergers and Acquisitions.* 36 (Dec): 36-42.

Gleason, Kimberly C.; Mathur, Ike; Wiggins, Roy A. 2003. "Evidence of Value Creation in the Financial Services Industries Through the Use of Joint Ventures and Strategic Alliances." *Financial Review*. 38 (May): 213.

Goold, Michael; Campbell, Andrew; Alexander, Marcus. 1994. *Corporate Level Strategy: Creating Value in a Multibusiness Company*. New York: John Wiley & Sons, Inc.

Goold, Michael and Campbell, Andrew. 1998. "Desperately Seeking Synergy." *Harvard Business Review*. 76 (Sep-Oct): 63.

Greene, Jay. 2003. "Small Biz: Microsoft's Next Big Thing? With New Software And An Army Of Resellers, It's Targeting 45 Million Companies Worldwide." *Business Week*. (Apr 21): 72.

Greene, Jay and Grover, Ronald. 2001. "Microsoft's First-Class Deal: It Sold Expedia For Cheap--But Gets Passengers For Hailstorm." *Business Week*. (July 30): 37.

Greene, Jay; Kerstetter, Jim; Hamm, Steve. 2003. "Microsoft: A Killer App That Could Kill The Competition: Its Entry Into The Antivirus Market Has Rivals Spooked." *Business Week*. (Sep 29): 48.

Green, Thad B. and Knippen, Jay T. 1999. *Breaking the Barriers to Upward Communications: Strategies and Skills for Employees, Managers, and HR Specialists*. Westport: Quorum Books.

Grimpe, Christoph. 2004. "When an R&D Site Closes." *Research Technology Management*. 47 (Jul/Aug): 56

Grobmyer, James E. 2002. "Putting Your Financially Based Strategic Plan Into Action." *Trustee*. (Jan): 30-32.

Guirdham, Maureen. 1999. *Communicating Across Cultures*. London: McMillan Press.

Guptara, Prabhu. 1992. "The Role of Culture Audits and Culture Portraits in Making Acquisitions Work." *European Business Review*. 92 (2): 1.

Guy, Robert. 2001. "USX to Split U.S. Steel and Marathon Oil: Breakup is Called Good For Oil Firm, Leaves Steel Entity Vulnerable." *Wall Street Journal*. (April 25): A.2.

Guyon, Janet. 2003. "The Man Who Mooned Larry Ellison." *Fortune*. 148 (Jul 7): 71.

H

Hahn, Avital Louria. 2002. "Global M&A Swoons 45%: Worst Quarter Since 1995 May Yield to Second-Half Pickup, M&A Chiefs Say." *The Investment Dealers' Digest*. (Apr 15): 1.

Hahn, Avital Louria. 2004. "Dizzying Growth for Online Due Diligence: More M&A Auctions and Hedge Fund Buyers Spark a Boom for IntraLinks." *The Investment Dealers' Digest*. (Nov 29): 1.

Haines, Leslie. 1997. "After the Honeymoon: Only the Right Post-Merger Integration Delivers the Promised Value." *Oil and Gas Investor*. (Second Quarter): 18.

Hakim, Danny. 2001. "Why Funds See Daimler as a Trade-In." *New York Times*. (May 20): 3.8.

Hall, Mark. 2002. "Integration: IT's Albatross." *Computerworld*. 36 (Jan 1): 22-24.

Hallinan, Joseph T. and Pacelle, Mitchell. 2002. "Conseco's Tale of Success Ends In Chapter 11 --- Several High-Profile Investors And Executives Are Brought Low; Insurance Unit Remains Sound." *Wall Street Journal*. (Dec 19): C.1.

Halperin, Michael and Bell, Steven J. 1992. *Research Guide to Corporate Acquisitions, Mergers, and Other Restructuring*. New York: Greenwood Press.

Halpern, Jennifer J. and Robert N. Stern. 1998. *Debating Rationality: Nonrational Aspects of Organizational Decision Making.* Ithaca: Cornell University Press.

Hambrick, D., and P. Mason. 1984. "Upper Echelons: The Organization as a Reflection of its Top Managers." *Academy of Management Review.* 9 (Apr): 193-206.

Hamel, Gary and Prahalad, C. K. 1994. *Competing For The Future: Breakthrough Strategies For Seizing Control Of Your Industry And Creating The Markets Of Tomorrow.* Cambridge: Harvard Business School Press.

Hamm, Steve; Engardio, Pete; Balfour, Frederik. 2004. "Big Blue's Bold Step Into China." *Business Week.* (Dec 20): 35.

Hammond, John S.; Keeney, Ralph L.; Raiffa, Howard. 1998. "Even Swaps: A Rational Method For Making Trade-Offs." *Harvard Business Review.* 76 (Mar/Apr): 137.

Hansell, Saul. 1998. "S.E.C. Crackdown on Technology Write-Offs." *New York Times.* (Sep 29): C.1.

Harding, David; Rovit, Sam; Milway, Katie Smith; Lemire, Catherine. 2004. *Mastering The Merger : Four Critical Decisions That Make Or Break The Deal.* Boston: Harvard Business School Press.

Hardman, David, Macchi, Laura. 2003. *Thinking: Psychological Perspectives on Reasoning, Judgment, and Decision Making.* Hoboken: Wiley.

Hargreaves, Pat and Jarvis, Peter. 1998. *The Human Resource Development Handbook.* London: Kogan Page.

Harrison, Joan. 2000. "M&A Time Line." *Mergers and Acquisitions Journal.* 35 (Sep): 24.

Harrison, J. Richard, March, James G. 1984. *Administrative Science Quarterly.* 29 (Mar): 26.

Harvard Business Essentials. 2002. *Hiring And Keeping The Best People.* Boston: Harvard Business School Press.

Harvard Business Review Paperback Series. 1998. *Harvard Business Review on Strategies for Growth.* Boston: Harvard Business School Press.

Haspeslagh, P. C. and Jemison, D. B. 1987. "Acquisitions--Myths and Reality." *Sloan Management Review.* (Winter): 53.

Haspeslagh, Phillippe C. and Jemison, David B. 1991. *Managing Acquisitions: Creating Value Through Corporate Renewal.* New York: The Free Press,

Hax, Arnold C. and Majluf, Nicholas S. 1984. *Strategic Management: An Integrative Perspective.* New Jersey: Prentice Hall.

Health & Technology. 2001. "Son of H-P Founder to File Proxy in Fight Against Compaq Deal" *Wall Street Journal.* (Nov 19): B.5.

Healy, Paul M.; Palepu, Krishna; and Ruback, Richard S. 1997. "Which Takeovers are Profitable? Strategic or Financial?" *Sloan Management Review.* 38 (Summer): 45.

Heitner, Mark. 1998. "The Thorny Business of Merging Rival Firms." *Mergers and Acquisitions.* 32 (Jan/Feb): 18.

Heller, Frank. 1992. *Decision Making and Leadership.* Cambridge: Cambridge University Press.

Hemp, Paul. 2004. "A Time For Growth: An Interview with Amgen CEO Kevin Sharer." *Harvard Business Review.* 82 (Jul-Aug): 67-74.

Henke, John W.; Krachenberg, A. Richard; Lyons, Thomas F. 1993. "Perspective: Cross-Functional Teams: Good Concept, Poor Implementation!" *The Journal of Product Innovation Management.* 10 (Jun): 216.

Hensley, Scott. 2000. "Pfizer Appoints McKinnell to Top Posts – Executive Who Carried Out Warner-Lambert Merger To Be Chairman and CEO." *Wall Street Journal.*

(Aug 11): B.10.

Hermie, Jon. "Capturing the most upside from the deal Rob Kaye." *Oil & Gas Investor*. 19 (May 1999): 51.

Herrick, Thaddeus. 2000. "ChevronTexaco Vows Not to Cut Output---In Accord for $34.2 Billion, Company Plans to Curb Exploration and Spending." *Wall Street Journal*. (Oct 17): A.3.

Hersch Warren S. 1997. "Quick transition, prioritizing are key to successful mergers and acquisitions." *Computer Reseller News*. (Aug 4): 48.

Hershey, Robert D. 2000. "U.S. Clears Deal for Warner-Lambert." *New York Times*. (Jun 20): C.2.

Heskett, James L.; Sasser, W. Earl; Sclesinger, Leonard A. 2003. *The Value Profit Chain: Treat Employees Like Customers and Customers Like Employees*. New York: The Free Press.

Hiatt, John T. 1994. "Crossborder Marriages Can Work." *International Business*. 7 (May): 22.

Hiday, Jeffrey L. 1998. "Most Mergers Fail to Add Value, Consultants Find." *Wall Street Journal*. (Oct 12): 1.

Hinterhuber, Andreas. 2002. "Making M & A Work." *Business Strategy Review*. 13 (Autumn): 7-9.

Hitt, Michael A.; Harrison, Jeffrey S.; Ireland, R. Duane. 2001. *Mergers and Acquisitions: A Guide for Creating Value for Shareholders*. Oxford: Oxford University Press.

Hitt, Michael A. and Tyler, Beverly B. 1991. "Strategic Decision Models: Integrating Different Perspectives." *Strategic Management Journal*. 12 (Jul): 327-351.

Hogarth, R.H. 1981. *Judgment and Choice: The Psychology of Decision*. New York: Wiley.

Holubec, Lev; Klee, John; Wathen, Michael. 2002. "The Deal Process That Never Stops." *Mergers and Acquisitions*. 37 (Jul): 24.

Hooke, Jeffery C. 1997. *M&A: A Practical Guide to Doing the Deal*. New York: John Wiley & Sons.

I

Ibrahim, Youssef M. 1999. "Daimler-Chrysler Merger Made an Art of Making a Case." *New York Times*. (May 26): 1.

International Energy Agency. "Monthly Market Report."

Ip, Greg. 2001. "Silver Lining: Amid Devastation, Many Still See Gains In Burst Tech Bubble --- Even Sufferers Cite the Value of Innovation and Base for Longer Growth --- Looking Again to the Fed." *Wall Street Journal*. (Mar 20): A.1.

J

Jacobs, Karen and Fairclough, Gordon. 1999. "As Honeywell CEO, Bonsignore's Task Is to Meld Diverse Corporate Cultures." *Wall Street Journal*. (Dec 2): 1.

Jacobs, Peter. 2002. "Reducing the Risk of Acquisitions." *MIT Sloan Management Review*. 43 (Summer): 16.

Jenkins, Holman W. Jr. 1999. "Just Another German Car Company." *Wall Street Journal*. (May 26): A.23.

Johann, Bernard; Macesich, Mike; Massoudi, Barry. 1998. "Enterprise-Wide IT Systems." *Oil & Gas Investor*. (Second Quarter): 7-12.

Johne, Marjo. 2004. "A Foreign Affair." *CMA Management*. 78 (May): 26.

Johnson, Hazel J. 1995. *Bank Mergers, Acquisitions & Strategic Alliances : Positioning &*

Protecting Your Bank In The Era Of Consolidation. Burr Ridge: Irwin.

Joint Proxy Statement/Prospectus dated March 22, 2002, Between Amgen Inc. and Immunes Corporation. Joint proxy statements can be obtained online from www.sec.gov.

Joint Proxy Statement/Prospectus dated October 21, 2002, Between Pfizer Inc. and Pharmacia Corporation. Joint proxy statements can be obtained online from www.sec.gov.

Jones, Chuck. 2000. "Conseco Bosses Quit as Ratings Drop from Sale Announcement." *Advisor Today*. 95 (Jun): 40.

Joyce, William; Nohria, Nitin; Roberson, Bruce. 2003. *What Really Works: The 4+2 Formula For Sustained Business Success*. New York: Harper Collins Publishers.

K

Kadlec, Daniel J. 1999. *Masters Of The Universe : Winning Strategies Of America's Greatest Deal Makers*. New York: Harper Collins Publishers.

Kaen, Fred R. 2003. *A Blueprint For Corporate Governance : Strategy, Accountability, And The Preservation Of Shareholder Value*. New York: AMACOM.

Kahaner, Larry. 1996. *Competitive Intelligence : From Black Ops To Boardrooms : How Businesses Gather, Analyze, And Use Information To Succeed In The Global Marketplace*. New York: Simon & Schuster.

Kale, P.; Dryer, J.H.; Singh, H. 2002. "Alliance Capability, Stock Market Response , and Long Term Alliance Success: The Role Of The Alliance Function" *Strategic Management Journal* 23 (August):747-768.

Kanter, Rosabeth Moss, Kao, John and Wiersema, Fred. 1997. *Innovation: Breakthrough Thinking at 3M, DuPont, GE, Pfizer, and Rubbermaid*. New York: Harper Business.

Kaplan, Nancy. 2001. "Assimilate, Integrate, or Leave Alone?" *Journal of Business Strategy* (Jan/Feb): 23-25.

Karp, Richard. 1993. "Fickle forecaster." *Barron's National Business and Financial Weekly*. 73 (Dec 13): 19.

Kasper, Larry J. 1997. *Business Valuation: Advanced Topics*. Westport: Quorum Books.

Keating, Peter. 1998. "When a Merger May Pay Off." *Money*. 27 (Jan): 62.

Keeney, Ralph L. 1992. *Value Focused Thinking: A Path to Creative Decision Making*. Cambridge: Harvard University Press.

Kelly, Eamon M. 1967. *The Profitability of Growth Through Acquisitions*. Pennsylvania State University.

Kempner, Matt. 2000. "Uncertainty Looms Over Atlanta unit AOL-Time Warner Merger: Turner Employees Wary of Changes." *The Atlanta Constitution*. (Dec 15): H.1.

Khermouch, Gerry. 2003. "InterPublic Group: Synergy – Or Sinkhole?" *Business Week*. (Apr 21): 76.

Kilmann, R., M. Saxton, and R. Serpa. 1986. "Issues in Understanding and Changing Culture." *California Management Review* 28 (2): 87-94.

Kim, W. Chan; Henderson, Bruce D.; Mauborgne, Renee. 1997. "Value Innovation: The Strategic Logic of High Growth." *Harvard Business Review*. 82 (Jan/Feb): 103.

Klammer, Thomas. 1994. *Managing Strategic and Capital Investment Decisions: Going Beyond the Numbers to Improve Decision Making*. New York: Irwin Professional Publishing.

Knowledge Management Study. Final Report. 1996. "The Partner Case Studies." *APQC's International Benchmarking Clearinghouse.*

Knox, Noelle. 1999. "MCI WorldCom Sprints Ahead." *The Associated Press.* (Oct 5):1

Koberg, C.S. 1987. "Resource Scarcity, Environmental Uncertainty, and Adaptive Organizational Behavior." *Academy of Management Journal* 30(4): 798.

Kotter, John P. 1990. *A Force For Change: How Leadership Differs From Management.* New York: The Free Press.

Kouzes, James M. and Posner, Barry Z. 1995. *The Leadership Challenge.* San Francisco: Jossey-Bass Publishers.

Kounalakis, Markos; Banks, Drew; Daus, Kim. 1999. *Beyond Spin: The Power of Strategic Corporate Journalism.* San Francisco: Jossy-Bass Publishers.

Krachenberg, A. Richard; Henke, John W. Jr.; Lyons, Thomas F. 1993. "The Isolation of Upper Management." *Business Horizons.* 36 (Jul/Aug): 41.

Kranhold, Kathryn and Fleming, Charles. 2003. "Leading the News – A Global Journal Report: GE Agrees to Pay Aegon $5.4 Billion for Finance Units." *Wall Street Journal.* (Aug 6): A.3.

Kuppinger, Roger. *Everything You Always Wanted to Know About Mergers, Acquisitions, and Divestitures But Didn't Know Whom to Ask.* Published by Roger Kuppinger.

L

Langreth, Robert. 2000. "Pfizer, Warner-Lambert Agree on Terms --- AHP Receives $1.8 Billion, No Other Compensation, To Exit Its Merger Pact." *Wall Street Journal* (Feb 7): A.3.

Langreth, Robert. 2000. "Behind Pfizer's Takeover Battle: An Urgent Need" *Wall Street Journal* (Feb 8): B1.

Langreth, Robert. 2000. "Pfizer's Warner-Lambert Purchase Contains Big Prize – Pipeline of Biotechnology Unit Agouron is Stuffed With Potential Blockbusters" *Wall Street Journal* (April 28): B4.

Langreth, Robert; Lipin, Steven; Burton, Tomas M. 2000. "After Drug-Firm Mergers, the Prescription Is on the Wall for More." *Wall Street Journal* (Feb 9): B.2.

Latour, Almar. 2001. "'IP' Sales: The Internet Can Still Coin Money." *Wall Street Journal.* (Dec 6): B.6.

Layne, Richard. 1992. "How Investors Should Analyze Bank Mergers." *American Banker.* (Apr 28): 1.

Lee, Steven James and Colman, Robert Douglas. 1981. *Handbook of Mergers, Acquisitions and Buyouts.* Englewood Cliffs: Prentice Hall, Inc.

Lessem, Ronnie. 1990. *Managing Corporate Culture.* Worcester: Billing & Sons Ltd.

Lessen, Ronnie. 1989. *Global Management Principals.* New York: Prentice Hall.

Levenbach, Hans and Cleary, James P. 1984. *The Modern Forecaster: The Forecasting Process Through Data Analysis.* Belmont: Lifetime Learning Publications.

Levinthal, Daniel A, March, James G. 1993. "The Myopia Of Learning." *Strategic Management Journal* 14 (Winter): 95.

Lipton, Mark. 2003. *Guiding Growth : How Vision Keeps Companies On Course.* Boston: Harvard Business School Press.

Lissack, Michael R. 2002. *The Interaction of Complexity and Management.* Westport: Quorum Books.

Lloyd, Bruce. Ed. 1997. *Creating Value: Through Acquisitions, Demergers, Buyouts, and Alliances.* Oxford: Elsevier Science.

Loftus, Peter. 2003. "Fragmented Computer Services Are Ripe for Mergers, Acquisitions." *Wall Street Journal.* (Jan 8): B.7.D.

Lohse, Deborah. 2000. "Conseco Board Forces CEO To Step Down." *Wall Street Journal.* (May 1): A.3.

Loughran, Tim and Vijh, Anand, J. 1997. "Do Long-Term Shareholders Benefit From Corporate Acquisitions? *The Journal of Finance.* 52 (Dec): 1765.

Lowell, Rebecca. 1999. "Lone Star Industries to be Purchased by Dykerfhoff AG for $1.19 Billion." Wall Street Journal. (Sep 3): B.3.

Lowenstein, Michael W. 1995. *Customer Retention: An Integrated Process for Keeping Your Best Customers.* Milwaukee: ASQC Quality Press.

Lowenstein, Michael W. 1997. *The Customer Loyalty Pyramid.* Westport: Quorum Books.

Luca, Joe. 2002. "Dissecting Banking's Bigness." *Mortgage Banking.* 62 (Aug): 68-73.

M

MacDonald, Elizabeth. 1998. "Deloitte & Touche Continues to Attack Two Merger Plans." *Wall Street Journal.* (Jan 29): A1.

MacDonald, Elizabeth. 1999. "U.S. Accounting Board Faults Global Rules." *Wall Street Journal.* (Oct 18): A1.

Mahaffy, A. Paul. 1998. "Look Before You Leap: The Need For Due Diligence When Buying Or Financing A Business." *CMA.* 72 (Jul/Aug): 21.

Mandel, Andrew D. 2003. "Benefits due diligence issues in a carve-out transaction." *Journal of Compensation and Benefits* 19 (Jan/Feb): 9.

Manganelli, Raymond L. and Hagen, Brian W. 2003. *Solving The Corporate Value Enigma: A System To Unlock Shareholder Value.* New York: American Management Association.

March, James G. 1981. "Footnotes to Organizational Change." *Administrative Science Quarterly.* 26 (Dec): 563-77.

March, James G. 1988. "Variable Risk Preferences and Adaptive Aspirations." *Journal of Economic Behavior & Organization.* 9 (Jan): 5.

March, James G. 1994. *A Primer on Decision Making: How Decisions Happen.* New York: The Free Press.

March, James G. 1996. "Continuity and Change in Theories Of Organizational Action." *Administrative Science Quarterly.* 41 (Jun): 278.

March, James G. 1997. *Understanding How Decisions Happen In Organizations.* Palo Alto: Stanford University and Cambridge University Presses.

March, James G. and Shapira, Zur. 1987. "Managerial Perspectives on Risk and Risk Taking." *Management Science.* 33 (Nov): 1404.

Markides, Constantinos. 2000. *All The Right Moves: A Guide to Crafting Breakthrough Strategies.* Boston: Harvard Business School Press.

Marks, Mitchell Lee, and Mirvis, Philip H. 1998. *Joining Forces: Making One Plus One Equal Three in Mergers, Acquisitions, and Alliances.* New York: Jossey-Bass.

Martin, Joanne. 1992. *Cultures in Organizations: Three Perspectives.* New York: Oxford University Press.

Massimillian, Dick. 2001. "Notes From the M&A Trenches." *Journal of Business Strategy* (Jan/Feb): 20-22.

Mathews, Anna Wilde. 2001. "E-Commerce (A Special Report): Cover Story --- Applause, Applause: What do Audiences Want? Entertainment Companies Are

Looking for Answers on the Web." *Wall Street Journal.* (Oct 29): R.8.

Matthews, Guy Robert. 2001. "USX to Split U.S. Steel and Marathon Oil: Breakup is Called Good for Oil Firm, Leaves Steel Entity Vulnerable." *Wall Street Journal.* (April 25,): A.2.

Maynard, Micheline. 2001. "Cutbacks by Daimler Leave a Bitter Residue at Chrysler." *New York Times.* (Apr 11): C.4.

Mazur, Laura. 2001. "The Trouble with Takeovers." *Marketing.* (Feb 8): 26.

McChesney, Robert W. 1999. *Rich Media Poor Democracy: Communication Politics in Dubious Times.* Urbana: University of Illinois Press.

McClam, Erin. 2001. "California; Coke Confirms Odwalla Buy; Soft Drinks: Purchase Would Mean a Bigger Piece of 'Good For You' Beverage Niche for Industry Giant." *The Los Angeles Times.* (Oct 31): C.2.

McDonald, Caroline. 2001. "Exposure Checklist Expanding in M&A's." *National Underwriter.* 105 (Nov 19): 16.

McEachern, Cristina. 2001. "The Economy May Be Slowing, But Retaining A Quality Tech Department Is Always Key." *Wall Street & Technology.* 19 (Jul): 43.

McKelvey, Peter. 1999. "The Ties That Bind In Roll-Up Plays That Work." *Mergers and Acquisitions.* 33 (May/Jun): 37.

McMillin, John. 1992. *Games, Strategies, & Managers – How Managers Can Use Game Theory To Make Better Business Decisions.* New York: Oxford University Press.

McNamara, Mary. 1999. "The Ultimate Betrayal of a Brand Loyalist; Commentary The Ford-Volvo Deal and Other Mega-Mergers Mean That we Can No Longer Define Ourselves by the Products to which We Paid Allegiance." *The Los Angeles Times.* (Feb 1): 1.

McWilliams, Gary and Tam, Pui-Wing. 2002. "H-P Battle Raises Bar for Proxy Costs." *Wall Street Journal.* (Mar 26): A.4.

Melloan, George. 1999. "The Central Economic Lesson of This Century." *Wall Street Journal.* (Dec 28): A.19.

Melloan, George. 1999. "Corporate Marriage Aren't Made in Heaven." *Wall Street Journal.* (Jan 5): A.23.

Merrick, Amy. 2000. "Fifth Third Bancorp Will Buy Old Kent For $4.74 Billion in Midwest Bank Deal" *Wall Street Journal.* (Nov 21): A.6.

Michaels, Adrian. 2002. "Pfizer Buys Breathing Space With Deal." *Financial Times.* (July 16): 18.

Michaels, Ed; Handfield-Jones, Helen; Axelrod, Beth. 2001. *The War for Talent.* Boston: Harvard Business School Press.

Michaelson, John. 2003. *Restructuring for Growth.* New York: McGraw Hill.

Michman, Ronald D. 1989. "Why Forecast for the Long Term?" *The Journal of Business Strategy.* 10 (Sep/Oct): 36.

Miller, James P. 2000. "Conseco to Unload Former Green Tree And Take a Charge." *Wall Street Journal.* (April 3): A.13.

Milligan, Jack. 2001. "Getting the Merger Formula Right." *Financial Executive.* (Jan/Feb): 23.

Mills, Roger. 2002. "Accounting and Finance: Mergers and acquisitions." *Manager Update.* 13 (Spring): 32.

Mintzberg, H. 1987. "Crafting Strategy." *Harvard Business Review* 65 (Jul/Aug): 66-75.

Mintzberg, H. 1989. *Mintzberg on Management: Inside Our Strange World of Organizations.* New York: The Free Press.

Mintzberg, H. 1996. "Musings on Management." *Harvard Business Review* 74 (Jul/Aug): 61.

Mintzberg, Henry, Bruce Ahlstrand, and Joseph Lampel. 1998. *Strategy Safari: A Guided Tour Through the Wilds of Strategic Management.* New York: The Free Press.

Mirvis, Philip H. and Marks, Mitchell Lee. 1992. "The Human Side Of Merger Planning: Assessing And Analyzing." *Human Resource Planning.* 15(3): 69.

Mirvis, Phillip H. and Marks, Mitchell Lee. 1992. *Managing the Merger: Making It Work.* Englewood Cliffs: Prentice Hall.

Montlake, Simon. 2002. "More Work Ahead." *The Banker.* 152 (Apr): 65.

Moon, Ronald W. 1968. *Business Mergers and Takeover Bids.* London: Gee & Co.

Morgan, M. Granger and Henrion, Max. 1990. *Uncertainty: A Guide to Dealing With Uncertainty in Quantitative Risk and Policy Analysis.* Cambridge: Cambridge University Press.

Morrall, Katherine. 1996. "Managing A Merger Without Losing Customers." *Bank Marketing.* 28 (Mar): 18.

Mozeson, Mark H.; Gretchko, Susan. 1998. "Realizing the Value of a Merger." *Pharmaceutical Executive.* 18 (02-01): 94.

Muolo, Paul. 2002. "The Worst B&C Deal of All Time." *National Mortgage News.* 27 (Dec 30): 1.

N

Nadler, David A.; Gerstein Marc S.; Shaw Robert B.; and Associates. 1992. *Organizational Architecture : Designs For Changing Organizations.* San Francisco: Jossey-Bass.

Nahavandi, A., and Malekzadeh, A. 1988. "Acculturation in Mergers and Acquisitions." *Academy of Management Review.* 13 (1): 79-90.

Nathans, Leah J. 1989. "Is Wasserstein's Star Tarnished?" *Business Week.* (Oct 2): 88.

Newman, Jerry M. and Krzystofiak, Frank J. 1993 "Changes In Employee Attitudes After An Acquisition." *Group & Organization Management.* 18 (Dec): 390.

Nolf, Brian and Wimer, Paul. 1998. "Global Supply Integration: A Methodology for Success." *Pharmaceutical Executive.* 18 (Mar): 94-106.

Noonan, Brendan. 1998. "Poking Holes in the Umbrella." *Best's Review.* 99 (Aug): 59-62.

Norton, Leslie P. 2000. "Fading Signal? After Nine Years of Stunning Growth, Clear Channel May be Facing Static." Barron's. 80 (Mar 6): 31.

Nutt, Paul C. 1986. "Tactics of Implementation." *Academy of Management Journal.* 29 (Jun): 230-261.

Nutt, Paul C. 2002. *Why Decisions Fail: Avoiding the Blunders and Traps That Lead to Debacles.* San Francisco: Berrett-Koehler Publishers.

O

O'Connor, W.E. 2001. *An Introduction to Airline Economics.* Sixth Ed. Westport: Praeger.

Oldfield, George S. and Santomero, Anthony M. 1997. "Risk Management in Financial Institutions." *Sloan Management Review.* 39 (September): 33-47.

O'Reilly, Charles A. and Pfeffer, Jeffrey. 2000. *Hidden Value: How Great Companies Achieve Extraordinary Results With Ordinary People.* Boston: Harvard Business School Press.

Ouchi, William G. and Price, Raymond L. 1978. "Hierarchies, Clans, and Theory Z: A New Perspective on Organizational Development." *Organizational Dynamics* 7

(2): 25-44.

Owen, Robert R.; Garner, Daniel R.; Bunder, Dennis S. 1986. *Arthur Young Guide to Financing for Growth – Ten Alternatives for Raising Capital.* New York: John Wiley & Sons.

P

Palepu, Krishna G.; Paul M. Healy; Victor L. Bernard. 2000. *Business Analysis & Valuation : Using Financial Statements : Text & Cases.* Cincinnati: South-Western College Pub.

Paulson, Ed. 2001. *Inside Cisco : The Real Story Of Sustained M & A Growth.* New York: Wiley.

Pavlou, Alex K. 2003. "Biotechnology M&A insight: Deals and Strategies." *Journal of Commercial Biotechnology.* 10 (Sep): 85.

Pekala, Nancy. 2001. "Merger They Wrote: Avoiding a Corporate Culture Collision." *Journal of Property.* 66 (May/Jun): 32-36.

Pellet, Jennifer. 2001. "Gary, Gary Quite Contrary." *Chief Executive.* (Jun): 26.

Perkins, Jody M. 1999. "The Economic State of the US Oil and Natural Gas Exploration and Production Industry: Long-Term Trends and Recent Events." *American Petroleum Institute.* (Apr 30): 1-16.

Peters, T., and Waterman, R. 1982. *In Search of Excellence.* New York: Harper and Row.

Peterson, Melody and Holson, Laura M. 2000. "Warner-Lambert and American Home Seek New Merger Suitors." *New York Times.* (Jan 20): C.1.

Peterson, Melody. 2000. "Pfizer Gets Its Deal To Buy Warner-Lambert for $90.2 Billion." *New York Times.* (Feb 8): C.1.

Peterson, Melody. 2002. "Wall St. Is Wary of Pfizer but Embraces the Target." *New York Times.* (Jul 16): C.1.

Pfeffer, Jeffrey. 1994. *Competitive Advantage Through People: Unleashing the Power of the Work Force.* Boston: Harvard Business School Press.

Pfeffer, Jeffrey. 1998. *The Human Equation: Building Profits by Putting People First.* Boston: Harvard Business School Press.

Pinkerton, Janet. 2001. "From Process to Profits." *Dealerscope.* 43 (Aug): 24.

Pol, Louis G. and Thomas, Richard K. 1997. *Demography for Business decision Making.* Westport: Quorum Books.

Popper, Margaret. 1994. "How Henkel Makes Its Takeover Decisions." *Corporate Finance* (January): 34 –36.

Porter, Michael E. 1980. *Competitive Strategy.* New York: Free Press.

Porter, Michael E. 1985. *Competitive Advantage: Creating and Sustaining Superior Performance* New York: The Free Press.

Porter, Michael E. 1996. "What is Strategy?" *Harvard Business Review.* 74 (Nov-Dec): 63.

Pound, John. 1985. "Are Takeover Targets Undervalued?: An Empirical Examination Of The Financial Characteristics Of Target Companies." *Investor Responsibility Research Center.*

Prahalad, C.K. and Ramaswamy, Venkant. 2004. *The Future of Competition: Co-Creating Unique Value with Customers.* Boston: Harvard Business School Press.

Prasso, Sheridan. 2001. "Is Service Worse After a Merger?" *Business Week* (Aug 6):10.

Pratt. Shannon P. 1989. *Valuing a Business: The Analysis and Appraisal of Closely Held Companies.* Homewood: Dow Jones-Irwin.

Pratt, Shannon P. 1998. *Cost of Capital: Estimation and Applications.* New York: John Wiley & Sons.

Pratt, Shannon P. 2003. *Business Valuation Body of Knowledge* Hoboken: J. Wiley & Sons.

Pratt, Shannon P.; Reilly, Robert F.; Schweihs, Robert P. 1998. *Valuing Small Businesses and Professional Practices.* 3rd Ed. New York: McGraw Hill.

Pritchett, Price; Robinson, Donald; Clarkson, Russell. 1997. *After the Merger: The Authoritative Guide for Integration Success.* New York: McGraw Hill.

R

Raab, David and Clark, Arthur E. Jr. 1992. "Cover Story: Mindful Management for Merger Mania." Bankers Monthly. 109 (May): 17.

Radford. K. J. 1977. *Complex Decision Problems: An Integrated Strategy for Resolution.* Reston: Reston Publishing Co.

Rappaport, Alfred. 1986. *Creating Shareholder Value: The New Standard for Business Performance.* New York: The Free Press.

Ravenscraft, David J. and Scherer, F.M. 1987. *Mergers, Sell-offs, and Economic Efficiency.* Washington, D.C.: The Brooking Institution.

Reading, Clive. 2002. *Strategic Business Planning: A Dynamic System for Improving Performance and Competitive Advantage.* London: Kogan Page.

Redstone, Sumner with Peter Knobler. 2001. *A Passion To Win.* New York : Simon & Schuster.

Reed, Stanley. 2000. "J.P. Morgan and Chase: Again, Europe is Left Out." *BusinessWeek Online.* (Sep 14)

Reed, Stanley Foster and Reed-Lajoux, Alexandra. 1999. *The Art Of M&A: A Merger Acquisition Buyout Guide.* New York: McGraw-Hill.

Reed-Lajoux, Alexandra. 1998. *The Art Of M & A Integration: A Guide To Merging Resources, Processes And Responsibilities.* New York: McGraw-Hill.

Reed-Lajoux, Alexandra and Elson, Charles M. 2000. *The Art of M&A Due Diligence: Navigating Critical Steps and Uncovering Crucial Data.* New York: McGraw-Hill.

Reed-Lajoux, Alexandra and Weston, J Fred. 1998. "Do Deals Deliver on Postmerger Performance?" *Mergers And Acquisitions.* 33 (Sep/Oct): 34.

Reichard, Robert S. 1972. *The Numbers Game: Uses and Abuses of Managerial Statistics.* New York: McGraw-Hill.

Reichheld, Fred and Henske, Brad. 1991. "The Only Sure Method of Recouping Merger Premiums." *Journal of Retail Banking.* 13 (Summer): 9.

Reichheld, Frederick F. and Teal, Thomas. 1996. *The Loyalty Effect : The Hidden Force Behind Growth, Profits, And Lasting Value.* Boston: Harvard Business School Press.

Reid, Samuel Richardson. 1968. *Mergers , Managers, and the Economy.* New York: McGraw-Hill.

Reigle, Ronda F. 2001. "Measuring Organic and Mechanistic Cultures." *Engineering Management Journal.* 13 (Dec): 3-9.

Reilly, Robert F. and Schweihs, Robert P. 2000. *The Handbook of Advanced Business Valuation.* New York: McGraw-Hill.

Rhoads, Christopher. 1998. "Deutsche Bank to Give BT `No Autonomy' --- Combination Will Result In Loss of 5,500 Jobs, Many From New York." *Wall Street Journal.* (Dec 1): 1.

Rigsby, Jeffrey A. and Greco, Guy. 2003. *Mastering Strategy: Insights from the World's Greatest Leaders and Thinkers*. New York: McGraw-Hill.

Roberts, Edward B. and Liu, Weynum Kathy. 2001. "Ally or Acquire? How Technology Leaders Decide." MIT Sloan Management Review. (Fall): 26.

Rock, Milton L.; Rock, Robert H.; Sikora, Martin. 1994. *The Mergers and Acquisitions Handbook. 2nd Ed*. New York: McGraw Hill.

Roman, Monica. 2002. "Conseco Throws In The Towel" *Business Week* (Dec 30): 52.

Rooney, Paula and Darrow, Barbara. 2003. "Novell's Linux Coup." *CRN*. (Nov 10): 5.

Rozemeijer, Frank A.; van Weele, Argan; Weggeman, Mathieu. 2003. "Creating Corporate Advantage Through Purchasing: Toward a Contingency Model." *Journal of Supply Chain Management*. 39 (Winter): 4.

S

Saaty, Thomas L. 1982. *Decision Making for Leaders*. Belmont: Lifetime Learning Publication.

Sackman, S.A. 1992. "Culture and Subcultures: An Analysis of Organizational Knowledge." *Administrative Science Quarterly*. 37 (2): 140.

Sackmann, Sonja A. Editor. 1997. *Cultural Complexity in Organizations: Inherent Contrasts and Contradictions*. Thousand Oaks: SAGE Publications, Inc.

Saffold, Guy S. 1988. "Culture Traits, Strength, and Organizational Performance: Moving Beyond Strong Culture." *Academy of Management Review*. 13 (Oct):546-58.

Samuelson, Robert J. 2000. "Merger Frenzy." *The Washington Post*. (Oct 12): A.25.

Sanborn, Stephanie. 2001. "Into the Integration Jungle" *InfoWorld*. 23 (Nov 26): 49.

Sathe, Vijay. 1985. *Culture And Related Corporate Realities: Text, Cases, And Readings On Organization Entry, Establishment, And Change*. Homewood: Irwin.

Schall, Maryan S. 1983. "A Communications-rules Approach to Organizational Culture." *Administrative Science Quarterly* 28 (Dec): 557.

Schein, Edgar. 1984. "Coming to a New Awareness of Organizational Culture." *Sloan Management Review* 25 (2): 3-16.

Schein, Edgar. 1985. *Organization Culture and Leadership*. San Francisco: Jossey – Bass.

Schein, Edgar H. 1993. "On Dialogue, Culture, and Organizational Learning." *Organizational Dynamics*. 22 (Autumn): 40.

Schein, Edgar H. 1995. "Dialogue and Learning." *Executive Excellence*. 12(Apr): 3.

Schein, Edgar H. 1996. "Three Cultures of Management: The Key to Organizational Learning." *Sloan Management Review*. 38 (Fall): 9.

Schein, Edgar H. 1998. "Commentary: The Family As A Metaphor For Culture: Some Comments On The DEC Story." *Journal of Management Inquiry*. 7 (Jun): 131.

Schein, Edgar H. 1999. "Empowerment, Coercive Persuasion and Organizational Learning: Do They Connect?" *The Learning Organization*. 6: 163.

Schein, Edgar H. 1999. *The Corporate Culture Survival Guide : Sense And Nonsense About Culture Change*. San Francisco: Jossey-Bass.

Schellhardt, Timothy D. 1999. "A Marriage of Unequals: When Executives at One Merger Partner Make a Lot More Than Their Counterparts, It Can Make for Some Rocky Times." *Wall Street Journal*. (Apr 5): R.8.

Schelling, Thomas C. 1960. *The Strategy of Conflict*. Cambridge: Harvard University Press.

Schneider, Greg and Drozdiak, William. 2001. "Lucent Merger Talks Collapse; Firm's Insistence on 'Merger of Equals' Kills Deal With Alcatel, Sources Say." *The*

Washington Post. (May 30):E.1.

Schneider, S.C. and De Meyer, A. 1991. "Interpreting and Responding to Strategic Issues: The Impact of National Culture." *Strategic Management Journal* 12(4): 307-20.

Schonfeld, Erick and Malik, Om. 2003. "GULP! The Tech Industry is Poised for a Major Eat-or-be-Eaten Phase." *Business 2.0.* (August): 89.

Schulman, Donniel S.; Harmer, Martin J.; Dunleavy, John R.; Lusk, James S. 1999. *Shared Services: Adding Value to Business Units.* New York: John Wiley & Sons.

Schwartz, R., and Davis, S. 1981. "Matching Corporate Culture and Business Strategy." *Organizational Dynamics* 10 (1): 30-48.

Schweiger, David M. 2001. *M&A Integration: A Framework for Executives and Managers.* New York: McGraw-Hill.

Segil, Larraine. 2000. "Fast Alliances Are the Key to Dot-Com Success" *The Journal for Quality and Participation.* 23 (Fall): 40-42.

Serwer, Andy. 2002. "Conseco's Colorful Crash." *Fortune.* 146 (Sep 16): 197.

Shapira, Zur. 1997. *Organizational Decision Making.* Cambridge: Cambridge University Press.

Sharpe, W.F. 1964. "Capital Asset Prices: A Theory of Market Equilibrium Under Conditions of Risk" *Journal of Finance* 19 (September): 425–42.

Sheehy, Barry; Bracey, Hyler; Frazier, Rick. 1996. *Winning the Race for Value: Strategies to Create Competitive Advantage in Emerging "Age of Abundance".* New York: Amacom.

Shenefield, John H. and Stelzer, Irwin M. 2001. *The Antitrust Laws: A Primer.* Washington D.C.: The AEI Press.

Sherer, Paul M. 1999. "1998 Year-End Review of Markets: The Lesson From Chrysler, Citicorp and Mobil: No Companies Nowadays Are Too Big to Merge." *Wall Street Journal.* (Jan 4):R8.

Sherman, Andrew J. Franchising & licensing : two ways to build your business. New York: AMACOM, 1999.

Shishkin, Phillip and Pasztor, Andy. 2001. "GE-Honeywell Deal's Problems Deepen: Europe's Antitrust Enforcers Push for Aerospace Sale That Undercuts Synergies. *Wall Street Journal.* (Jun 12): A3.

Shull, Bernard, Hanweck, Gerald A. 2001. *Bank Mergers In A Deregulated Environment : Promise And Peril.* Westport: Quorum Books.

Sidel, Robin And Hamilton, David P. 2001. "Amgen Signs a Deal to Buy Immunex; Pact Could Inspire More Consolidation." *Wall Street Journal.* (Dec 17): A.4.

Sidel, Robin and Williams, Molly. 2001. "Deals & Deal Makers: Hewlett's Fight on Compaq Turns Heads; H-P Director's Stance Is Unusually Strong" *Wall Street Journal.* (Dec 31): C.1.

Silver, A. David. 1993. *Cashing out: How to Value and Sell the Privately Held Company.* Dearborn: Dearborn Trade.

Simon, Julian L. 2000. *Developing Decision Making Skills for Business.* Armonk: M.E. Sharpe.

Sirower, Mark. 1999. "Manager's Journal: What Acquiring Minds Need to Know." *Wall Street Journal.* (Feb 22): A.18.

Slywotzky, Adrian J. 2002. *The Art of Profitability.* New York : Warner Books.

Smith, Alvie L. 1991. *Innovative Employee Communication: New Approaches to Improving Trust, Teamwork, and Performance.* Englewood Cliffs: Prentice Hall.

Smith, Gregory P. 2001. *Here Today, Here Tomorrow : Transforming Your Workforce From*

High-Turnover To High-Retention. Chicago: Dearborn Trade Pub.

Smith, Roy C. 1990. *The Money Wars: The Rise and Fall of the Great Buyout Boom of the 1980s.* New York: Dutton.

Snowden, Richard W. 1994. *The Complete Guide To Buying A Business.* New York: American Management Association.

Srikonda, Susan L P. 1999. "How the West Was Won." *Industrial Distribution.* 88 (Jul): 62-65.

Staff. 1987. "Acquisition Strategies: The Primary Objective Must be to Satisfy a Need" *Small Buisness Report* 12 (Jan): 30.

Staff. 1993. "M&A Due Diligence That Leaves Nothing to Chance." *Mergers and Acquisitions.* 28 (Jul/Aug): 11.

Staff. 1996. "Growth Through Acquisitions Has Consequences." *Quality.* 35 (Apr): 26.

Staff. 1997. "The Big Five?" *The Economist.* 344 (Sep 20): 69.

Staff. 1998. "Managing Alliances: Skills For the Modern Era." *Alliance Analyst.* (Mar)

Staff. 1999. "Sustaining Profitable Growth: Strategies for Enterprise-Wide Innovation." *Economist Intelligence Unit.*

Staff. 1999. "Surge in Mergers Likely." *The Atlanta Constitution.* (Apr 22): E.8.

Staff. 1999. "Daimler in Distress." *Wall Street Journal.* (Sep 22): A.22.

Staff. 2000. "Managing the Merger Process." *Strategic Direction.* 16 (Jan): 19.

Staff. 2000. *Mergerstat Review Quarterly Report.* Los Angeles: Houlihan, Lokey, Howard & Zukin.

Staff. 2000. "India: Victory for Warner-Lambert Shareholders." *Businessline.* (Jan 23): 1.

Staff. 2000. "Equilon Enterprises LLC." *Wall Street Journal.* (Mar 7): C.14.

Staff. 2000. "Business Brief – TOSCO CORP.: Agreement Is Set to Buy Refinery for $420 Million." *Wall Street Journal.* (Apr 7): C.14.

Staff. 2000. "Hanging on to Value After the Deal Closes." *Mergers and Acquisitions Journal* 35 (Oct): 19.

Staff. 2001. "M&A News and Trends." *Mergerstat.* (Dec): 1.

Staff. 2001. *Mergerstat Review Quarterly Report.* Los Angeles: Houlihan, Lokey, Howard & Zukin.

Staff. 2001. "Chrysler's Troubled Marriage." *New York Times.* (Jan 9): A.18.

Staff. 2001. "U.A.W. Chief Says Daimler Saved Chrysler." *New York Times.* (Apr 6): C.5.

Staff. 2001. "Merger Helps Pfizer Exceed Expectations." *New York Times.* (Apr 19): C.7.

Staff. 2001. " Business: Sheltering From the Storm; Hewlett-Packard and Compaq." *The Economist.* 360 (Sep 8): 63.

Staff. 2001. "Executive Perspectives: Fred Salerno CFO, Verizon." *Risk Management.* 48 (Sep): 12-15.

Staff. 2001. "Business: Coming of age; Biotechnology." *The Economist.* 361 (Dec 22): 88.

Staff. 2001. "Conoco, Phillips Latest To Announce Merger Plans." *World Refining.* 11 (Dec): 16.

Staff. 2002. "EU, Canada Approve $15B Conoco-Phillips Merger." *The Daily Deal.* (Mar 7): N.A.

Staff. 2002. "Mergerstat's M&A Roundup: Year in Review 2002." www.mergerstat.com. (Dec 30).

Staff. 2002. "Pepsi to Distribute Gatorade to Schools, Vending Machines." *Wall Street Journal.* (Aug 20): A.8.

Staff. 2002. *Mergerstat Review Quarterly Report.* Los Angeles: Houlihan, Lokey, Howard & Zukin.

Staff. 2002. "Union of Conoco, Phillips Creates U.S.'s Largest Refining Company." *Octane Week.* 17 (Sep 9): 1.

Staff. 2002. "Chronology – Milestones for HP, Compaq Merger Plan." *Reuters Business Report.* (03-19)

Staff. 2002. "IBM Consulting Aims for Growth in Energy Sector." *Energy Network.* (Nov 28): 1.

Staff. 2003. "ConocoPhillips, Williams Ink Wichita Throughput Agreement."*Octane Week.* (Jan 27): 1.

Staff. 2003. "The Return of The Deal." *Economist.com/Global Agenda.* (10 Jul): 1.

Staff. 2003. "Business: Now it's Novell; Open-Source Software." *The Economist.* 369 (Nov 8): 81.

Staff. 2003. *Mergerstat Review Quarterly Report.* Los Angeles: Houlihan, Lokey, Howard & Zukin.

Staff. 2004. "Conseco Inc.: Settlement Is Set With SEC On Probe of Mobile-Home Unit." *Wall Street Journal.* (Mar 11): 1.

Staff Reports. 1998. "Keeping Score On the Key Drivers In M&A's Future." *Mergers and Acquisitions Journal* 32 (Jun): 10.

Standard & Poor's Industry Surveys.

Steinberg, Steven B. 2002. "Due Diligence for Mergers and Acquisitions." *Rough Notes.* 145 (Dec): 14-16.

Stern, Erik, Hutchinson, Mike. 2004. *The Value Mindset: Returning To The First Principles Of Capitalist Enterprise.* Hoboken: John Wiley & Sons.

Stern, Joel M. and Shiely, John S. 2001. *The EVA Challenge: Implementing Value Added Change in an Organization.* New York: John Wiley & Sons.

Stewart, Thomas A. 2002. "How to Think With Your Gut." *Business 2.0.* (Nov): 98.

Stires, David. 2003. "Ready to get swallowed." *Fortune.* 148 (Jul 21): 148.

Strage, Mark. Ed. 1971. *Acquisitions and Merger Negotiating Strategy.* New York: Presidents Publishing House, Inc.

Strickland, Gordon. 1980. "How an Investment Banker Prepares a Company for a Tender Offer." *Management Accounting.* 61 (Feb): 26-28.

Stuart, Scott. 2002. "Conoco Closer, But FTC Still Working." *The Daily Deal.* (Jun 21): N.A.

Stuck, Bart and Weingarten, Michael. 1997. "The Death of Innovation?" *Business Communications Review.* 27 (04-01) 59.

Sturges, John S. 1989. "A Method for Merger Madness" *Personnel Journal.* 68 (Mar): 60-9.

Suhr, Jim. 1999. *The Choosing by Advantages Decision Making System.* Westport: Quorum Books.

Sutton, Robert I. 2000. *The Knowing-Doing Gap: How Smart Companies Turn Knowledge into Action.* Boston: Harvard Business School Press.

Swisher, Kara. 1998. "On-Line: When Bill Met Steve: A Showdown That Shaped AOL." *Wall Street Journal.* (Jun 22): B.1.

Swisher, Kara. 2002. "Hewlett, Fiorina: Can the Marriage at H-P Be Saved?" *Wall Street Journal.* (Mar 18): B.1.

Swoboda, Frank. 2001. "A Model Comeback? Chrysler, in 3rd Crisis in 3 Decades, Hopes to be Profitable by End of 2003, But it Won't be Easy." *The Washington Post.* (May 13): H.1.

Symonds, William C. 2001. "The Most Aggressive CEO." *Business Week.* (May 28): 69-

77.

T

Tam, Pui-Wing and Williams, Molly. 2002. "E-Business: Hewlett Visits H-P Investors to Make Antimerger Case." *Wall Street Journal*. (Jan 7): A.15.

Tam, Pui-Wing. 2002. "The Chief Does Double Duty — How H-P's Fiorina Manages to Run Global Corporation While Waging Proxy Fight." *Wall Street Journal*. (Feb 7): B.1.

Tam, Pui-Wing. 2002. "Walter Hewlett's Counterplan — His H-P Scenario Emphasizes Printer and Imaging Unit, Pointedly Excludes Fiorina." *Wall Street Journal*. (Feb 11): B.1.

Tam, Pui-Wing. 2002. "H-P Credit Rating Is Cut by S&P; Risks of Compaq Acquisition Cited." *Wall Street Journal*. (Mar 8): B.5.

Tam, Pui-Wing. 2002. "H-P Deal Vote Pits 'Growth' Against 'Value'" *The Wall Street Journal*. (Mar 13): C.1.

Tam, Pui-Wing. 2002. "Divided Electorate: For Fund Managers, Hewlett-Compaq Vote Is Agonizing Choice — Personal Lobbying by Fiorina Helped Turn a Rout Into a Very Tight Race — Early Results Possible Today." *Wall Street Journal*. (Mar 19): A.1.

Tam, Pui-Wing. 2002. "Proxy Battle Proves Distracting, H-P Internal Documents Suggest." *Wall Street Journal*. (Mar 28): C.1.

Tam, Pui-Wing; McWilliams, Gary; Thurm, Scott. 2002. "Tough Challenges Face H-P: Customers and Opponents of Compaq Deal Need to Be Reassured." *Wall Street Journal*. (May 2): B.5.

Tam, Pui-Wing. 2002. "H-P Hails Cuts, Says Growth to Ebb" *Wall Street Journal*. (Jun 5): B.2.

Tam, Pui-Wing. 2002. "H-P Designs Workshops to Break Post-Merger Ice." *Wall Street Journal*. (Jul 11): B.6.

Taub, Stephen. 2002. "Conseco Adds Its Name To The List Of Billion-Dollar Busts; Green Tree Acquisition Did Company In." *CFO.com* (Dec 19)

Taulli, Tom. 2002. *The Complete M&A Handbook: The Ultimate Guide to Buying, Selling, Merging, or Valuing a Business*. Roseville: Prima Venture.

Temple, John E.; Veal, Thomas G. Jr.; Smith, William K. 1981. "Strategic Growth Through Merger and Acquisition: Careful Screening of Candidates for Merger or Acquisition can Help Ensure Successful Diversification." *Financial Executive*. 49 (May): 23.

Thornton, Emily. 2004. "Dragging Heels, Canceling Deals: Skittish Investors And Executives Are Making Managers Harder To Pull Off Then Ever." *Business Week* (Oct 18): 114.

Thurm, Scott; Tam, Pui-Wing; McWilliams, Gary. 2002. "Nail-Byter: H-P Claims Victory on Compaq Merger; Foe Doesn't Concede —Both Sides Agree Margin Is Slim in Bitter Proxy Fight; Final Tally to Take Weeks — A Delay and Boos at Meeting." *Wall Street Journal*. (Mar 20): A.1.

Trotta, Raymond J. 2003. *Translating Strategy Into Shareholder Value : A Company-Wide Approach To Value Creation*. New York: American Management Association.

Trottier, Richard M. 1998. "How the Successful Acquirer Keys On Market Power: The Best M&A Due Diligence Probes the Qualities of a Target That Provide Sustained Competitive Advantage To The Acquirer." *Mergers and Acquisitions*

Journal. 32 (Jan/Feb): 30.

Tully, Shawn. 1999. "A Deal Too Far." *Fortune.* 140 (Nov 8): 131.

U

Uchitelle, Louis. 2000. "As Mergers Get Bigger, So Does the Danger." *New York Times.* (Feb 13): C.4.

Umbenhaur, Rexford E. III. 1999. *Selling Your Business Successfully: Tips, Strategies, and Tools.* New York: John Wiley & Sons, Inc.

United States Securities and Exchange Commission web site: http://www.sec.gov. Information and forms are available at http://www.sec.gov/info/edgar/forms.htm

V

Van Mannen, J.; Schein, E.; Staw, B. Ed. 1979. *Toward a Theory of Organizational Socialization: In Research in Organizational Behavior.* Greenwich: JAI Press.

Velayutham, S. and Perera, M. H. B. 2004. "The Influence of Emotions and Culture on Accountability and Governance." *Corporate Governance.* 4 (1): 52.

Velocci, Anthony L., Jr. 1998. "Efficiency Gains Elude Biggest Merger Survivors; The Most Competitive Companies Are Focusing Mainly On Supply-Chain Management Issues, Not Major M&A Activity." *Aviation Week & Space Technology.* 149 (Aug 10): 45.

Vestal, Katherine W. and Spreier, Scott W. 1997. "More Than Art, Less Than Science." *Healthcare Executive.* 12 (Jul/Aug): 22-27.

Vlasic, Bill and Stertz, Bradley A. 2001. *Taken For A Ride - How Daimler-Benz Drove Off With Chrysler.* New York: Harper Business.

W

Wagner, Jan F. 2002. "Are Dresdner's Days Numbered?" *The Banker* 152 (Sep): 130-132.

Waldholz, Michael; Tanouye, Elyse; Harris, Gardiner. 1999. "Rx for Drug Companies: Get Hitched, Stat! --- With Executives Aging and Patents Expiring, Industry Is Ripe for Megamergers." *Wall Street Journal.* (Nov 4): B.1.

Wall, Stephen J. 2001. "Making Mergers Work." *Financial Executive.* 17 (Mar/Apr): 34.

Walker, M. Mark. 2000. "Corporate Takeovers, Strategic Objectives, and Acquiring-Firm Shareholder Wealth." *Financial Management.* (Spring): 53-66.

Walton, Mark S. 2004. *Generating Buy-in: Mastering the Language of Leadership.* New York: Amacom.

Warwick, Ben. Ed. 2003. *The Handbook of Risk.* Hoboken: John Wiley & Sons.

Wasserman, Noam; Nohria, Nitin; Anand, Bharat. 2001. *When Does Leadership Matter?* Boston: Harvard Business School Press.

Wasserstein, Bruce. 1998. *Big Deal: The Battle For Control Of America's Leading Corporations.* New York: Warner Books.

Wasserstein, Bruce. 1998. *Big Deal – Mergers and Acquisitions in The Digital Age.* New York: Warner Business Books.

Weaver, Samuel C.; Harris, Robert S.; Bielinski, Daniel W.; Mackenzie, Kenneth F. 1991. "Merger and Acquisition Valuation." *Financial Management.* 20 (Summer): 85.

Weber, Joseph. 1998. "The Year of the Deal; Merger Power Drives the Global Leaders of the Top 1000." *Business Week.* (July 13,): 52.

West, Thomas L. and Jones, Jeffrey D. 1999. *Handbook of Business Valuation.* New York: John Wiley & Sons.

Weston, J. Fred; Mitchell, Mark L.; Mulherin, J. Harold. 2004. *Takeovers, Restructuring, and Corporate Governance.* New Jersey: Pearson.

Weston, J. Fred and Weaver, Samuel C. 2001. *Mergers & Acquisitions: Tax and Accounting Guidelines, Includes Valuation and Structuring Models, Guidelines for Postmerger Integration.* New York: McGraw-Hill.

Weston, J. Fred, and Brigham, Eugene F. 1993. *Essentials of Managerial Finance.* Fort Worth: Dryden Press.

White, Gregory L. 2001. "GM Finally Nails Down Deal With Daewoo --- U.S. Auto Maker Will Pay $400 Million for Assets, But Is It Getting a Lemon?" *Wall Street Journal.* (Sep 21): A.21.

Wiener, Y. 1988. "Forms of Value Systems: A Focus on Organizational Effectiveness and Culture Change and Maintenance." *Academy of Management Review* 13 (4): 534-545.

Williams, Carol J. 2001. "DaimlerChrysler Woes Fuel Merger Second-Guessing; Automobiles: Firm Will Post $269-Million Loss and Details a Chrysler Turnaround Plan, But Some Analysts Question Feasibility." *The Los Angeles Times.* (Feb 27): C.1.

Williams, Molly. 2001. "H-P's Deal for Compaq Has Doubters As Value of Plan Falls to $20.52 Billion --- Companies' Stocks Decline Amid Fear That Fiorina Can't Make It All Work." *Wall Street Journal.* (Sep 5): A.3.

Williams, Molly and McWilliams, Gary. 2001. "Packard Group Opposes Compaq Deal — Being Largest Shareholder, Family Foundation Vote Could Influence Others" *Wall Street Journal.* (Dec 10): A.3.

Williams, Molly. 2001. "Walter Hewlett Urges Boards to Drop Deal." *Wall Street Journal.* (Dec 14): B.8.

Wingfield, Nick. 2001. "E-Commerce (A Special Report): Cover Story --- The People Behind Sites: Ebay: Alawys Looking For the Next Trade." *Wall Street Journal.* (Dec 10): R.6.

Wojcik, Joanne. 2004. "Consumer-Driven Plan Model Enters Fast Lane; UnitedHealth's Purchase of Definity Gives Approach Momentum." *Business Insurance.* 38 (Dec 6): 1.

Woodall, Pam. 2000. "Survey: The New Economy: Untangling E-conomics." *The Economist.* 356 (Sep 23): S.5.

WSJ Research. 2002. "Corporate Accountability." *WSJ Market Data Group* (Updated July 11).

Y

Yates, Brock. 2000. "Daimler Drives Chrysler Into a Ditch." *Wall Street Journal.* (Nov 8): A26.

Yates, Frank J. 2003. *Decision Management: How to Ensure Better Decisions in Your Company.* San Francisco: Jossey Bass.

Yergin, Daniel. 1991. *The Prize – The Epic Quest for Oil, Money & Power.* New York: Touchstone.

Yoffie, David B. and Kwak, Mary. 2002. "Family Feud: How to Avoid Another H-P Battle." *Wall Street Journal.* (Mar 25): A.18.

Yost, Mark. 2000. "From Motor City to Autobahn." *Wall Street Journal.* (Jun 12): A28.

Young, Shawn and Perez, Evan. 2002. "Finance Chief of WorldCom Got High Marks on Wall Street." *Wall Street Journal.* (Jun 27): B.1.

Z

Zingheim, Patricia K. 2000. *Pay People Right!* San Francisco: Jossey-Bass Publishers.

INDEX

ABOUT THE AUTHOR

Barry Massoudi is founder of Cubicon LLC, a management consulting firm based in Seattle, Washington. Barry has over eighteen years of experience in project management, human resource management, and management consulting. He has consulted with many multinational Fortune 500 companies in the U.S., Europe, and Asia. He is an expert in business process thinking and has extensive experience working with senior managers on mergers and acquisitions and other management issues. Barry holds a master's degree in engineering and an MBA.